ALL THEM CORNFIELDS AND BALLET IN THE EVENING

BY

JOHN MILLER

First published in Great Britain by Hodgson Press 2010

Hodgson Press
PO Box 903^A
Kingston upon Thames
Surrey
KT1 9LY
United Kingdom
enquiries@hodgsonpress.co.uk
www.hodgsonpress.co.uk

A CIP catalogue record for this book is available from the British Library.

ISBN: 978-1-906164-12-6

Printed in Great Britain by Lightning Source Ltd.

ALL THEM CORNFIELDS AND BALLET IN THE EVENING

BY

JOHN MILLER

Hodgson Press

Dedication

For Brenda, Dodik, Zhenya, Timosha and all our grandchildren

© Photograph by Dod Miller

John Miller co-authored *The Day we almost Bombed Moscow* and collaborated on *The Cruellest Night* –the story of the sinking of the William Gustloff, the world's worst sea disaster. His novel *The Chamdo Raid* is set in Tibet. He lives in Southwold, Suffolk, with his wife and has produced two local books: *The Best of Southwold* and *Southwold in Old Photographs*.

Contents

List of Illustrations

xi

Preface

I had the title of this book – *All them Cornfields and Ballet in the Evening* – long before I sat down and wrote it. It was a mouthful, I agree, but I thought it was just right. For there is a scene in *I'm All Right, Jack*, the classic British trade-union satire and Boulting Brothers film box-office success of 1957, where Peter Sellers, a tragi-comic shop steward, by the name of Fred Kite, is talking about the Soviet Union as a workers' paradise. His young lodger, Windrush, listens patiently and asks if he had ever been to Russia. 'No, not yet,' Sellers replies. His eyes glaze. 'I've always wanted to though... all them cornfields and ballet in the evening.'

It is a memorable line, encapsulating a Sellers-Kite view of the Soviet Union once quite commonly held by people who were intelligent enough to have known better. And this book is about that country as I saw it over forty or so years. But, you will not be surprised to hear, I discovered there was a lot more to Russia than cornfields and ballet.

By the title, and some of the chapter headings, it will quickly be perceived that this is not a profound book about a country that has dominated my adult life, as well as, course, the lives of millions throughout the world. It is not a history of the Soviet Union, or of Russia. Nor a Who Was Who? of the Soviet leadership. Nor a travel book. Only occasionally does it touch on high politics and usually only if I found something ridiculous about them. And dear old Gorby and poor old Boris Yeltsin and young President Vladimir Putin (incidentally some of my 'best friends' in the Soviet Union were rat-faced KGB colonels) hardly get a look in – they are Ivans-come-lately.

And if there should be any Fred Kites still living on this planet I warn that my personal panorama of Soviet history bares little or no resemblance to the fairy tales purveyed over the years by apologists of the regime. It is definitely not a solid volume about Five Year Plans being fulfilled and over-fulfilled, granaries overflowing with grain, apple-cheeked dairy maids milking plump contented Soviet cows, and of course the sublime bliss brought about by an evening at the Bolshoi.

This book, unashamedly, is a period piece. It is about the vanished world of the USSR. Like the parrot in the Monty Python sketch it is a late, expired, former, ex, deceased, etc., USSR. I can assure you it cannot be revived. It ain't coming back... ever.

Yet, as the reader will hopefully see for himself I believe I still could entitle this book The Real Russia or The Russians as People or Putting Up with the Russians or Russian Prospect or Russia Perceived. For the Russians were, and are, a funny old lot.

Because I am not a profound man – I had a lot of laughs in Russia – this book contains little gloom, no deep analysis, not much pontification. Nor is it doom-laden. But I lived and worked in that wonderful, extraordinary country for quite a few years and I saw and heard a lot of things. I had a better idea than many Kremlinologists (whatever became of them? what are they doing now?) of Russia's real life: the *poshlost* (banality), the drunkenness, the bureaucracy, and not forgetting the desperate shortages of food, services and ideas. And I kept a lot of cuttings – in what my family persisted, and not without some justification, called 'crap books' – and made not a few notes.

I have talked to a great many Russians (when they were officially 'citizens of the USSR') and I use some direct quotations. It would be daft of me to claim I recorded them all on the spot – the miniature tape recorder was not a tool of the trade when I started in journalism, nor, come to that, were mobile phones, laptops and e-mail. But I think I fairly faithfully report the content of what I said to them and they said to me.

Deliberately, because this not, I repeat, not, a history book there are only a few dates in these pages. The death of Uncle Joe Stalin is an important one – March 1953. But to me the Big Question is not where were you when President Kennedy was assassinated, but what were you doing when you heard that Stalin had died. And the dates that really matter to all of us now are August 1991 when Gorbachev dissolved the Soviet Communist Party because its leaders failed to defy the coup against him, and December of that year when Yeltsin announced that the Soviet Union had ceased to exist.

I think two abbreviations are in order to describe one of the most momentous events of our life time: BCC – Before the Collapse of Communism; and ACC – After the Collapse of Communism. You will meet these abbreviations from time to time in this book so do not worry about them.

And, if you didn't already know it, we won. And that's a fact.

ALL THEM CORNFIELDS AND BALLET IN THE EVENING

1 – Nikita's Knickers

The Viscount flew low over anti-aircraft guns ringing the airfield, thumped down on the ground, skittered along the icy runway and taxied to the terminal at Vnukovo, Moscow's international airfield. It was late afternoon and dark, and when the plane came to a stop, it was suddenly fixed by the light of several powerful arc lamps.

Two military trucks, and soldiers armed with those stubby little machine guns that took Berlin, raced across the tarmac and surrounded the aircraft. There were only a few of us flying on it – in those days comparatively few people went to and from the Soviet Union – and we got up to collect our things. 'Sit down!' the stewardess ordered: disembarking at Moscow airport was a slow business.

We did what we were told: excellent training for living and working in the USSR. But I was excited. Stories and headlines were already dancing in my mind. Moscow, the Kremlin, Khrushchev, the Cold War, the Red Army, the Sino-Soviet split, the Spy Game. I was on the threshold of a new world. I was working for a great news agency. Russia was the big one and I had got it. Russia was a story I could handle.

A staircase was moved up to the aircraft's exit door and two men wearing fur hats and heavy, grey overcoats came up the steps and into the plane. They were called *Pogranichniki* – or border troops – and you learned to recognize them by green epaulettes on their uniforms and their green hats.

And their grim faces. They were an arm of the KGB, and if they weren't at the airport, they would be guarding and patrolling many thousands of miles of the nation's frontiers with the aid of dogs, watchtowers, electronic sensors and strips of no-man's-land. Officers had the job of going aboard Western aircraft to count the number of arrivals. How they scowled!

They scowled at us that night when they took our passports, scowled when they stared at us and compared our faces with our photographs and scowled when they handed them back, as if to say, 'We know who you are and what you are up to, so ... watch it!' They went on scowling for the next thirty or so years, whenever I had anything to do with them, arriving or leaving the country. Of

3

course, there was nothing for them to laugh about. They had to be on guard twenty-four hours a day, protecting the Motherland from spies, diversionists and saboteurs, who apparently came in droves on Western aircraft, disguised as journalists, businessmen or tourists. At the same time, they had to catch traitors and others trying to escape from the paradise. Woe betide being trapped in a queue behind a family, because after their humblest and most personal possessions were gone through on the grounds they might be national treasures, their passports and visas were minutely examined in the apparent belief they could be forgeries.

Later, much later, when a huge new airport was built at Sheremetevo, the *Pogranichniki* became overwhelmed with the number of aircraft flying to and from Moscow, so such security measures were relaxed. And they stopped carrying machine guns because it was no way to welcome foreign visitors flocking to the land of peace and friendship, bringing much-needed hard currency. And then one day, Russia became a 'normal' country and there were green and red channels, duty free shops and all the rest of it.

But in those days we left aircraft and were fearful... and then it hit me. How cold it was, so cold it seemed to burn. I was grateful for Reuters, the world's greatest and meanest news agency, buying Brenda and me new sheepskin coats, *de rigeur* for a Russian winter. And as we shuffled across the snow to the airport terminal – marshalled by the gun-toting *Pogranichniki* and picked out by the arc lamps – it was suddenly all familiar. I had been here before, many times. I had read about it in books. I had dreamt it. This was sinister, exciting, scary, huge and unfathomable Russia. Mother Russia.

Dark Communistic Russia. The land of fur caps and vodka. Natasha, and hungry wolves bounding across the frozen steppe. Troikas and samovars. Red Square and St Basil's Cathedral, sticks of peppermint rock mixed up with pineapples. Tolstoy and Dostoevsky and Pushkin and Chekhov. And me, from Enfield, skyrocketed into the middle of all this.

They counted us again as we entered the airport terminal – just in case one of us had done a runner and disappeared into the snowy wastes of the USSR to spy on missile sites or carry out acts of sabotage

4

against armament factories. We queued to present our passports to the border guard sitting in a small, glass-fronted booth.

Later, there were banks of booths to deal with foreigners and the process was considerably speeded up to prevent disgorging Jumbos from swamping and suffocating the airport. But for years, Moscow airport was Hades, with every passport and customs official a Cerberus guarding its gate.

Young border guards were the worst offenders. They were extra-specially careful about vetting visitors and I never met one who was jolly and welcoming. As though off a conveyor-belt, they were pimply-faced with vacant eyes and 'short back and sides' and they took so long new arrivals almost felt that their arrest was imminent. Looking through the passport. Studying the Soviet visa. Comparing the photograph in the passport with your face. Staring stony-faced at you for a long second or two. And from time to time tossing a question, designed to catch you out. Barking out in Russian: 'How old are you?' or 'What year were you born in?' and then comparing what you said with the date in the passport. Sometimes they would speak into the telephone, but so quietly you couldn't hear what they were saying. Were they phoning their mums to say they would be late for supper? Or reporting that *neki* (a certain) Miller had just arrived from London and should he be let in or thrown out?

They even had a measuring place outside the cubicle and you could be asked to stand up against it. They would look at your height in the passport and compare it with the measurements, but it was a ludicrous exercise because your height was in feet and inches and their measurements were metric. No matter. The slogan of the time was 'Be Vigilant', and that's what they were.

The customs officers, many of whom were also KGB or ready to act like them when necessary, didn't really want to let you enter the country either. Cases would have to be opened and rummaged through – fingers lingering, it seemed to me, over women's underwear – but the worst thing you could do then, and right up to the collapse of Communism, would be to bring books into the country.

Any books in English worried Moscow customs, but particularly 'anti-Soviet' books or books they were not sure about. I had a copy of Lenin's unreadable work *What's to be Done?* confiscated, although it was returned later when I wrote about what had happened. And *Playboy* was definitely out – you couldn't bring tits and bums pictures into the USSR because the Party's cultural watchdogs didn't approve. But you knew that after such magazines were taken, they would be passed around among the boys and eventually reach the desk of a party or a KGB official, who would then sell them for a bundle of roubles.

Perhaps it has always been thus. The Marquis de Custine arrived by ship at St Petersburg in 1839 with letters of introduction to the mightiest in Tsarist Russia. And a fat lot of good it did him. The ship was unable to dock for the best part of a day while formalities were completed and customs confiscated a trunk here, a parasol there. With characteristic venom, the Marquis commented: 'What has man done to God that 60 million of the human race should be condemned to live in Russia?'

It was bitterly cold that January in 1960. A couple of days it reached minus thirty degrees celsius and the trams stopped running and schools were closed. We stayed for several weeks in the Ukraine Hotel, one of Stalin's so-called wedding cake skyscrapers with its hideous and wonderful confection of mock-Gothic spires and walls as thick as a medieval fortress, magnificently built 'heritage' kitsch that made your jaw drop. I have heard it suggested that Stalin's architects were influenced by Dracula and Batman, but I doubt they had heard of either of them. All they appreciated was that if they strayed towards un-Soviet Modernism, they would join the forced-labour gangs that worked on many of these titanic projects of architectural fantasy and political propaganda.

Wickedly cold outside but hot and stifling in the hotel, and unpleasant – we British were used to living in houses without central heating. If you opened the *fortochka*, the little inset double window, to let in air, the room could take hours to heat up again. And leaving the hotel to go to work or for a walk was a monumental task on its own. It was commonplace to wait half an hour for a lift to arrive, and when it did, it was packed, as the Russians say, like herrings in a barrel, with people all wearing heavy overcoats and fur hats. You needed to enter the lift headfirst to find room in this stinking warmth, if you were ever going to get anywhere that day.

Out through the massive wooden revolving doors of the Ukraine Hotel and you gasp. You go on gasping at minus thirty degrees and you try and narrow your nostrils to give your lungs a chance to get used to the cold. At first I thought my nose was actually freezing, certainly the longer hairs got ice on them. Eyebrows and moustaches could also grow an icicle or two, but you could cope with that. The main thing was to make sure you didn't get frostbitten ears – and you could prevent that happening by lowering the ear-flaps of the *shapka*, the fur hat.

My first *shapka* was rabbit with black imitation leather and I wore it with pride for months until being identified as a lorry driver. The *shapka* provided material for my first feature-article: about winter … the drabness of Russian clothes … and how they were bought for utility rather than for looks. And I vowed to draw the line on wearing fox or wolf on my head. You needed soft boots with fur inside, too, to keep frostbite from your toes, or the pressed-felt boots called *valenki* that have kept Russian feet warm since long before the days of Peter the Great. They reached up to the knees and looked big and clumsy but they were the most effective winter footwear known to Russian man and the *babushkas*, connoisseurs of cold.

On these days a walk of half an hour was an afternoon's exercise. The tops of legs soon began to tingle unless long johns were worn. When you could bear it no longer, you took a taxi – usually it was easy to get one. Except during ferocious snow blizzards, life went on surprisingly well in Moscow.

Under Communism the snow ploughs were always at work, enabling cars and lorries to do without chains, rolling the ice gradually into waves and hummocks. And taxis, I recall, may have looked beaten-up and smelling of cheap petrol, tobacco, sweat and cabbage soup, with a pool of melted snow on the floor, but they were warm and cheap, and they worked.

The first taxi told me something about life in the Soviet Union. I hailed it near the hotel and as I got in a drunken Russian staggered up and knocked on the driver's window. It was clear the drunk had wanted this taxi too and intended to find out where it was going so as to share it. The driver, a tough-looking lady smelling more of garlic than perfume, lowered the window very slowly. For a moment or two she listened to the man rambling on. Then she spat accurately in his eye, wound up the window and drove off at speed.

I couldn't resist expressing surprise at what she had done to her comrade, although I conceded he could have handled it better. 'Comrade Driver,' I said as politely as an Englishman could manage. 'Now why did you do that? All he wanted to do was to share the taxi and get himself home.'

'Maybe,' she said and there was the trace of a smile on her face, 'Maybe. But you could see for yourself that the whoring fucking drunken son-of-a-bitch was uncultured.'

There was a campaign on in Russia at that time – there were always campaigns of some kind or another especially against alcoholism – for people to behave in a *kulturno*, a 'cultured' or civilized way. What was being demanded was more humaneness, kindness and tact in human relations, and indeed I was constantly struck by the rudeness and lack of civility revealing the antagonisms of Soviet life.

While the Russians were lovely people and disarmingly kind in their private lives, once they put on a uniform – and it seemed as though most of them did – or stepped into a job in which they dealt with the public, so they became as brusque and as rude as any ill-tempered traffic warden.

For foreigners it was irksome. A colleague took his raincoat to a newly opened dry cleaning shop and when, after queuing for twenty minutes, he reached the counter, an assistant told him they didn't accept garments with buttons on because they might get damaged. 'Should I cut them off?' he asked. 'Yes,' she said and handed him a razor blade. When he had carefully amputated all the buttons, he rejoined the queue and, as the assistant took the razor blade back from him and put it in a drawer, she looked him straight in the eyes and said coldly: 'We don't accept that kind of raincoat for dry cleaning.'

Learning to cope with unprovoked rudeness was one of the great challenges of living in the USSR, but of course most foreigners were cocooned, living in their exclusive flats and hotels, being able to buy imported food, make special travel arrangements for hard currency, as well as having the God-given right to jump queues for theatres and tourist spots ranging from the Bolshoi theatre to Lenin's Mausoleum.

8

Similar privileges, it should not come as a surprise, were available to the Soviet ruling class, and the bosses seized them with both hands.

But Ivan Ivanovitch Ivanov and his wife had a hard time of it. Their lives were one long, jarring rebuff. I was often shocked by the high-handedness with which saleswomen dominating the service sector – low wages and the labour shortage had taken the men elsewhere – dealt with customers who had suffered enough by the time they reached the counter from the pushing, swearing, queue-jumping and general boorishness. And there they would be met by indifference, barked commands and grosser negatives. They were left in no doubt they were a nuisance.

On Moscow's streets it was a common sight to see bus drivers deliberately roaring away from stops as little old ladies scurried towards them, while drivers of ubiquitous black saloons – usually a sign they were party or government cars – would delight in making pedestrians scatter from their path or would drive through the deepest of puddles to splash them with slush and mud. And in restaurants, where again there was low pay and prestige and no incentive, waiters served food but not the customer.

In time I realized why this was happening in the first workers' and peasants' state, a land run by Russians, a kindly and warmhearted people who addressed each other as 'Comrade'. Rudeness had become a matter of habit created by shortages, traditions of authority and the Soviet way of life.

Statistics fell like confetti, but one of the most interesting and revealing I ever ran across was that in GUM, the huge departmental store on Red Square which – ACC – was given a new capitalist look and is now, arguably, the Harrods of Russia, one assistant sometimes served 800 or more customers a day, all clamouring to buy the few goods on offer. A cashier would deal with as many as 1,400 customers. No wonder that under a system involving queueing to choose, queueing to pay and finally queueing to collect the goods, stores became a seething mass of angry and sweating customers and shop assistants.

I never got to know shop assistants, but I always assumed they acted like they did because they spent their lives arguing with their neighbours in their communal flat, cursing their drunken husband, shouting at the loutish and spoilt children and they simply carried on the same way when they arrived at work. And the Soviet people were tired. They were tired of destruction and of wars. They were tired of the gigantic social, industrial and agricultural experiments that had taken place and to which no end was in sight. They were tired of the queues and the ceaseless shortages. And they were tired of being kicked around.

I did my best to shame bloody-minded Russians with a word of thanks or a smile or a well-timed one-liner. But I always thought then that only a revolution would change things…

∗≈⋇≈∗

The Reuters office was one room attached to the Bureau Chief's flat in Tverskaya Yamskaya, a long road running parallel to Gorky Street which – ACC – reverted to its pre-revolutionary name of Tverskaya. Maxim Gorky, it turned out, was not only a crony of Stalin's and pre-eminent in extolling all aspects of Stalinism, but he had toured the GULAG, cracking it up as an admirable way of constructing Communism.

It was an oddity, a tiny Western enclave of just four flats the other three of which were rented by Dutch diplomats. One of them told me that when they 'swept' their flats for bugs, they found as many as fourteen. Reuters must have been bugged too, as the KGB was still a power in the land and did what it liked – and it liked to keep a close eye on Western journalists. Then, and for years afterwards and until Moscow became swamped by embassies and media organizations and businesses, and ultimately the collapse of Communism, there was a box outside the main entrance and a policeman would telephone your arrival and departure to some unknown headquarters. But it was possible to establish a relationship with these chaps – you smiled at them and wished them good morning – and they saluted you.

That first year when we living in Prospekt Mira, I would take the tram to the Reuters office. The number 15 ran clanking and clunking from Rizhsky Voksal (Riga Station) to Byelorusski Voksal (Belarus Station) and it was always full. The tram drivers were women and I loved the journey because of the sound of the ding ding ding bell and the motion, and I felt I was riding in a relic of a bygone age, although in fact trams are still common near the big Moscow stations. You boarded the front of the tram and bought your five-kopeck ticket from the driver and forced your way through passengers to find a seat. When it was bitterly cold, you tried to clear the frost on the window with your gloved hand to make a peephole so you knew where to get off. The trams were all beaten-up and rusty and needed painting, but they did the job, unless of course, the overhead line came down, but that was not often.

The tram ran though mean streets with very few cars and lorries and down the hill to Novoslobodskaya ulitza. I soon learned that the forty-foot high wall running for some one hundred yards on my right side was the huge Butyrka prison, the transit camp for the GULAG, now still overcrowded with some 7,000 detainees, including 500 women, and where executions are carried out.

One morning when I was walking to the office, I came up behind an old man who was suddenly attacked by a snarling dog. He lashed out with his stick as I passed him and he whacked me on the arm. Fortunately, I was wearing a then-fashionable sheepskin overcoat which took the blow, but I swore at him in English. He stood there looking at me quizzically because he had not understood. I realized that if I wanted to get on in the Soviet Union I had to learn a few Russian swear words...

The departing bureau chief was Vincent Buist, a veteran correspondent. He had been a prisoner-of-war in Germany and given to black moods, making life a misery for those working for him. He had scarcely welcomed me to Moscow and wished me well before asking me if I had any hard currency; when I said I had £15, he told me it was no use to me and to hand it over. The official exchange rate was four roubles to the pound – forty or so years later, ACC of course, it reached several thousands – but the black-market rate was four times that.

'Of course, Old Boy,' said Vincent as he took my banknotes. 'You must appreciate I can't do anything illegal and give you anything else but four roubles to the pound.' And off he went, handing over Reuters Moscow to Bob Elphick. Vincent returned to Moscow once more before he died and behaved disgracefully by failing to support two bright young journalists on his staff who had been targeted and blackmailed by the KGB.

Bob Elphick was a hard taskmaster but he was a first-rate correspondent, and fair. We worked well together for two years, producing a file highly regarded in London. But by and large, the stories I wrote for Reuters in the first months were hardly earth-shattering.

Knickers, in fact, was the first subject I wrote about, and those in question could easily have been purchased from Marks and Spencer. What warranted a Reuters news story about knickers was that the Soviet prime minister, Nikita Khrushchev, had a thing about them, or rather, he was concerned that the Soviet Union was not producing enough good-quality knickers and in pretty colours. He raised the problem in a major three-hour speech in the Kremlin, attacking Soviet writers who had visited Britain and then wrote articles when they got home about how foreign knickers were better and came in many more colours than Soviet ones.

Khrushchev was a wonderful old windbag and he used the Russian word *pantaloony* which really meant the old-fashioned bloomers – the only kind that Soviet women were then able to buy. And indeed, there really was only one design – the Soviet bloomer was made of cotton, long in leg, with elastic at the top and bottom, and it came only in blue and purple, or so I was told. But of course, in London the writers had bought knickers. And he promised: 'Give us time, Comrades, and we shall produce knickers for your wives of the highest quality and in colours which cannot be seen anywhere else in the world.'

It was another of his many boasts that was not achieved until the collapse of Communism when Marks and Spencer and many other Western influences got to work...

But that day in 1960, Nikita's knickers went round the world. Reuters report said this 'popular bright' was front-paged in Canada, Australia and the United States and, curiously, a leading Japanese University requested a copy of the dispatch!

I quickly appreciated that people wanted to read something more than who was who in the Communist Party hierarchy or statistics on the output of ball-bearings. And in those Soviet newspapers that I despised for their lies, distortions and half-truths, and for being dull, boring and unreadable, there were, now and again, what we like to call human-interest stories. Thus I became a compulsive reader of Soviet

12

newspapers – eventually getting to read one after the other in bed in the morning with a cup of tea.

There were some good yarns about that extraordinary country, which scored in newspapers across the world just as often as did the big political and diplomatic stories that concerned governments and moved stock markets, such as the following example from *Krasnaya Zvezda* (*Red Star*) – the Soviet Defence Ministry organ – compulsory reading for the officers and men of one of the world's biggest, most powerful and threatening armies.

For weeks an argument raged in the newspaper about housework: should a soldier, especially an officer, roll up his sleeves and get into the kitchen to cook a meal or wash up? *Red Star* could not bring itself to remind readers that Russian men were among the laziest in the world, preferring to drink or watch television when they got home from work while the women returned from their jobs to spend several hours doing the housework and queueing. It may well be that young couples are now beginning to share domestic chores more equally, but Russian women will confirm that theirs is the greatest burden in the Russian family.

The Red Army's male chauvinist pigs had a field day in their organ. Housework, said one, reflected badly on the 'glory of the soldier's greatcoat'. Another said it violated 'the dignity of the traditions of the Soviet armed forces'. The newspaper concluded its debate with a comment that it was wrong to divide housework into clean and dirty jobs, with women doing the dirty ones, because 'all work in our country is honourable'.

There were quaint crime stories. Cakes and pastry, I reported, had led to the downfall of twenty-stone Nikolai Kudriatsev, but not through eating them. Chief pastry cook at the Peking Restaurant, infamous for its execrable Chinese food, he had also worked *na levo* – literally 'on the left', but in this context meaning 'on the side' – providing cakes to Moscow's top shops.

And how did he do it? Instead of using twenty eggs for every one hundred cakes, he used only ten; he diluted the milk and ordered kitchen staff to cut down on the sugar and butter they used. He made so much money from pastry sales to his outside customers that he bought himself a *dacha* and a large foreign car for his girlfriend. For this classic example of private enterprise, the fat man got ten years in a pastry-free labour camp. If he had hung on for another thirty, until Boris Yeltsin took power, he would have been hailed as one of the new breed of Russian entrepreneurs.

Another crime story was about a forty-five-year-old woman who walked into a Moscow police station and pleaded to be sent to a labour camp. She confessed to being a confidence trickster but complained that her victims wouldn't leave her alone. Could they please put her away for, say, two years, so that when she got out they would have forgotten her?

In those days the 'queue' to buy a car was at least five-years long – the few hundred thousand cars which were made in the Soviet Union going to party and government organizations. Private ownership of cars scarcely existed. Somehow the lady persuaded several dozen men that she knew how to jump the queue and would get them a car quickly for a substantial deposit. They paid, but she didn't deliver and now they were after her. The police duly arrested her for fraud but instead of getting two years inside, she got twelve.

My conception of young love in the Soviet Union was summed up by the story of the boy and girl sitting on a park bench in the moonlight. At last he summons up enough courage to tell her he loves her. 'Comrade,' he says. 'Yes, Comrade,' she says, hoping to hear at last some words of love. But his courage deserts him. 'Nothing Comrade… ,' he says, '… just Comrade, Comrade.'

But I soon found stories about love and sex and young people. I told of a lovely champion pig-breeder who had been inundated with love letters after her photograph had appeared in a newspaper. But some of the writers were more interested in her bust measurements and her attitude to sex than in learning the secrets of successful pig rearing. Then I spotted the first Soviet agony column in *Yunost* (Youth), a youth magazine which revealed that it was getting sacks of letters every day from young people being 'bruised by the facts of life'. It is worth recording that it took another twenty-five years and glasnost before sex was discussed openly in the Russian media. In what seems today to be quaint language *Yunost* told the story of Tanya who was sweet sixteen when she fell in love and loved too much. After getting

14

her into bed, her boyfriend stopped seeing her and she was now in a 'difficult position'. What should she do?

Yunost suggested that young girls should keep away from dance floors and spend more time in libraries and youth circles. 'Young people should be thinking not only of searching for fun and pleasure, but also of searching for knowledge.' And it couldn't resist making propaganda for the Soviet way of life:

'Whereas in the West, young people are tired of the senselessness of their lives because they live in a society deprived of greatness and of hope, in the Soviet Union there is work for all. Everywhere young hands, clear heads and honest hearts are needed. Everywhere there are good Soviet people with whom one can be friends.'

But this was the other world, the bits and pieces of Russian life, away from the cardboard façade the Cold War had erected. Life was not as pale and as pasty as *Pravda* painted it. This was the Russia of flesh and blood – as one particular story underlined.

Two young medical students were lovers, then he took up with another student. The first girl friend persuaded him to spend one last night together and plied him with vodka laced with morphine. He woke up in terrible pain: she had attacked him with a pair of surgical scissors and cut off his testicles. A court sentenced her to ten years in a labour camp.

By a coincidence, I had no sooner written this story, than I was presented with a heart-wrenching tale of love across the Iron Curtain, played out in front of me. An Oxford graduate by the name Francis Anderson, met a girl at the World Youth Festival held in Moscow three years before, corresponded with her by letter and went back to Moscow to marry her. It shouldn't have been difficult, but it was. ZAGS, the Soviet marriage registration office, turned them away. Officials were not going to let a nice Russian girl marry a foreigner.

When his visa ran out and he moved in with the girl, the KGB arrested him. I was tipped off about the story and went out to Sheremetevo with a feeling in my water that he was going to be put firmly on a Soviet flight to London.

I watched the plane load up with passengers and suddenly saw four border guards marching him across the tarmac. What happened next was straight out of a Hollywood film. A beautiful red-haired

Russian girl came out of a crowd of people watching the aircraft depart and ran across the tarmac, arms wide open and screaming 'Francis! Francis, I love you, I love you.' He slipped his guards and ran towards her crying her name.

I also raced across the tarmac ignoring shouts from policemen who set off after me, and got near to the couple as they flew into each other's arms, crying, hugging and kissing. The sun came out. Somewhere, bringing a lump to the throat and tears to the eyes, violins sobbed a tune straight from Prokofiev's *Romeo and Juliet*. This took place before television cameras were let loose in the Soviet Union, but it was a highly emotional and moving moment and it is locked in my memory. Even the border guards and the police were taken back by the scene and stood there for a minute or two watching the couple, before dragging them apart.

The wide use of the story in Britain embarrassed the Soviet authorities. They began to make it easier for Russian women to marry foreigners and to leave the country with them. It was about time too.

～☙❧～

I worked every day that first year in Moscow, sometimes for an hour or two on a 'day off', and it was fun. Yet it was not all work. We played hard too, and devised 'broomball' a game which almost defies comprehension. The British Embassy had a tennis court in its compound which in winter was frozen over and became a skating rink. Ice-hockey was out to British diplomats and the handful of journalists and businessmen, since few of us could ice-skate. But we could play hockey wearing running shoes or boots, and instead of sticks we could used brooms of twig, bought for a few roubles from the Russian markets and bound with sticky tape.

So broomball came about, providing camaraderie for the transient British community, whose tour of duty was two or three years. The game was dangerous: we wore only jeans, pullovers and fur hats. The idea of the game was to hit the ball into goals at both ends of the rink and you achieved that by sliding, kicking and pushing. But chasing after the ball created it own problems. Sometimes it was as though you were running on the spot or chasing the wrong way on a moving beltway. And like a dodgem car, you would crash into your opponents or those on your own side or into the fencing surrounding the court.

Fractured or sprained ankles, legs or back injuries were common and players were flown to London or Helsinki to have plaster casts set.

Later the game became serious. Other embassies formed teams. Players 'padded up' like American footballers and wore helmets. The protective gear ensured that players could survive to play the following Sunday, and a league was formed. Teams of women emerged, and they practised, played seriously and seldom lost.

True to form the British have insisted over the years on remaining amateurs. A team of stray journalists and businessmen who called themselves the Pits – some said the name was linked to their poor performance, others because it stood for 'Piss In The Snow' – kept the flag flying. They prided themselves on almost never winning. It did not matter who won or lost. What mattered was the spirit in which the game was played. Or so they said.

2 – Cockroach Whiskers Croaks

Uncle George set me on the road to Russia.

Not that he meant to and not that he ever knew what he had done. I was thirteen when I first heard him hail Joseph Stalin, the Red Army and Communism. And when my father told him he was stupid and that now we had beaten Hitler and the Nazis, the Soviet Union was our enemy.

Uncle George was not a card-carrying Communist – he voted Labour, or said he did; my father was a Conservative. Uncle George worked in a munitions factory during the War; my father was in the Royal Air Force, an intelligence officer. There was sibling rivalry. Uncle George insisted he was a member of the 'working class', trade unionist and a shop steward. He didn't like what he called ca-pita-lists all of whom, apparently, were 'fat and bloated'. My father worked for the *Financial Times*, the paper of the bosses, the capitalists.

Every weekend my uncle, who had a small monkey-like face and a Douglas Fairbanks' moustache, would walk the one-hundred yards from his semi-detached house in Enfield to our semi round the corner and knock on our door. He would be invited in and within minutes the two brothers would be arguing at the top of their voices.

Invariably, uncle would start the row by attacking Winston Churchill, a hero in our house, the wartime prime minister who had lost the first peacetime general election. My uncle knew how to get my father's goat.

'Churchill was a bloody old war monger', he would shout, 'who spent the War in a Whitehall bunker swigging brandy and smoking big fat cigars, while the valiant Red Army took on the Nazis single-handed and, despite terrible losses, smashed their way to Berlin and brought peace to the world.'

He would say it without stopping for breath. More than that, he would continue, Churchill had delayed opening the Second Front because he wanted the Soviet Union to bleed to death. And now Churchill, who, we were reminded, had tried to strangle the USSR at birth, was stoking up a Cold War. In this he was being aided and abetted by the Yanks, cowards who had been as late entering the Second World War, as they had been in joining in the first.

In my second year at the local grammar school I was beginning to get interested in history and learning about the Roman period. At home I had lessons in modern history, or at least, I had my father's and my uncle's versions of it.

The same 'facts' – different interpretations. But facts were never just facts to my uncle. They were always 'stone-bonker' ones. Thus he would say: 'Stalin won the war. It's a stone-bonker fact.' Or, 'All them Poles and that lot love the Red Army. That's why they are voting Communist. It's a stone-bonker fact.'

My father did his best to deal with the pro-Soviet propaganda. In those days it wasn't easy knocking 'Uncle Joe' (Stalin). The Russians were still held in tremendous popular affection. For years they could do no wrong. They had been our allies in the War, when we had stood shoulder to shoulder to defeat the Fascists. And my father had met Russian officers – he was with an American unit that reached the River Elbe in Germany and linked up with Red Army troops. There was a great deal of hugging, backslapping and smiling, and cigarettes were exchanged, and he saw straightaway that not all Russians stood twelve-feet tall in huge, black thigh boots and ate babies.

But in that March in a sombre speech in Fulton, Missouri, Churchill warned that from 'Stettin in the Baltic to Trieste in the Adriatic an Iron Curtain has descended across the Continent,' and that the growing Soviet menace was aimed at the whole free world. My father believed him, and he was right to.

My uncle said Churchill was starting a Cold War. It was the first time I had heard the expression; for the next forty years or so I was to hear it used frequently. And from that day on, there was an ongoing argument in our house between the two brothers over who had started the Cold War. The Russians who were gobbling up country after country in Eastern Europe? Or Churchill, aided and abetted by America's president, Harry Truman?

One day this row became so heated that the two brothers decided to settle it in the back garden, and with boxing gloves. I watched as they sparred and then thumped each other until my uncle's nose bled, and my father's face was flushed with blows. They called a halt only when my mother screamed at them that they would kill each other.

That fight was the beginning of a 'cold war' which lasted between the brothers for the rest of their lives. And I learned just how controversial Stalin and the Soviet Union were. But who was right? I was at that age when I was beginning to question some of my father's opinions such as Jews and Communists being 'behind' jazz, so as to 'indoctrinate' British youth. Or that Hitler was a genius – if pressed he would add the word 'evil' – and that Adolf would have beaten the Russians easily, but for greedy Father Winter. But what had happened to cause him to change his mind about Russians?

It was he who told me that the Battle of Stalingrad, one of the most terrifying conflicts ever known, and where half a million Soviet troops died, was the turning point of the War. For some 300,000 German troops and their allies were surrounded there, and Hitler's war machine never recovered.

I started reading about this man Stalin, the USSR and Communism. But the first book I got my hands on was *I Choose Freedom* by a Soviet defector, Viktor Kravchenko. At the time the book was a sensation, probably because it was the first to appear in the West after the War, saying the USSR was a hell on earth. This blistering indictment of the Soviet system sold hundreds of thousands of copies and generated a barrage of Soviet-instigated invective against Kravchenko, who later committed suicide. I read Arthur Koestler's *Darkness at Noon* a terrifying book about a man and the Stalin Purges. I tried to read Karl Marx's *Das Kapital*, and failed.

Does anyone, anywhere, read it now, I wonder?

I read an extraordinary book about a Soviet spy ring in Switzerland during the War run by an Englishman, Alexander Foote. Somebody told me to read George Orwell's *Animal Farm* – they said it was an allegory for the Soviet Union, but I only appreciated how good it was many years later.

And then in an Enfield cinema, I heard the Soviet National anthem. It was played as background music to a grainy black and white newsreel of a November parade on Red Square. Solid phalanxes of Red army soldiers goose-stepped across the square, followed by squadrons of T-34 tanks and artillery, and on the Lenin Mausoleum stood Stalin and his cohorts, taking the salute. A massed band crashed out the anthem and there was a salute from a battery of guns out of sight in the Kremlin. And there was a commentary about the Soviet Union continuing to maintain a huge army.

But it was the music that gripped my attention. This was a magnificent, stirring tune. By comparison, all other anthems I knew – including 'God Save the King' – were thin, poor and uninspiring.

Surely there must be something special about a country with such an anthem, I thought. With a tune like this, how could Stalin and Communism fail?

I bought the record. On the flip side was the song of the Soviet air force. The composer was Alexander Alexandrov who – though I didn't know it then – had just died. The choirmaster at a Moscow cathedral, he lost the job after Stalin dynamited it to the ground – Moscow's huge outdoor swimming pool was built on the site (and – ACC – has once again become a cathedral). So he founded the Red Army song and dance ensemble, and among his many patriotic compositions was a Cantata to Stalin.

Stalin ordered the anthem to be written and demanded an epic theme for an epic endeavour – to smash the German army and sweep on to victory. Sergei Mikhalkov was told to get on and write the words. Prokofiev and Shostakovich were also roped in by Stalin, but it was impossible for the three composers to work together. The Soviet Union's two greatest composers pretended they were ill, leaving Alexandrov to get on with it. With hindsight the words were fatuous. There were references to the 'Unbreakable Union of freeborn republics' and 'nowhere else on earth where one can breathe so freely' and 'to Communism's triumph lead us on'. Mikhalkov twice rewrote the words to accommodate the changing political landscape before dying in 2009, aged ninety-six. But was there ever such a tune as this to rally a great people?

I bought a book in the popular Teach Yourself series and began my struggle with the Russian language. Although I never got anywhere even remotely near mastering it, it did lead me into other fields of Russian literature, history and politics. And military intelligence.

My call-up papers arrived when I was eighteen, it was time to do my bit for King and Country. National Service, they called it, and every young man who was physically and mentally fit spent two years in the armed forces. I was ready, had read a lot about World War II,

1. Called up for National Service in 1951 John Miller learned Russian at the Joint Services School for Linguists at Bodmin, Cornwall. His group included Clive Bull, John Clease, Martin Carter and the Ukranian tutor, Dani Bondarenko.

and heard more from my father. By now I knew very clearly who was the enemy – the Red Army – and because I saw myself taking on the Tartar hordes in the front-line in Germany, I got myself assigned to the Royal Armoured Corps.

There were six weeks of square bashing – drill, PT, polishing boots and buttons, until you could see yourself in them, and physical discomfort aimed at ironing out independence or self-assertion, followed by a month learning how to drive a Centurion tank and handle its radio.

We were destined for Korea, where there had been the first direct post-war confrontation between Communists and the West. In June 1950 North Korea, backed by the Russians and the Chinese, invaded South Korea. A United Nations force turned a successful Communist invasion into a massive defeat. Ceasefire talks began in July 1951, but there was still sporadic fighting and British tank units were sent there to beef up the Commonwealth contingent.

I never got to Korea. But with that war the world had come nearer to total conflict than at any time since Potsdam. Stalin was at his most expansionist. There were fears he might have decided to break through in Germany and start World War III. And suddenly Britain's defence chiefs grasped that if war came, hundreds of Russian-speaking soldiers would be needed – for interpreting, for translating, and for a wide range of intelligence duties. Crash courses in the Russian language were created overnight. Any National Servicemen who had learned French or German at school were pulled out of their units and sent to the newly-created camps to be taught Russian by the few dozen émigrés, defectors and others who knew it as their first language.

For a year we learned Russian. If we were gifted and natural linguists, we were sent to Cambridge University to become interpreters. If not, we were reassigned to the Intelligence Corps. One day I knocked at the door of the War Office in Whitehall to take up a post as a Russian language clerk in MI10, the intelligence branch dealing with Soviet military equipment.

Now I began to read Soviet newspapers, especially *Krasnaya Zvezda*, and a great deal of much more fascinating material about 'the enemy'. In those times thousands of German POW's were being

2. From Bodmin in 1952 John Miller went to Maresfield, the Intelligence Corps Depot in Sussex, where the intake was prepared for intelligence duties. Miller is in the centre of the front row.

freed from Soviet camps. On their return to West Germany they were interviewed by intelligence officers and told stories of their years in Russia. The reports of these interviews were sent to the War Office to be 'tasted' for any intelligence on military subjects. But to me, their chief interest lay in the wealth of material about life in the Soviet Union. They spoke not just about the labour camps they were held in, but also about the towns and villages around them, not only about their guards but also about the Russian women they met and with whom they had a 'quickie' in cookhouse cupboards.

When these intelligence reports began drying up, a package appeared in my in-tray and I found a new source of information about Stalin's Russia. The package comprised dozens of letters written on paper of different sizes. Grey, brown and stained, from all over the Soviet Union, they were written largely by mothers and girl friends to Red Army soldiers serving in Germany.

But they were not just about family matters, about deaths and births and weddings; they also told in very general terms of conditions in towns and villages, of the state of the crops, the production of a factory, shortages and of personalities, like the local mayor or Communist Party boss.

Some of these hand-written letters were hard to read. And for an unusual reason. Forty years ago or more, toilet paper was in short supply for the front-line troops of the Red Army – in this particular case, a huge tank base in East Germany. In its place Ivan Ivanovitch wiped his backside with newspaper, or any other kind of paper, and that included pages torn out of his training manuals and exercise books, or his letters from home.

This bum paper found its way to a sewage farm, and British Military Intelligence had decided that it should, and could, be recycled. A night-shift worker at the sewage farm was bribed to do the job. From his sewage pits he removed every bit of a paper he could get his hands on. He put the paper in sacks and left them at a certain place. They were collected and delivered to British Intelligence officers in West Berlin. The paper was washed and baked and sent to the War Office for the attention of Private Miller 22588340. My job was to read the letters, or pages torn from tank manuals, for intelligence. And with the aid of a razor blade and a scalpel (to remove portions of baked shit obscuring a word or a sentence) and a fine brush and magnifying glass, I worked out my time in the army. I never read anything of military value, but some of the 'Dear Ivan' letters from home about the new man in a young girl's life, or sister Olga becoming pregnant by a drunken good-for-nothing tractor driver, could be heart-rending.

Predictably, the sewage worker responsible for salvaging the letters fell in it himself, so to speak. East German police were tipped off that he was fishing things out of the sewage. He was arrested, interrogated, charged with treason and shot.

One March morning in 1953, as I emerged from a former underground station off Tottenham Court Road, which had been taken over by the army and where I collected my pay, I heard a newspaper seller shouting: 'Stalin dead! Read all about it.'

The unthinkable had happened. The man who for a quarter of a century had been unquestioned master of life and death over every citizen of the USSR, who had wielded greater power than anyone else in history, was dead. Dead. Stalin, all-mighty, all-seeing, indestructible, was dead. He who started the Cold War, and was thus responsible for my being in the army, was dead. I was convinced the world was going to change. And it did… and so fast it made your head spin. To start with, Stalin's name disappeared. Before 5 March, 1953, it would appear in the front page of *Pravda* perhaps 200 times. By the end of the month, it was seen once or twice a week, and then as one half of the adjective 'Leninist-Stalinist.'

The newspapers I was getting at the War Office – I still have those reporting Stalin's death and funeral – showed pictures of Russians weeping openly, as did those British intellectuals and academics who had been unwilling or unable to face the truth about the Soviet Union, who had been ready to give it the benefit of the doubt, ready always with an apologetic explanation for anything that Stalin did.

But millions in and out of the GULAG were hoping for a miracle, and it happened. 'Old Cockroach Whiskers', as they called him in the labour camps, had croaked. I cheered with them because it meant that before long I would be seeing Russia. Four years later the opportunity presented itself, when Nikita Khrushchev opened the Kremlin that Stalin had closed and staged the Greatest Propaganda Show on Earth, the World Youth Festival.

We got there for next to nothing; Communists, Socialists, university students, Scots wearing kilts, Little Woodcraft Folk, Young Conservatives. The train, endlessly playing *Kalinka, Kalinka, Kalinka, my dear*, took us through Ukraine where at every station we were met by young people throwing flowers and shouting '*Mir*' and '*Drouzhba*' – 'Peace' and 'Friendship'. For three weeks we forgot about sleep. There were exhibitions, mass celebrations, excursions, concerts, seminars, parties and shows. The Kremlin was the stage for a carnival and beneath the window where Stalin had his office a platform was set up for British ballroom dancers to perform, along with Egyptian belly dancers, Chinese singers, Turkmenistani jugglers. Stalin wouldn't have liked it at all. For around the cobblestone courts and rambling lawns ran, at times somewhat drunkenly, the youth of the world. A great deal of sexual intercourse between Soviet citizens and foreigners took place on the grass and in the bushes of the Alexander Gardens. Later girls suspected of being 'too friendly' were rounded up, had their heads shaved and were sent to the Virgin Lands project in far-off Kazakhstan. Girls who gave birth to coloured babies were also disgraced. A newspaper claimed that the Festival had introduced venereal disease to the Soviet Union!

More than anything else, however, the World Youth Festival gave me an opportunity to talk to Russians. On Red Square you were surrounded by hundreds, not just dozens, of people who would fire questions at you. Had my government tried to stop me visiting the USSR? How much did my suit, shoes, shirt, cost? Why did Britain invade Egypt? Did I prefer Moscow to London? Did it always rain in England? One such session lasted nearly two hours. And of course among the crowd were men and women who had only recently been freed from labour camps. We were the first foreigners many had ever seen, let alone talked to, and they were both shy and frightened.

Other Russians weren't. A young man speaking fair English stopped me in the street outside the hotel and introduced himself. 'My name's Tolya Yuglov,' he said. 'I am a reporter for Moscow Radio.' Indeed he was, he was sweating profusely from lugging around a large box strapped around his neck. It was a Soviet tape recorder.

'Now,' he said, shoving a large black microphone in my face, 'we are going to do an interview. You will tell our listeners how happy and

28

3.   The World Youth Festival, a Soviet Communist jamboree,
opened in Moscow in August 1957. Miller was there having
met two Russian stewards on the train from Prague who
brought him innumerable glasses of tea.

glad you are to be in the Soviet Union, about the wonderful people you have met and about how impressed you are with Soviet achievements.'

I was street-wise even in those days and asked: 'One, who is this for? And two, how much are you paying for the interview?'

He looked genuinely hurt. 'Dzhon, Dzhon,' said Tolya. 'I do not know, but I think that if it is a good interview it will be used both for Soviet listeners and for those millions around the world.' He winced. 'As for money... alas we haven't much at Moscow Radio. We may pay or we may not. It depends on whether we use the piece.'

'Tolya,' I said. 'I don't think you will. Because I have bad news for you. You don't want a piece from me. I might say bad things about your country.'

'Don't worry, Dzhon,' he said, 'we can take criticism in our country. On Moscow Radio we often use criticisms of our reality.'

'You joke,' I said. 'Now bugger off! Get your propaganda from someone else. There are thousands of Britons here who would give you a super interview.' And off he went.

The next morning he was outside the hotel waiting for me. We went through the whole performance again. 'All right,' he said, 'then let's be friends and I will come around Moscow with you and perhaps do my own story.'

And that was what he did, which worried me, because he was *always* around when I was talking to anybody. Four years later, shortly after I arrived in Moscow for Reuters, he telephoned me. He never said where he got my number from, but he was still with Moscow Radio although not writing for them. He came to see me in my flat – which was a daring thing to do – and we had a few drinks. Had he become my KGB 'minder', I wondered.

Suddenly Tolya went over to the gramophone, turned it up loudly and then came close to me and said: 'Did you know, Dzhon, that we have nuclear submarines?'

Now that was provocative and I told him straightaway that I couldn't care less. Tolya shrugged. 'Well,' he said, 'I must be going now. Any chance of me taking with me some good English gin.' And he went over to the drinks cabinet, took a bottle and put it in his overcoat pocket.

✧❀✧

Before I left for the World Youth Festival, I had been called to the War Office for a talk. I had signed the Official Secrets Act and had to tell my former bosses I was going to the USSR. A colonel said: 'Normally we don't think much to such trips, but in your case we are not going to tell you to keep away. Whatever we say, you are going to go there, aren't you?'

'That's right,' I said.

'Anyway,' said the colonel. 'It just so happens you might be able to be of some use.'

'How's that?'

I'd already got an inkling.

'The T-54 tank,' he said. 'It has replaced the T-34. Much better. Faster, and the bastards pinched some of our technology from one of our tank parks in Germany. So it's a good tank and we need to know a lot more about it.'

'What is this to do with me?' I asked.

'We are rather hoping you might see one somewhere on your trip.'

I was curious.

'And if I do?'

'Well,' he said, absolutely straight-faced. 'It would be terribly useful if you could give us some idea of the thickness of the armour. It will help us with the research and development of the armour-piercing shell.'

Even more intrigued, I asked: 'And how do I go about this extraordinary exercise in intelligence gathering?'

His answer was not what I expected. Having spotted a T-54, preferably, of course, unmanned and unguarded, I was to climb onto the front of it. Then I was to stick a pencil through the tank's front window, or where the gun pops out, and, using it as ruler, mark the pencil at the point where it cannot be pushed further.

31

That had to be worth a medal.

I saw plenty of Russians at the World Youth Festival. I saw that there was little freedom of any kind, that the economic problems of capitalism and the sufferings they caused were mild when compared with the poverty of Russia, and that far from being peace-loving, the Soviet Union was maintaining its armies at wartime strength. But I didn't see a single T-54.

⁂

When I turned down a chance to join the *Daily Express* in favour of working for Reuters, I was ready for Russia. In those days the international news agency had 250 staff correspondents, it paid rotten wages, and there were no bylines and little glory. But it was a synonym for speed, accuracy and impartiality, and that was what I had to learn. I started to do that on Central Desk, where stories filed by the dashing, even distinguished, correspondents in the field were subbed and fed to teleprinters across the world. There were other desks and later I worked on some of them, but Central Desk was the nerve centre of a highly organized, nerve-jangling confusion.

But the very first day I had a shock. I was given a seat and told to read the file of news processed that day. I got talking to the man seated next to me. He introduced himself; he was Don Dallas, the first full-time correspondent in Moscow after the War who had been withdrawn partly in exasperation and partly for reasons of economy. Dallas had written a riveting book about the Soviet Union which influenced me greatly and fired my enthusiasm to work in Moscow. Now he was sitting on Central Desk subbing stories like the newest recruit.

It transpired he was being cut down to size, a Reuters routine, favoured by executives who couldn't touch him as a correspondent. But there were some characters who took the big decisions in what was the world's oldest and busiest news factory.

Sid Mason, the chief news editor, was one. He had been a docker and he wore braces and a thick leather belt to remind you of it. He talked tough but he was straight, and he cared. One day he called me over. There was no chair so he told to sit on the waste-paper basket.

'Do you want to go to Moscow, Cock?' he asked.

32

'You bet,' I said.

'There's a good chance then,' he said. 'Keep it under your hat. I'll let you know very soon. Now bugger off!'

I was nearly there. But not quite. A month later I heard that someone else was going to Moscow. It was Gerry Ratzin, now a good friend, but on the day I heard he had got the job I had set my heart on, I did not wish him well.

But fate (for better or for worse) played a hand. For reasons still obscure, the Russians would not renew his temporary visa. He stayed only six months and returned to London, later to make his name in the even nastier situation in the Congo.

'All right, Cock,' said Sidney Mason. 'You were disappointed last time. But this time the job's yours. It's a big one. And because I like you, I'm going to give you some advice about how to handle it.'

'Yes, Mr Mason,' I said, leaning forward so as not to miss a single word.

'Keep well away from Soviet pussy. Don't touch it. It's trouble'. And that was all he said.

Not a word about writing quick, hard prose, being accurate – or dying.

3 - Floppy and Co.

In place of serious political information, there were always animal stories to be written, and the Soviet Union could produce some humdingers. Take one of the first I wrote for Reuters.

In a one-room communal flat in Moscow lived a couple, their two children and a mother-in-law. Which would have meant it was crowded enough. But the man also kept several dozen parrots housed in cages in the flat and on the balcony. Like parrots everywhere, they made a noise, and had even been taught their names and a few phrases, such as 'Good morning' and 'Shut up!'. They insisted on showing off their knowledge by squawking at all hours of the day and night. And of course, parrots crap too.

The family's neighbours in the flat neither liked the noise nor the smell of the parrots and their droppings. They complained to a newspaper which carried a major article – it, too, was apparently short of hard news – and called for the parrot-owner to be arrested. For why? Not because keeping parrots in a flat was antisocial, but because the man was breeding the parrots and selling them. He was a capitalist, making money, profiteering, etc. So off with his head!

Given Soviet life at the time, it was a believable story. But how about this one spotted by Stanley Johnson, an American colleague who worked for Associated Press, and a very bright writer. Johnson and his wife lived in the Metropol Hotel where they consumed vast amounts of alcohol because they were missing the tobacco plantations they owned back in Alabama.

Many a time Mrs Johnson told me that she was always kind to her slaves and, however poor they may have appeared, everyone had a 'goddam icebox in the shack', which is more than could be said for millions of Russians living under Communism.

Their greatest moment in Moscow came when they took delivery of the biggest and most expensive Cadillac ever seen in the Soviet Union – including the car used by the American Ambassador – and they parked it outside the hotel. The vehicle drew enormous crowds who stood around it, gawping, and when Stanley and Josephine staggered down to the car to drive away, it would be like the arrival of two stars at a Hollywood film première. Police had to protect the car from drunks and souvenir hunters – in those days, metal parts on Western cars were often removed, sometimes, it would appear, ripped off by vandals using steel wire and a lorry.

Stanley's other claim to fame during his Moscow stint was when he found a story on the back page of the *Literaturaya Gazeta* (*Literary Gazette*), and decided to give it the full treatment. A Muscovite who worked at the circus and was involved with elephants had taken a baby elephant home to care for and train as a pet. The man lived on the sixth floor of a new prefabricated block – familiarly known as 'Khrushchev boxes'. Weeks passed and a jumbo-sized problem came along: the elephant grew rapidly and suddenly it was physically unable to get through the door.

Moscow City Council became involved. A giant crane was put up near the block and the elephant was brought out in a harness through the window, safely lowered to the ground and returned to the circus.

Stanley's story was used widely throughout the United States and elsewhere, and it was indeed a good story. But newspapers wanted more, such as a photograph of the elephant with its owner. When Stanley chased up the story with the newspaper they pointed out it was on their humour page, and, of course, it was an invention. Stanley kept his cool. He acted decisively and dispatched the AP photographer to Moscow circus, under instructions to take a picture of the smallest elephant they had. Wired to New York, it won widespread interest and there were more 'hero-grams' for Stanley.

I, too, became involved with a Soviet elephant some ten years later. This was the famous Batyr, then aged thirteen, and the star of the Karaganda Zoo in the southern republic of Kazakhstan. Batyr could talk. It did not know many words, but it could pronounce its own name and used phrases such as 'Batyr is beautiful', and 'Give me'. He spoke by putting his trunk in his mouth and sounding off with a deep male voice. A trick he had picked up when he found that his keeper and visitors threw him buns after shouting his name and praising him.

It was impossible to ignore the potential of a talking elephant. But the *Daily Telegraph* was unenthusiastic about me flying down to Kazakhstan – Karaganda, formerly the centre of a huge GULAG, was closed to westerners – to interview Batyr, since it did not take the story seriously. So I telephoned the director of the zoo and asked him if they was any way he could get Batyr into his office and put him on the line. He couldn't, but I have to report that while we were talking, there was some kind of a trumpeting sound in the background, which the director said was Batyr. Who was I to argue?

Many years later the Karaganda Zoo was in the news again. Batyr was still alive and the news report referred to his famous imitation of human speech. But it was a sad story. The food shortages of the perestroika era were posing real problems for zoos. Karaganda's monkeys were starving and living on carrots. There was no meat for the lions and tigers, who were being fed pigeons instead.

Batyr was also going hungry and so the zoo had begun killing off its wild boars one after the other, looking around for other animals suitable for fodder. Batyr survived, but in a remarkably slimmed-down zoo.

Sadder was the fate of Masha, another elephant of the Volgograd zoo. Faced with empty shelves and hungry families, her keepers started stealing her food, leaving her with far less than the 350 lb a-day she needed to stay healthy. When it was noted she was looking thin, a desperate rescue effort was made to stuff her with fresh vegetables and a home brew of vodka, red wine and sugar. Too late. She died of malnutrition aged thirty-two, half the elephant's average life-span. The story lent itself to a cartoon of an elephant looking at a sign saying, 'Your dinner is in the keeper'.

Another talking-animal story the *Daily Telegraph* declined to use involved a pet raven living near Minsk, who used to go fishing with its owner. It hopped from catch to catch cawing in Russian 'r-r-oach' and 'p-p-erch'. The first time he saw a pike he commented 't-t-terrible.' More, he would steal items from other fishermen such as buttons, knives and cigarette lighters and when being made by his owner to give them back would ask: 'Who-o-o are y-you?'

Even serious Soviet media outlets were responsible for barely credible non-political stories. Moscow Radio once announced that a dog swimming across a river in Siberia had been swallowed by a giant pike some six feet in length. The pike was subsequently hooked by a fisherman who, on forcing open its jaws, came across the dog's tail. He pulled the dog out and it ran off barking.

My first reaction to that was, 'Pull the other one Mikhail Gorbachev, its got Kremlin bells on it!' I was somewhat surprised Moscow Radio had not insisted the dog's name was Jonah. Fishermen do tell tall stories, but this was a skyscraper of one.

Pikes, of course, are greedy and can grow to a considerable length; they are known to have seized rats and ducklings. But this dog was not a chihuahua. Nor, if the story is true, does it appear to have put up much of a fight. As the dog was unhurt and unmarked, could the pike have left its false teeth in a glass on the bedside table that very morning?

The story failed on several accounts. We should have been told the size of the dog and its breed. As for the pike, exactly how wide could its jaws stretch? What size hook did the fisherman use? Did he boil or grill the pike for supper or have him stuffed? Perhaps it was, in fact, an alligator? We should also have been told about what they drink at Moscow Radio and if they export it.

Moscow Radio could do well to recall the story about the Duke of Wellington and the time a leaf was found in a bottle opened in the mess for dinner. They went round the table recounting similar discoveries – beetle, twig, mouse – until the Duke topped the lot by claiming he had found a rat in a wine bottle.

Impulsively, a young subaltern said: 'Well, it must have been a very small rat.' Which prompted the Duke to retort: 'It was a damned large rat.' Anxious to put things right, the officer stammered: 'W-w-ell then, I suppose it was a very large bottle.' To which the Duke, glaring ferociously at the wretched man, shouted: 'It was a damned small bottle.'

Over the years the only animals I became closely acquainted with – apart from rodents and insects – were cats and a rabbit by the name of Floppy, naturally on account of its ears. Floppy lived in the *Daily Telegraph*'s ground floor flat in Sadovo-Samotechnaya, a ghetto for Westerners, and it belonged to Nigel Wade, the newspaper's Moscow correspondent, and his wife Christine. It is not, of course, unusual to have a rabbit as a pet. My daughter kept one in the garden of our house in Dulwich for years. But it is rare to have a rabbit living with you in a flat in the capital of the Soviet Union. Apart from anything else, it lent itself to jokes, such as the possibility that Floppy was working for the KGB whose code-name for their agent was Bugs Bunny.

Floppy was certainly a conversation stopper. Visitors to the flat took little notice when one of the cats strolled into the living room or slept on the sofa. But when Floppy hopped in, guests unaware of his existence were gobsmacked. 'Bloody hell! That's a rabbit, isn't it?' was one reaction.

Many was the time I wanted to reverse James Stewart's 'Harvey' role and say: 'Rabbit? What rabbit? I see no rabbit.' And to suggest it was the guest who was seeing things, perhaps having drunk too much or been working too hard. A consummate actor could have pulled it off.

Floppy was entertaining in his own right. He would hop around the room, disappear under the sofa, pop out again and hop off. What a lovely little character he was. He crapped with the cats in a litter box kept in a small store cupboard, and he ate grass and nettles brought once a week from the country by Marsha, the Russian maid, who was very fond of him. She would cover the kitchen floor with his food and ignored my complaints that I was not up to eating breakfast in the morning in a kitchen ankle deep in grass being munched by a hungry rabbit.

I never made much of a fuss of him when standing in for Nigel Wade during his holidays. There were reasons. Such as the day I found a handful of rabbit droppings on the telex machine installed in the flat for sending stories to London. I bollocked him for that, suspecting he was trying to tell me what he thought about my copy, but of course you cannot punish a naughty rabbit by smacking him.

A week later a strange thing happened. The telex went dead and as I feared an electrical fault, I summoned the Russian mechanic who serviced the machine on a regular basis. Meanwhile, I told the *Daily Telegraph* of the fault and suggested we communicate by telephone until further notice. The mechanic took the machine to pieces but couldn't discover why it wasn't working.

He then spent time carefully tracing the course of the wiring. He found a break; the wire had been bitten clean through. Floppy's work. The first telexed message to London for several days read:

'Pro-Eastwood Ex-Miller telex restored after being sabotaged by rabbit'. They were on the telephone from London very quickly: 'Got your telex, old boy. Are you all right? What's all this about a rabbit? You haven't been hitting the old vodka, have you?' They didn't know about Floppy and the problems of living in Moscow. Again I reprimanded him, but I always felt he wasn't taking it on board. After all, he was Chinese – the Wade's bought him in a Peking market when he was destined for the pot.

He had a pretty good life for a few years – at least he never got myxomatosis before he died in his sleep, just before Christmas. There was a shortage of meat in Moscow at the time but I am assured his death at that festive time had nothing to do with it.

Floppy was one thing. Tackling the bedbugs, cockroaches and mice that make their appearance in Moscow flats was another. The bedbugs were around in our first flat in Prospekt Mira and I wasn't surprised by their arrival, since Russia had always had bedbugs. We only had a few, but it was a nasty experience to wake up one night and to know that something was feasting on your body. I got out of bed and went into the bathroom, put on the light and took off my pyjama jacket. I shook it violently over the bath and a couple of bedbugs fell out. Back in the bedroom, two or three others, bloated with my blood, were scuttling up the wall.

Living below us in a basement flat was the Ghanaian Ambassador to Moscow, John Banks Elliot, his wife and seven children ranging from a few months old to eleven. The family had been living in a few rooms for several months. The delay in finding them an embassy or at least some decent accommodation was a mystery , since Kwame Nkrumah, the Ghanaian leader, was at that time the Soviet Union's best friend in Africa.

But here he was, living in some squalor. The flat adjoined the area where the rubbish mounted as it came down a chute from other flats – the breeding ground of the bedbug, cockroach and other vermin. I always suspected it was done deliberately because Russians are outrageously racist, and they might have thought this was the way he had lived in Ghana and was therefore happy.

The ambassador publicly had nothing but praise for the Soviet Union as a 'a bastion of anti-colonialism' and a 'generous friend of

4.   A view from the living room in the first foreigners-only ghetto
      in Prospekt Mira where the Millers lived. They later moved
      to Sadova-Samotechnaya ulitza, shortened to 'Sad Sam' by
      generations of Moscow expats, and built by German prisoners
      of war.

Africa' – neither of which was true. But he did tell me several times that the Russians were uncultured, incompetent and not to be trusted. In the end he got his embassy, but within a few months Nkrumah was toppled in a *coup*. He was ordered home and thrown into prison, which must have been a lot more uncomfortable than anything he'd experienced in Moscow.

I am not blaming John Banks Elliot and his family for the bedbugs that came up from his flat and into our bedroom. I never told him about them and we dealt with the problem in the time-hallowed fashion of standing the legs of the bed in small tins of paraffin and keeping the bed away from the wall. So when the bedbug smelt your blood he would try and climb up the bed's legs, fall into the paraffin and drown.

We never saw a bedbug after we moved to Sadovo-Samotechnaya. But this block of flats for foreigners was cockroach country. Again, their appearance did not surprise me – long before I went to Moscow I had heard that *tarakany* (cockroaches) were part of the Moscow scene, a hazard on a par with being arrested for taking photographs of railway stations, anonymous telephone calls and having one's windscreen wipers stolen.

Never having seen one in Enfield, I had the bizarre idea they were indestructible, plated in black armour and, if let loose in a larder, had the appetite of piranha fish. In the event they were no more than about three-quarters of an inch long, brown and shiny, like acorns. As they scurried here and there, the long whiskers protruding from their heads waved frantically when light was suddenly thrown upon them. If threatened, they scuttled away as fast as their many little legs could carry them.

Frequently they would pop up in the kitchen and if spotted run for cover under the washing machine and the cooker or scuttle off into the bathroom. Once I saw a few lurking with their tiny offspring under my office typewriter. They must have been millions in Sadovo-Samotechnaya and how I would have liked a kopek for every one I crunched under foot.

Their numbers certainly embarrassed those Russians who worked for us, and Masha told me that there never used to be cockroaches in Russia until they were brought into the country by Indians. Russian homes rarely had cockroaches, said she. They existed in the flats of Westerners because of all the uneaten food left about in kitchens and thrown down the waste shoot. She had a point.

They seemed immune to being wiped out. There were several remedies, such as soaking balls of cotton wool in a solution of boracic powder, using a bait that looked like white putty, and foul-smelling oils. UPDK, the organization looking after foreigners, would send round a fumigator. But if you had cats, you wouldn't dare try out any of the repellents they put down, however much assured that both you and your pets were safe.

Nowadays, the Japanese have a way of luring cockroaches to their deaths with little boxes containing a sweet, sticky substance, which they cannot resist. The Americans have the state-of-the-art technology in the war against them – small triangular trays, called roach motels. Apparently they check in, but they don't check out.

Given that the cockroach is nature's supreme survivor – it dates back 300 million years and can sire some 400,000 family members in a year, I doubt that it will ever be beaten. Campaigns and crackdowns appeared successful because these invincible insects would disappear for a while, having sought sanctuary in a neighbouring flat. When the coast was clear, they would be back and in greater numbers.

Once the gigantic Cosmos Hotel, which at the time contained more than a third of all beds for foreign tourists in the city, was suddenly closed down for 'sanitary reasons'. There was a plague of *tarakany*, and the Moscow press referred to a new breed of cockroach, four or five times larger than normal, which had somehow reached Russia from the United States. This cockroach was said to be as big as a man's fist, able to munch its way through doors and furniture and, if touched, hissed like a snake.

The report caused some panic until experts said that although the *tarakany* were voracious, they were nowhere near as fearsome as was made out. Muscovites were warned to keep their flats clean and tidy because that was what the *tarakany* hated the most.

Probably the most important news about cockroaches is that cockroach racing, an old, pre-revolutionary pastime, has returned to Russia with the collapse of Communism.

Mice were always treated differently. I used to chase them with a black Finnish ski boot, but you were encouraged to call UPDK who would send round a Mouse Lady for a few roubles. She would seal up any cracks or holes in the floor with cement and newspaper – not *Pravda* I noted – but it never worked. The mice came along the pipeways and through the badly-built walls somewhere else. Traps did better, but we rarely caught any mice.

I wrote about the problem for the *Daily Telegraph*'s 'Women's Page' and was astonished by the response. Whereas, day after day, stories and articles about Soviet politics, personalities and developments would not produce so much as a squeak of response, I got a post-bag of a dozen letters about the mice of Moscow, including several from readers, saying what lovely, lively intelligent little creatures they were.

One lady writing from south London told me of how she would sit in her living room and call to the mice to come and eat. They would appear from out of the floorboards, run up her legs and sit on her lap to be stroked and fed. Her daughter had been affected by her mice-worship and had become a well-known illustrator of mice for children's books. She enclosed some drawings and indeed the mice looked quite endearing, which is more than I can say for their Soviet brothers, as they popped in and out of the gas cooker in our kitchen in Sadovo-Samotechnaya, effectively putting two fingers up to us.

4 – The Flight That Never Was

Moscow had its rats too. And some of them were forever pretending to be mice. With one exception, they are now dead: the traitors, defectors, Soviet dupes and Communist sympathizers I knew, and sometimes harried, over the years in Moscow for the sake of 'The Story'. Almost without exception they croaked miserably in some rundown Soviet hospital without benefit of families and friends at their bedside. As they joined the Great Party Congress in the skies did they think of England? When the end came did they regret having embarked on a career of spying and treachery, which ultimately meant they had to do a bunk?

When I arrived in Moscow in the winter of 1960, there were several 'grey men' one could meet, but the two really interesting and newsworthy traitors were Guy Burgess and Donald Maclean, both late of Her Majesty's Foreign Office, and they did their best to keep well out of sight from nosey, sensation-seeking journalists.

Inexorably twinned in the public mind as Marks and Spencer or Fortnum & Mason, the duo had boarded the Southampton-St Malo steamer *Falaise* at midnight on 25 May 1951, and disappeared just when MI5 were about to close in. They had emerged briefly in 1956 for Soviet propaganda purposes, then effectively gone to ground, although it was known they were living in Moscow and from time to time were visited by trustworthy comrades who approved of their betrayal of British interests in the greater cause of Stalinism and the glorious Soviet Union.

One gloomy March day, I was about to hand over two kopeks for a newspaper at a booth on Prospekt Mira where we lived, when my eye fell on a stack of large books. I looked at the top one out of curiosity and could hardly believe my eyes. It was a phone book, listing personal telephone numbers. So what?

You should know, Dear Reader, that this was a collector's item. It was the first telephone directory published in the Soviet Union, certainly since the end of World War II. There were probably about four million private telephone subscribers in the capital, but no directories, not even in telephone booths or post offices. Russians jotted down handy numbers in notebooks.

I bought three copies of each of the two heavy volumes and bore them triumphantly back to the Reuters office. Here was a feature which would put an end to the conventional wisdom that the Soviet Union was so backward or uncaring about consumer demand, that it was not prepared to publish a decent telephone directory. It was also interesting reading – counting the number of Khrushchevs, Molotovs, Mikoyans and others who had names similar to those in the Soviet establishment. There were, of course, no Stalins because none would have dared use it for all sorts of reasons – not least the fear of the '3 o'clock knock' and, after 1953, obscene telephone calls. For the same reason neither were there Lenins or Trotskys. But there were tens of thousands of Ivanovs, the Smiths of Russia, and a great many Stroginovs and Loginovs (there is a faintly rude Russian joke about an organ being Stronginough and Longinough).

I looked up the Millers and found there were quite a few of them, probably because of the strong Scottish links that exist with Russia. Thinking of the Scottish connection, I looked to see if there were any Frazers. There was one... and that was when the hairs on my neck rose because I was on to a 'Good Story'.

It was that simple. It was common knowledge that Donald Maclean had a Russian name – Mark Petrovich Frazer. And the entry was Frazer M.P., living at Bolshoi Dorogomilovskaya 4, Moscow. There was neither a block nor a flat number, but there was the telephone number 234-05-48. Wow! Got the bastard! And he's mine, all mine. With hands trembling ever so slightly I dialled the number...

Over the years the story of the treachery and defection of Maclean and Burgess has been well documented. From time to time the wretched tale has been given an added whirl or two by such equally dramatic events as the defection to Moscow of Kim 'the Third Man' Philby, and later the unmasking of Anthony 'the Fourth Man' Blunt.

Yes, it *is* old history now. Who cares that a couple of duplicitous, homosexual and often drunken diplomats took up with Uncle Joe and flogged a few secrets to his police force? In the end, they got it badly wrong, didn't they? Indeed they did, but at the time it was a hell of a 'Story', part and parcel of the Cold War, material for a thousand thrillers. And I suppose lifting the stone on Donald Maclean was my first Moscow scoop.

Mimsie, his six-year-old daughter – who eventually broke with her old Dad and the USSR by marrying a French doctor and clearing out – clinched it by nervously denying the name Frazer and putting down the telephone. Poor little thing, she couldn't have understood what it was all about; why the family was always on the run; why papa was so strange.

It was enough. I had him. But I left it for a week, telling nobody, thinking about the approach. 'Donald Duart Maclean, I presume' was not bad. Better, perhaps, was: 'Good evening, Comrade. I wonder if I could have a word with you?' Should I do a Fleet Street and put my foot firmly in the door? More, should I say who I was – after all, he might report me to the Ministry of Foreign Affairs, and have me expelled for intrusion.

But I hesitate to ring his doorbell – some hard work needs to be done. All I have is the name of the street and the *Dom* (literally house or the whole block of flats) – the number of the whole complex. I do not know which *korpus* (or block) he lives in or the number of his flat. Travelling anywhere in Moscow is a matter of navigating by numbers. Thus, you take the 43 bus for 5 stops for Building 60, Block 4, Entrance 7, Floor 15, Flat 61. In fact, it turns out there are five blocks, each with several entrances and, fortunately, each with a *dvornik*, or concierge, sitting by the lift, knitting, dozing or watching all who come and go. To each in turn I ask, authoritatively: 'And where does the tall English comrade live?' Three *dvorniks* shake their heads and carry on knitting. The fourth says 'Flat 88.'

Getting warmer. Into the lift… get out at what I think is the right floor… find I am wrong… and walk down to the sixth… up to the door, glancing at the blue post box – which is empty – and a firm ring of the doorbell. It has to be Mimsie who opens it – big eyes on a very small girl.

Cranking up a crafty smile I ask, in English: 'Is Mr Maclean at home?'

Mimsie looks just a little scared. 'Papa,' she shouts, and the traitor and spy, runaway diplomat, father of three, looms over her shoulder. Perhaps, not unsuprisingly, he scowls at me. He is not minded to invite me in, steps out into the corridor, pulling the door almost closed behind him.

'What do you want,' he asks. He is wearing tartan carpet slippers and is still recognizable as every inch the British diplomat. I offer him a hand because that is how gentlemen should behave. He gives me a limp handshake and when I tell him who I am, he runs a tongue over his lips.

He trots out the old Foreign Office line as though he is still in the business. 'I've no comment to make. Nothing to say. Absolutely nothing. I have nothing against you personally – you are doing your job. But I have decided not to give interviews.'

I hear myself saying I fully understand. But the conversation has to keep flowing so I ask him if he is settling in all right, which is not very clever given that he has been living in the Soviet Union for ten years. He may have thought it to be sarcasm, because he replies: 'Yes, very nicely, thank you.'

Did he know what is going on in the world? Is he getting British newspapers? 'Just *The Times*,' he says, and for a moment I think the man is going to open up, having decided I am not like all the other rascals.

Instead, he says, absolutely deadpan: 'We have made our lives here now and we would prefer not to have any kind of intrusion. I may say that I have been following in *The Times* the progress of the bill in the Lords to haul reporters into court if they pester people.'

It is an obvious threat. Nonetheless, I ask him what work he is doing – rumour has it that he writes briefs on British foreign policy for the Soviet Ministry of Foreign Affairs with copies, no doubt, to the KGB. He confirms the bit about writing articles on foreign policy, but nothing more. Then he says goodbye, and – just then – there is nothing more to say.

So Maclean was found, and more than two decades later, shortly before he died, he talked at length with Mark Frankland, the outstanding and perceptive *Observer* journalist, referring to the time I had called on him. He said it was instrumental in his decision to drop the pseudonym of 'Frazer' and get his own name back. It was not easy and it involved a long legal process, because it signified that he wanted to live a much more normal life and the authorities – particularly the KGB – were not happy. But Maclean claimed that he never regretted it because it meant that his children too could keep their real names.

Maclean wanted to live openly in the Soviet Union but he most certainly did not want to be bothered by journalists. By and large, he wasn't. I only called on him if there was a news peg to hang on what he said. A year later there was one, and it remains a curious event to this day.

In April 1962, a warrant was taken out in a closed court at Bow Street for the arrest of Burgess and Maclean. Predictably it caused excitement boarding on hysteria in Fleet Street, as editors smacked their lips in anticipation of a good espionage serial. Rumours flew thick and fast and it soon became a 'fact' that the two were not only returning to Britain to face trial, but that they had already left Moscow, reached Amsterdam and were going to be on a KLM flight to London. Men and resources were thrown at the story like there was no tomorrow. ITN, for example, had 120 people working on it and were planning, for the first time in British television history, to interrupt broadcasts with live inserts from Amsterdam and Heathrow.

We got the snaps and the 'urgents' on our wire in Moscow, as Fleet Street whipped itself into a frenzy. To us it was madness. It could not be true. But there was one problem: Burgess was not at home. Tolya, his Russian boy friend and a former coal-miner, was living in his flat and said Burgess was on holiday and would not be back in Moscow for three weeks. That did worry me. Moreover Maclean's telephone was always engaged. So we could not write categorically that the whole story that Britain's and the West's two most famous defectors were on their way home to face the music was a load of codswallop. As hundreds of journalists and cameramen descended on Amsterdam, I was driving through Moscow streets to Maclean's flat. Up on the eighth floor, I rang the bell. Maclean opened it and, as I expected, he told me to clear off. 'Hang about a bit,' I said, 'do you know there is a warrant out for your arrest in London?' He did, because he listened to the BBC's World Service to tell him what was really going on, as opposed to the lies and nonsense of Moscow Radio. But he wasn't going to let on, was he? All he could manage in reply was: 'I've asked you before not to come here. I have nothing to say. I never will have. Please, go away. Goodbye.'

I didn't really need any more. We 'urgented' the story to Reuters in London, where it was sent to every newspaper office… and ignored.

For the, then, British European Airways knew better and said the two men were flying into London from Amsterdam on BEA Flight 439, timed to touchdown at 10.10 p.m. Meanwhile the KLM flight had arrived and neither Burgess nor Maclean were on it. And when the BEA plane landed and came to a halt, dozens of camera-men surged forwards, shouting and pushing. A man with an overcoat pulled over his head and shoulders came down the steps and was stopped at the bottom by waiting police. It was a *Daily Mirror* reporter who had caught the plane expecting to interview the spies on the flight, and was now playing a joke on the media pack and the police. He was lucky not to have been lynched.

Reuters in Fleet Street was now being plagued by questions from its clients, the British press, about our story that Burgess was on holiday somewhere in Russia, and Maclean was still holed up in his Moscow flat. Apologetically, they asked us whether anything had changed. So once again I rang his doorbell.

This time his door was opened by a woman who was a British Communist, probably acting as some kind of courier for the traitor and former Soviet spy.

'Bugger off,' she said, when she saw me standing there. 'He is not going to talk to you people.'

'So he's still here?'

'Of course he's fucking here! Where do you think he is?' (Many years later I bumped into her by pure chance in Sainsburys in south London and once again she used a swear word or two while remaining unhelpful and unforthcoming.)

I handed her the piece from Reuters about the airline spokesman saying Maclean was on his way to Amsterdam. 'I'd like to know what he thinks about that.'

Maclean must have been listening to what we were saying because he suddenly loomed up behind his friend, bellowing, 'Shut the door. Shut the door on that chap.'

I could tell he was not a happy man. And I knew this was the time for some foot-in-the-door journalism, so I got my size seven into position and did my best to look determined, even menacing.

50

'I would have thought a small quote saying that you are not flying to London tonight, tomorrow night or any other night would fit the bill,' I said. 'Then you might get a bit of peace and quiet.'

Maclean blinked. 'Go away,' he said. 'I've told you never to come here. This is an unwarrantable intrusion into my private life.'

Given that he had passed onto the Soviet KGB every major diplomatic secret he could get his hands on, and had done quite a few sneaky and intrusive things in his time, it was a pathetic response. He slammed the door with such force that it must have been heard all over the building.

I went back to work and wrote that Maclean was still alive, well, if angry, and living in Moscow. It must have landed with a unpleasant thud on the desks of editors of newspapers, who would have been smacking their lips with anticipation of a tremendous front-page story. But at least the fiasco had given newsroom hacks a night out in Amsterdam, Stockholm, Paris and several other cities, and I bet their expenses made good reading.

So, how did it happen? Why was a warrant for the arrest of Burgess and Maclean taken out in the first place, thus prompting an extraordinary stampede? The conspiracy theory is that Whitehall got wind that Burgess couldn't stand Russia anymore and wanted to come home. But his many homosexual friends in high places feared he would be an embarrassment to them, so they got Scotland Yard to warn him off.

Not bad. But as I heard it several years later, the story began in Havana, Cuba, where the British Minister, Keith Oakshott, who had gone there from Moscow, was tipped off that Burgess and Maclean were about to visit 'Castroland' for a holiday in the sun. In those days Soviet aircraft did not have the range to reach Cuba non-stop and would put down at Prestwick. The Foreign Office told the Home Office and the Home Office felt it would be severely embarrassed if it emerged that the two men had passed through. Hence the warrants.

A few days later, Burgess got back to Moscow and gave me an interview. When the *Evening Standard* telephoned him to get him to amplify on what he had said, he replied: 'It's all in my statement to that lovely young man from Reuters.'

You can ignore the innuendo.

5 - Death Of The Dastardly Duo

As is well known – to use a familiar Russian-English phrase – it is possible for a person to be both charming and awful. And the Guy Francis de Moncy Burgess I knew in Moscow was a perfect example of this. Eton. Dartmouth College. Cambridge. The BBC. The Foreign Office. The KGB. Moscow. And all the time, frivolous, witty, amusing, disreputable, drunk and homosexual.

Alan Bennett, in his masterly play *An Englishman Abroad* got very near to showing what life was like for Burgess in the last few years of his life in the Soviet Union. The cadging of drinks, petty stealing of cigarettes, and general seediness came across very well but it was a lot worse than that.

Russia was all wrong for Burgess. He cared not at all for the Russians, had no interest in their culture, and never got past '*da*', '*nyet*' and '*spasibo*' with the language, despite his intellectual brilliance. Unlike Maclean and Kim Philby, he never tried to make a go of it. More than that, from the day of his arrival in Russia in June 1951, he was terrified of his hosts, the KGB; at the back of his mind was the fear that he would end his days not in Wormwood Scrubs, as might have happened had he not fled the country with Maclean, but in the GULAG.

He told me the story. Immediately after their arrival in Moscow via Paris and Prague, he and Maclean were debriefed by senior Soviet intelligence officers. The subject matter was British foreign policy and the atmosphere was friendly, with lots of laughter, back-slapping and toasts.

But one day they were suddenly told they were going to Kuibishev, a city on the Volga, closed to foreigners. There they were put in a small house, guarded night and day by KGB troops. To all intents and purposes, they were under house arrest. The debriefing became an interrogation.

This went on for several months and it quickly dawned on the two runaway diplomats that their hosts suspected they were in fact double agents. So they had to be broken – before being sent to a labour camp. Burgess claimed that after Stalin died in 1953, they were told that Lavrenti Beria, the sinister chief of security police, had been pressing for a 'confession'. He took a close interest in the case, ruled out making propaganda by publicizing their arrival and insisted they were given pseudonyms. But he suddenly lost interest in them. The atmosphere improved. They were allowed to leave the house. Burgess, offered male lovers, said he preferred to find his own. But on his first expedition he was badly beaten up and lost most of his teeth. His hosts found his experience amusing, but had dentures made and fitted for him. Unfortunately they were so stained and uneven that Burgess hated them for the rest of his days.

Not until 1955 were they allowed to leave Kuibishev and live in Moscow. Burgess had some idea that they would be allowed to find their own accommodation and suggested that he be allowed to take over an outhouse in the former nunnery of Novodevichy, and turn it into a cosy flat for himself and his lovers.

The Russians did their best and he got a flat in a newly-built block with a view of the Novodevichy churches, the cemetery and Moscow River. It was a desirable property and he soon found a flatmate who played the accordion in a band and whom he happened to meet in a toilet near the Metropole Hotel – the same place where Tom Driberg, chairman of the Labour Party, would pimp for him on his visits to Moscow.

I met his lover Tolya once or twice. He was a short, cheerful, broad-shouldered Russian, who came from Yasnaya Polyana, south of Moscow, famous as the home of Lev Tolstoy. Burgess would have it that Tolstoy had slept with Tolya's grandmother, and who's to say it wasn't true?

But at the end, Burgess was probably the loneliest man in the Soviet Union. He never saw Maclean and Kim Philby, who had recruited him and to whom he was much closer, had only just arrived after fleeing from Beirut, and the KGB was keeping him under wraps. The other 'grey men' thought him a slob, a bore and an appalling establishment name-dropper, and, of course, he didn't like Russians because they couldn't talk about the Reform Club and the bars of London. His friends could be counted on one hand and some of them were British correspondents.

One was Jeremy Wolfenden of the *Daily Telegraph*. They had a lot in common – both old Etonians with brilliant minds, homosexuals,

5. Jeremy Wolfenden, the brilliant, but wayward, homosexual *Daily Telegraph* correspondent in Moscow, hands over to John Miller on the steps of the British Embassy along with Keith Morfett of the *Daily Mail*. Aged 31, Wolfenden died a year later, in 1965, having drank himself to death.

chainsmokers, and, effectively, alcoholics (drink was to kill Wolfenden within a few years when he was thirty-one). Wolfenden could get Burgess to open up and provide a few quotes when needed. After a bottle of Armenian cognac had been uncorked and the room stunk of cheap Russian tobacco – and if it were before midday – Burgess would be in full steam, exhilarated and confident.

He might also get an offering from one of the hampers his mother sent him several times a year from Fortnum & Mason. Burgess attacked these hampers like a Billy Bunter, first gobbling up everything that took his fancy, such as the pate and the chocolate biscuits, and finishing up with the items he didn't particularly care for, such as the dried prunes and tinned fruit. Everything was washed down with slugs of cognac and squeaks of 'goody-goody gum drops! What's next?'

Burgess lived in a curious flat containing naff Soviet furniture, and odd items of antique furniture, including a bed, which he claimed had once belonged to Stendhal, a portable organ, and a rather nice little dressing table that had belonged to his mother. At one time he had a magnificent set of Imperial Russian china which – when it disappeared – he insisted he had presented to the Hermitage Museum in Leningrad 'in grateful thanks' for being allowed to live in the USSR. A likely story!

He also had a great many books which his mother had had sent to him after his defection. I found it ironic that, although both Burgess and Maclean were officially guilty of treachery and vilified, they had no difficulty receiving money or anything else they wanted from Britain. Or that although they had chosen Soviet communism, they were not adverse to sending off for creature comforts from the Old Country. Burgess loved to show off his books, including a volume of Churchill's *History of the English Speaking Peoples*, inscribed by the author 'To Guy, with grateful thanks'.

Another book he once showed me was a modest volume about his flight with Maclean. As I flicked through the pages, I was surprised to see several passages had been underlined. There were also exclamation marks in the margins and cryptic notes, such as 'Rubbish!' and 'Not A.C. but K.P.' Burgess whipped the book away when I attempted to read it properly.

When I heard he had died, I went to the flat to talk to Tolya. And I looked at his books to find the one about his defection. It had gone. The KGB and probably Philby, too, had gone through the flat removing anything that might have been of benefit to British intelligence. In fact, Philby was the sole benefactor of Burgess's will, taking the furniture and his clothes to sell on the black market.

That day, I suppose, I should have returned two books Burgess had lent to me and in which he had written his name. One was David Benedictus's *The Fourth of June*, a classic of its kind about life at Eton. The other was one of a limited edition of *The Black Diaries*, an account of the life of Roger Casement. Published in France, it was what used to be known as a dirty book, the sort of thing teenagers smuggled into Britain in the fifties, along with Henry Miller. Casement was hanged in 1916 as a traitor. He was also a homosexual whose diary about investigating atrocities in the Congo became one of the most explosive and mysterious documents in modern Anglo-Irish history. To the Irish, Casement was a patriotic hero. To the English, he was a German sympathiser and an abject pervert. Burgess's favourite book at bedtime?

I did not put them back on the dead man's shelf. Perhaps I should have left Philby a note offering to take them round to his place and drop them off...

In the year before he died, Burgess seldom left his flat and spent most of the day lying on a chaise longue in pyjamas and dressing gown. Four times a day a nurse came to give him injections in his backside. Once when I called on him, she hadn't been, and the first thing he said, was, 'I say, old boy, would you give me an injection?'

'Where?' I asked, suspecting trouble.

'In the bum, of course, where I am badly pricked.' He laughed.

'I'm not good at doing things like that and might faint,' I said. I wasn't kidding. He dropped the subject which was a lot better than him dropping his trousers.

John Mossman, the *Daily Mail*'s first correspondent in Moscow, a lovely man and a lovely writer, cultivated Burgess for the story and once persuaded him, without too much difficulty, to accompany him to a reception in a private room in the Prague restaurant on the Arbat. Their arrival was a staggering sight in more ways than one, as both had been drinking heavily. Burgess had tried to smarten himself up. He had put on his double-breasted English suit and was wearing his Old Etonian tie, of which he was immensely proud. The effect was somewhat spoiled by his Order of the Red Banner on his chest, which he said helped him in getting taxis and his expensive, but now badly-stained, dirty camel hair coat. At the time there was not a dry-cleaning establishment in the whole of the Soviet Union.

There was a sudden stampede by journalists away from the diplomats and their wives when Burgess appeared. He was plied with drinks and questions, some of which he fielded with the sort of remarks he would have used when he was working for the Foreign Office News department. But he was enjoying himself, he was swaying and belching and grinning and asking for more whisky. Suddenly he said: 'Chaps, I desperately need to urinate. Must I do it in the fireplace?' and pointed to a huge inglenook in the middle of the room.

We laughed, but the hostess didn't think it at all funny. She screamed hysterically: 'Will nobody get that filthy pederast out of here? The bugger is ruining my party.'

Mossman took the hint and went off into the night with the protesting Burgess.

One of the last interviews of any consequence I had with Burgess was shortly after the nonsense about him being on his way home to face the music. These days, it would have been recorded and every word used. Then we used to get it down in some kind of bastardized Pitmans. The *Guardian* gave the interview a good run and there were some arresting lines, such as when he poured himself a vodka and tomato juice declaring, 'This is the Queen's favourite drink, you know' and 'I like living under socialism in the Soviet Union. I would not like to live in expense-account Britain.' This sort of stuff was much more entertaining than the nonsense he had to come out with about Kim Philby, his old Cambridge friend, whose career in the British Secret Service was fortunately finished by his defection.

Burgess denied Philby was the 'Third Man' and produced an unlikely tale about how he and Maclean had been in a taxi when a car carrying some Special Branch officers bumped into it. Maclean suspected they were on to him and the game was up, so they made a run for it all the way to Stalin's Russia.

Clearly lying, he said: 'There was no 'Third Man'. No unnamed diplomat. No Philby. Nobody in Washington told me what was going on.' It was too much to expect that I would have been privy to the truth, the whole truth and nothing but the truth of the wretched story of the handful of men who betrayed a generation and became a minor part of twentieth-century history.

This interview brought me to the attention of readers of *Izvestia*, the Soviet government organ which published a typically propagandistic and ludicrous piece of journalism under the title *An exploded sensation – facts are stubborn*.

Izvestia said that Burgess – Soviet readers must have asked themselves 'Who he?' – gave me an interview that other sensation-seeking colleagues had been trying to obtain for three days. Within a few minutes, I had realized that London's fairy tale had dissolved into thin air. I began to look like a boxer hit again and again by knockout blows. Blow after blow hit its target. Figuratively speaking, the whole face of Western propaganda was bruised. And so on and so forth.

The reader was never told who Burgess was, why he was saying what he did, or even what he said. It took nearly thirty years for glasnost to sweep away such tripe.

❦

Jeremy Wolfenden burst into our bedroom at three in the morning to tell us the news. In the Moscow ghettos in which we lived, one never bothered to lock the door on the principle that no Russians would dare to break in and burgle the flat of a foreigner. Also, if the lock jammed as easily as it did, the door would have to be broken down. 'Guy's dead, Guy's dead!' he shouted, and he was clearly distressed, and it was not only because he had had a monumental call-back.

'Who says?' said I, because it was not unknown for newspapers to prematurely kill off personalities. 'Driburg in the *Sunday Express*,' said Wolfenden mournfully.

It sounded plausible; he would have heard it from Maclean, and was making a bob or two from the *Express*. I was not disposed to do anything about it at that time of the morning, such as driving Wolfenden to the flat. He had telephoned, but there had been no reply. 'Go on, match it,' I said. 'It must be true.' He did. It was. Burgess was fifty-one. A lifetime's drinking, smoking and so on, had caught up with him.

The funeral took place at Donskoi Crematorium on a warm September morning. Maclean had organized the event and had tried to keep it secret from the tiny British press *corps* who wanted to attend, if only to see if the disappeared Philby would want to say farewell to an old friend and fellow traitor.

But of course, his bosses in the Lubyanka would not have sanctioned that. Till the end of his days, he was never going to be his own man.

Maclean offered me a limp hand when I turned up early, before the lorry bringing the coffin had arrived. He asked Jeremy and me, 'as Guy's friends' to walk behind the coffin, each carrying a wreath.

I was attending a traitors farewell in order to write a story, not as a relative, family friend or virtual pallbearer, but I did not feel I was presented with a terrible moral dilemma. I now suspect, however, I was carrying a wreath from the Communist Party of the Soviet Union. I would have been very uncomfortable if it had been from the KGB.

The ceremony for Comrade Guy was held in a somewhat ghoulish hall, notable for the number of urns and plaques around the wall featuring members of the Soviet Secret police who had died on duty(!) right back to the early 1930s, when it was built. And only a hundred or so yards from the crematorium there is a small white gravestone marking the place where the ashes of thousands of nameless victims of Stalin's purges were dumped.

An inscription says: 'Communal grave No 1. Burial place for unclaimed ashes, 1930-42'. It is now a place of pilgrimage for the families of victims of the Great Terror, who were shot in the Lubyanka and brought to Donskoi at night, still warm, bullet hole in the head, a statistic of Stalin's conveyer-belt of death.

Maclean, Burgess's brother (who had broken all contact with him when he defected), a handful of journalists and a few Russians, stood around the coffin to hear Maclean's few words – Burgess had come to the Soviet Union with idealism which many people had not understood. He had been a gifted and courageous man who had stuck

6. Funeral of Guy Burgess at Donskoi Crematorium, Moscow. Donald Maclean is a pall-bearer. Miller helped carry a wreath from the Soviet Communist Party.

to his principles and dedicated his life to the cause of peace and the struggle for a better life for the people. Which of course was twaddle.

Someone, said to have been a colleague of Burgess but who was probably from the KGB, said something on the same lines in Russian. And then, as the coffin rolled forward to pass through a red curtain, a small brass band crashed out the Internationale, the international communist anthem, written by a French woodworker set to music by Pierre Degayter, a Belgian composer, and a haunting piece of music, surely now destined to be consigned to the archives of musical history.

We went out into the sunshine with some difficulty, as a large group of mourners were trying to get into the hall behind another coffin containing the body of an old woman – this time in accordance with Russian Orthodox rite, it was open and we could see her wizened, white face.

Maclean stood near the door like a village parson shaking hands and saying, 'Thank you for coming. Goodbye.'

Twenty years later, I returned to the same crematorium for his funeral.

⁂

There must be some bulky files on Burgess, Maclean *et al.*, held by MI5 and MI6, setting down the case against them, and they will, in all likelihood, remain closed for ever. Some other Foreign office files have reached the Public Record Office and will be open for public scrutiny in the next century. I suspect that the security services know almost precisely what 'secrets' the two men passed to the KGB. I hazard a guess they wouldn't have added up to much, not changed the course of history by an iota, although Maclean once boasted that secret information he gave the Russians on American intentions during the Korean War had influenced Stalin's decision-making.

I doubt if Maclean or any of the bunch at the end of the day concluded that it had all been worth it. The Soviet Union was a rotten place with an evil system when they arrived and it did not improve much before it collapsed in the early nineties. They all had an aching nostalgia for England and, despite what they say, none of them found happiness in a stark, friendless city. Certainly thirty years in the USSR was not much fun for Maclean. Philby managed the ultimate betrayal of his comrade-in-arms by persuading Mrs Maclean to move in with him. Although she left Philby after a year, she never went back to Donald.

All three of his children decided that the West had a lot more to offer than the twilight world their father was living in and they cleared out as soon as they were able. And as year followed year and he surveyed, alone, the wreckage of his life, he must have seen just how much the Soviet Union had failed to come up to his ideals.

Any chance of getting to see him to talk about his life in Russia disappeared when I broke a story in the *Sunday Telegraph*, that he was ill and had gone into hospital indefinitely. It was not quite right – he came out of hospital after a few weeks and, because he knew he had lung cancer and only a short time to live, he gave an interview on the record, his first and last, to Mark Frankland.

Maclean came across as rather a sad, lonely and ill old man, now much more a down-at-heel Soviet professor than an urbane, retired British diplomat. The flat he managed to keep me out of for more than twenty years exuded an atmosphere of cultivated, slightly bohemian comfort. The furniture was simple and Russian, except for a small, semicircular sideboard and a French-looking occasional table, which must have been the one belonging to Burgess. He had one of those huge Soviet televisions which can only be lifted by four men, an old record player with one speaker, an item or two of Staffordshire china and a few unframed photographs of children and grandchildren, and on the wall, some old prints of Cambridge.

Maclean was old and bent, deaf in one ear, white-haired and walked badly, wearing down the edges of his carpet slippers.

So what did he think of the Soviet Union? 'Where I think this system is fairer is in the distribution of wealth. You can't build up fortunes here. It may be a creaking inefficient system, but in that sense it's fairer.'

He referred to Stalin, the monster, as 'Uncle Joe' and described those who had made up the Old Guard in the Kremlin over the years, tenaciously hanging onto power with its perks and privileges, as 'sort of Ernie Bevins'. Now Ernest Bevin was an honest, democratic and formidable Labour Party politician and foreign secretary who stood up to Stalin and Soviet imperialism after 1945. He had nothing at all in common with the Communist Party gang that had sat on the necks of millions of Russians, denying them basic freedoms.

And my goodness, he was critical of aspects of Soviet life! Wingeing like a pensioner, he complained about the increase of one kopek in the price of a stamp for a postcard, and he was disgusted to learn that his gas bill was to go up from sixteen kopeks a month to forty-two.

About his treachery he had nothing to say but this: 'People call me a traitor. But I was never a traitor to my beliefs.'

So that's alright then.

As happened before, the news broke in London and was relayed to Moscow. Malcean had died, aged 69. Straightaway, we went round to his flat. This time nobody answered the doorbell. Outside the door there was an empty carton as though someone was starting to clear out the place. We rang the bell of the neighbouring flat. After a while a voice from behind the door says: 'What you do want?' There was real fear in the voice, as though this was the old days and we were Beria's men – they, of course, would have beaten on the door with their heavy fists and boots.

'We wondered', I say, 'if you could tell us where we can find Mr Frazer?' It was the wrong question, much too English and polite, to ask a Russian. We should have said something like – 'Your neighbour has croaked. Right?'

From behind the door: 'I know nothing. Nothing at all.' So we went away and wrote stories about 'unconfirmed reports' of Maclean's death. But he was dead alright, and had been for several days until found by his housekeeper when she came in to 'do' for him, after a national holiday. The KGB had gone through his flat too, just in case.

Once more I paid a visit to the Donskoi Crematorium. It was a bitterly cold day, temperatures minus 8°C and we dressed in heavy overcoats and fur hats. This time there were many journalists and many more Soviet mourners, mostly from the Institute of World Economy and International Relations, where he had worked analyzing British foreign policy. Not one member of the family turned up. Nor did Philby or Blake. But the KGB did, and they were surly, sour and unhelpful.

'Do you happen to know where he died?' I asked one of them. 'None of your business,' he replied. 'It is enough that you know he was one of the finest men in Moscow, that he was a great man and friend of the Soviet Union and its people.'

Many more wreaths than Burgess had followed the coffin into the crematorium. There were his rewards for selling his soul to the 'Cause' – the Red Banner of Combat, the Red Banner of Labour and the Lenin Medal for 'glorious labour' dished out in 1969 on the centenary of the Soviet leader's birth. But there was no brass band, only Bach played on an organ. There was a short tribute from a woman colleague: 'The Fatherland bids farewell to a dear man, a faithful son, a citizen of the Soviet Union, Donald Donaldovitch Maclean.' And she forecast, wrongly as it turned out, that his memory would survive for many, many years.

Small bunches of tulips, roses and mimosa, that must have cost a fortune in the local market, were laid on the coffin. Maclean's housekeeper alone wept as it slid from sight.

We went out into an icy wind. For me, the Burgess and Maclean story was over. At last.

6 – Khrushchev's Raspberries

I met Nikita Khrushchev for the first time at a British trade fair in Moscow's Sokolniki Park. He had turned up, with little notice to the British organizers, along with several other members of the ruling Politburo as part of his drive, despite the Cold War, for making friends and influencing people in the West. Compared to him, Stalin, and even Lenin, were hermits, emerging heavily guarded from the Kremlin only for Party conferences or state occasions. Not Nikita. He was like the Monkey King in the Chinese fable, popping up here, there and everywhere, breathlessly, hands waving, piggy eyes flickering, little upturned nose poking into everything. And my goodness! He liked parties, especially those thrown by Western ambassadors, and more especially those given to celebrate national days. On his arrival, we would drop like a hot brick whoever we were talking to and swarm around Khrushchev, in a hurry to corner him before his host did, because an impromptu give-and-take was in the offing, the nearest thing to a press conference the Soviet Union had known at that time, and much, much more entertaining than any government hand-out or organized trip. We also had the opportunity to observe the Soviet leadership from a few feet, sometimes inches, to see what they wore and how they ate and drank – I was always impressed by the way Khrushchev nibbled on a piece of ham expertly balanced on a knife – and what their wives looked like – for they, too, were beginning to emerge from Stalin's closet.

Khrushchev was one of those roly-poly, stout little men. He was fast on his feet. When he talked, and he did that a great deal, he leaned forward, as if he were on tiptoes. His mouth was always a tiny bit open, as if he could hardly wait to devour what he was being told. Upturned nose, three small chins, small dark eyes, two gold teeth and two warts, one next to his nose on his left check, the other under his right eye – they made Khrushchev instantly recognizable, as did the way he talked – straight out, bluntly, indiscreetly, and sometimes with a coarseness unequalled for a world leader.

Take an exchange as he toured the British exhibition.

Me: 'There is a story going around that the Soviet Union is interested in buying a complete plant from Britain to manufacture cars. Is it possible?'

Khrushchev: 'We know how to make cars. We have our own factories. Why should we need to buy one from you?'

Me: 'One reason is that it is widely accepted that Soviet cars are... well, not up to world standards.'

Khrushchev, with a grin: 'Maybe, but if it's your own shit, it smells like raspberries.'

There is another Khrushchev story concerning the same substance – in Russian, *govno*. This time the subject came up in a conversation he had with Richard Nixon, then US Vice-President at a Kremlin meeting. Both men were banging on about how poor they had been in their youth, how they went barefoot and the hardships they suffered.

Khrushchev said one of his first jobs was to clean horse shit out of stables. 'I've done that too,' said Nixon. 'Oh yes?' said Khrushchev. 'Well, I've also had to shovel cow shit and that was a lot worse!' Nixon insisted that he had done the same. 'OK,' said Khrushchev, 'let's get down to it. I've had the worst job of all – as a small boy I was given the job of shovelling human shit.'

Nixon said nothing more.

Khrushchev's boyhood had indeed been as close to poverty as he always suggested and his life followed the familiar, even blatantly trite, Soviet pattern: Peasant stock; little formal education; worker with his hands; then Party activity and advancement by slow stages. When I saw him in action, he had become by far the most important man in the Soviet Union, having survived under Stalin by obeying the old tyrant's whim and playing the fool. He also licked Stalin's boots in his speeches: 'Stalin – our hope. Stalin – our desire. Stalin – the light of advanced and progressive humanity. Stalin – our will. Stalin – our victory.' But later he recalled: 'Sometimes a man goes to see Stalin in the Kremlin and he does not know whether or not he will come home again.' Khrushchev always managed to.

Khrushchev was himself a kind of a monster, but not an unattractive one. He was what we would call a 'bit of a card'. And so quotable. At one of the few formal press conferences he gave, he came up with a wonderful line on the Berlin crisis, which at one time was permanently on the diplomatic agenda. Berlin, said he, exposed the testicles of the West, which 'I will grab and squeeze whenever it suits me'.

But stories abound about his good-humoured lack of taste. At a French embassy reception I overheard him talking to members of a high-powered delegation from Paris. One of them commented on the fact that most Russian women seemed to work, and to do heavy jobs, too.

Cheerfully, Khrushchev said: 'Yes, that's right. Our women do work, and they do honest work. Not like women in France who, I'm told, are all whores.'

He was capable of truly embarrassing miscalculations, the result of the many distortions of political life in the Soviet Union. There was his celebrated appearance at the United Nations when he pounded the table with his fists. My theory about this is that he had heard that this was how things were done in the Duma, the parliament shut down by the Bolsheviks, and thought it would go down well with Third World countries, which, he liked to think, were grateful for the Soviet Union's help in throwing off the colonialist yoke. But he went too far when he pulled off his shoe and banged that on the table as well. This was a gesture which backfired. Some people in the West may have thought it amusing, and it was, if only to catch the look of shock and horror which crossed the usually stoney face of Andrei Gromyko, the Soviet Foreign Minister, sitting right next to his boss. But many Third World politicians, nothing if not formal themselves, were not impressed and thought the Soviet leader gauche. For years after, whenever the incident was raised in conversation with Russians, the reaction was that his shoe-pounding was a vulgar act which did not reflect well on the Soviet state. 'We became a laughing stock through that sort of thing and other such antics,' they said, and with some justification.

Indeed the members of the Soviet intelligentsia that I knew deplored Khrushchev's manners, his scruffy Russian, his ill-fitting suits, and later, when he tried to do something about his image, his too-tailored Italian ones. To many of them he was rude, crude, vulgar and ignorant. Only when he had gone and was replaced by dreary Brezhnev and his awful cronies did they realize what a great character he had been, how much he had tried to get things moving.

Few political leaders have been less honoured for the good they did than Nikita Khrushchev – for nearly thirty years nothing favourable about him was published in his own country, and in the West he is remembered, if at all, mainly as a blustering adversary who tried to turn Cuba into a Soviet missile base. But Mikhail Gorbachev and Khrushchev have one thing in common: their legacy is their bold reformation of the Soviet system. They were both *velikie reformatori* – 'great reformers'. Under Khrushchev, twenty-five years of mass police terror ended. Millions of people were freed from prisons, labour camps and exile. Millions who had perished were rehabilitated so their families could regain full citizenship. Political life became more open and accessible. Censorship was relaxed, official ideology made less dogmatic. Intellectual and cultural activity grew freer. He took on and harried Russian bureaucrats – pushing their noses into dirty, disordered, backward local conditions, the sort of things that still exist today, such as poor housing and shoddy, inefficient agriculture. In the end, they cost him the support of every power élite. The result was a *coup*, his 'early retirement' and defamation, and the onset of eighteen years of conservative rule under Brezhnev.

But he was the journalist's dream, and so entertaining with it. After his historic space orbit, the cosmonaut, Yuri Gagarin, was honoured in the Kremlin with an award of Hero of the Soviet Union. We watched Khrushchev trying to pin the gold medal on his chest but, despite his best efforts, the pin would not penetrate the tunic. There was an embarrassed silence as Khrushchev pushed and prodded, followed by a titter, then outright laughter. Gagarin grinned as Khrushchev persevered. Finally the Soviet leader gave up, slapped the medal in the cosmonaut's hand and turning to the audience said, with a grin: 'There you are, Comrades, see how solid our Soviet cloth is. Even a pin cannot pierce it.' He knew, as we all did, that the problem was not Soviet cloth. It was shoddy workmanship of the pin on the country's highest award for valour.

He loved such occasions, and it is not difficult to understand why. The barefoot shepherd boy had risen to head a whole nation, and he wanted you to know he was now undisputed master of the Kremlin. Having started life in a straw-thatched hut with a beaten-earth floor, he was now dispensing hospitality in the name of one of the two most powerful – i.e. nuclear-armed – countries the world had ever seen. Moreover, these receptions in the St George Hall were also a recurring celebration of Russia's own progress from rags to riches.

They were a shop window intended to impress, very much a part of his personal pattern of rule.

The St George Hall would be a blaze of white and gold under the six, huge, gilded-crystal chandeliers, the white marble walls and pilasters carrying, in gold lettering, the roll-call of battle honours of Tzarist regiments. The entire diplomatic *corps* was there, along with the top brass from *apparatchiks* to academicians, often as many as a thousand men and women. In the minstrel gallery a guards' band, many of the musicians with fine flowing moustaches, played fanfares and national anthems. Long tables ranged down both sides of the hall, laden with yard-long sturgeons, gleaming hams, red and black caviar, bottles of vodka, Georgian wines, and mineral water. A host of waiters scurried about with trays of lobster from Kamchatka, ice-cream, coffee and champagne. And the nation's brightest and best devoured everything in sight as fast as they could, as though they hadn't had a square meal for days.

Khrushchev and the rest of the government and the Marshals would be behind a long table in front of the stage, at one end of the massive hall. It didn't take too long for them to get stuck into the vodka, raising their voices, their faces flushed, a scene which never failed to remind me of the end of George Orwell's *Animal Farm* where the pigs and the farmers are celebrating together. Then came the toasts and speeches: to the victory of Communism throughout the world; to the happy life of the Soviet people; to Peace and Friendship, – all coupled, of course, with warnings to the West's warmongers not to push the Soviet Union too far, because the Party and the People were one, and the USSR's military might would continue to be perfected. I would like a rouble for every time I've heard the USSR threatening to deliver a decisive rebuff to the aggressor.

Khrushchev, so extraordinarily articulate and well informed about so many things, was at the same time a prisoner of dogma. Even he would have to read a speech written for him in reply to a toast from some jumped-up African tinpot dictator, sucking up to the Russians.

And then he would do something so completely in character. We would get together after the speeches to compare notes on what was said, or snatches of gossip overheard or picked up from the Russian VIPs or diplomats. Once I shared a glass of vodka with General Ivan

71

Serov, who was involved in the massacre of 22,000 Polish officers in 1940 in the Katyn Forest and two other prisons, who played a major role in the bloody crackdown in Hungary after the ill-fated uprising in 1956, and who was responsible for deporting whole nationalities from Eastern Europe to Siberia.

I couldn't resist talking to him because our paths had crossed in a very minor way. In 1956, as head of the KGB, he organized security for the goodwill visit of Khrushchev and Marshal Bulganin to Britain and the *Norwich Mercury* had told me to cover the whole event. As it happened, the British media became aware of Serov's visit and predictably and justifiably demonized him as 'Ivan the Terrrible' and 'the Butcher.' So he never came with B and K, and now he was head of the GRU, the military intelligence directorate.

I was tempted to commiserate with him for not being given the chance to visit Norfolk, but decided that would be insincere as he was certainly the most evil man I had met. He was standing on his own, eating and drinking – perhaps his comrades also thought him a nasty and dangerous bastard – so I went and stood by his side, pretending to look at the food on the table. There was smoked salmon and a bowl of mushrooms. I tasted them and said to him: 'These are really tasty, don't you think?' He looked at me somewhat suspiciously, but we talked about the unseasonable weather and he told me of its effect on the mushroom crop. He went on about how to spot the *pogangka* toadstools, and it was clear he knew a thing or two about mushrooms, as he did about putting people up against a wall and shooting them. He came to a rather sticky end.

Serov had been the boss of Oleg Penkovsky, the best spy the West ever had. And when Penkovsky was shot, Serov was fired. It is said he was given a minor job in the Volga Military District, but being Russian, he took to drink in a big way and the day they told him he was kicked out of the Communist Party he walked out of his flat on the Arbat, went out into the street, shouted out something unintelligible and shot himself in the mouth with his service revolver. Nobody was impressed.

On one occasion the Kremlin reception was for Sékou Touré of Guinea, who suspected the Russians were laughing at him by sending him snow ploughs – in fact they were road-sweeping vehicles, but with the snow-clearing shovels still in place. Khrushchev, but more likely some Soviet bureaucrat, may have been intending to do just that, but it was decided to make it up to the Guinean leader by throwing a big bash for him in the Kremlin and promising him every assistance in his efforts to maintain independence and sovereignty, i.e. to keep him in the peace-loving Soviet camp. It wasn't much of a story, but we gathered in a small circle and leafed through our notebooks.

Khrushchev cottoned on to what we were doing and, to my astonishment, he abandoned Sékou Touré and advanced stealthily towards us, like a Red Indian chief on the war-path, until he emerged in our midst. Deadpan, he mimed writing in a notebook and said: 'Well then, lads, what was the old bastard rambling on about? Come on, give us a sentence or two.'

I saw Khrushchev in action once more before I left the country after my first tour there. It was a remarkable and unique occasion in the true sense of the word – for it was never again held in the Palace of Congresses or elsewhere in the Kremlin. Khrushchev, for some reason – a premonition, perhaps – arranged a huge New-Year reception. The new Palace of Congresses was thrown open to several thousand handpicked people and those attending read like a *Who's Who?* of Soviet society. I was lucky to be sent an invitation by the Press Department of the Soviet Foreign Ministry: by rights it should have gone to the Reuters Bureau chief, Peter Johnson. But I deserved to get it. I had spent three hard years in the country covering one of the great stories of the twentieth century – the emergence of Russia as a superpower.

But more important was that my wife Brenda had just given birth to twins in a Moscow hospital.

They were the first British twins born in the USSR since the Revolution, and there were pictures of mother, Jane and Timothy, in most London newspapers under headlines such as 'Red Star Twins'.

When they were born, I was covering the opening of the Supreme Soviet, the so-called parliament; but the cigars and Georgian champagne came out later. I have often wondered if that was why we got the invitation – the story underlined what my father had told me, that they did not eat babies in the USSR, at least, not British ones.

73

The Palace of Congresses was another result of Khrushchev's energy and impatience. Since 1930 they had talked of building a Palace of Soviets in honour of the first Five-Year Plan and intended it to be the largest building in the world, but had never got around to it. Khrushchev threw his weight behind the Palace of Congresses and it was built in sixteen months, inside the Kremlin, without any important buildings being demolished. Unlike Stalin, who insisted on throwing up those massive, wedding-cake monstrosities that disfigure the Moscow skyline, Khrushchev cannot seriously be accused of committing cultural vandalism. The Palace of Congresses does not interfere with the age-old and magnificent panorama of cupolas and bell towers that make the Kremlin so magical.

Now he laid on a reception to end all receptions. The Palace of Congresses, which was used for major Party conferences and as a theatre for ballet and opera, was packed. Again the country's élite descended like locusts on the feast. Here there was fine caviar – not only was none to be had in Moscow shops, there were queues outside for bread. Here there were plates of tongue, whereas across the country there were meat shortages. Here were many different kinds of sausage. All you could buy on Gorky Street was a boiled sausage called *doktorskaya*, which contained so little meat and so much starch that a joke circulated about the man who over-indulged for breakfast with the result that, although he had trouble breathing, his collar got a good starching. There were heaps of smoked salmon that night in the Palace of Congresses. All you could get in the city's fish shops was frozen cod, and it didn't look very nice either. I saw crab that night – for the first time in three years.

Khrushchev and the entire Politburo were behind a table at the end of the hall, feeding their faces and waving their crystal goblets in the air at any one who gave them a friendly smile. I wrote down their names. This was operational rule number 1 – you had to keep checking on the line-up just to see if somebody was missing, i.e. demoted or ill. Kremlinology they called it, and the Kremlinologists who practised it didn't know then that within thirty years, they would be out of a job because Russia was fast becoming a normal country. That night the *bolshiye shishki* – the 'big zits' – were all there: Brezhnev, Voronov, Kozlov, Kosygin, Kussinen, Mikoyan, Podgorny, Polyansky, Suslov, Khrushchev, Kirilenko, Shvernik, Grishin, Rashidov, Mazurov,

74

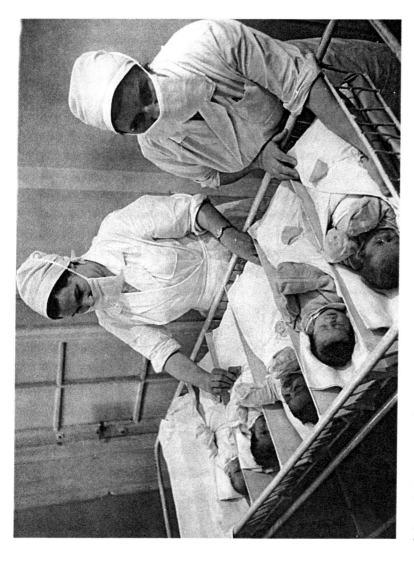

7. Two of these babies nursed in the Moscow Maternity Hospital in Bolshaya Pirogskaya ulitza (Big Pie Street) are Jane and Tim Miller. They were the first British twins born in the Soviet Union.

Mzhavanadze, and Shelest. Three decades later all but one of these self-appointed leaders of the USSR were dead, and the country with that name no longer existed.

At midnight the Kremlin chimes rang out the Old Year and brought in the New. '*S Novym Godom*' we shouted to each other, and kissed and knocked back the champagne which TASS once proudly reported was made by a secret Soviet formula in twelve minutes flat. Now those of us who wanted to shake the hands of all the men who ruled the Soviet Union could do so, and this was a chance too good to be missed. We joined a queue, mostly made up by ambassadors, to file past the table where they stood. But I had a special reason for wishing Nikita Sergeyevich a Happy New Year: a few months previously, after a good lunch of blinis and caviar and, of course, 'Stoli', a few of us had decided that if we could not form a Foreign Correspondent's Association – the Soviet Foreign Ministry said it was *nelzhya*, forbidden – we would at least have an identifiable tie to show who we were. So we designed one – dark blue with a golden motif of a Kremlin dome and a sickle crossed by a quill pen. Several dozen were made up by a London firm. They sold like hot blinis for two roubles a tie to the Western press *corps*. And now I had my chance to present one to a man who deserved to be our honorary president. I had a smile and a greeting for each of those grey, hard men, but when I got to Khrushchev, I delivered a little speech in Russian. 'Your sputniks, the Western correspondents, have designed a tie. We look upon you as our President. And we want you to have one.'

So saying, I reached into the inside pocket of my jacket. The square man behind Khrushchev stiffened and stepped forward and only relaxed as I produced the tie and gave it to Khrushchev.

'*Spasibo*,' said he, and held it up, studying the motif.

'Perhaps you will wear it at your next press conference?' I asked, optimistically.

'*Konyeshno*,' said Khrushchev. But of course, he never gave another press conference; most, if not all, of the gang with him that night soon got rid of him and he disappeared into Trotsky's dustbin of history, taking, I would like to think, our tie with him.

At 1 am the liquor was still flowing and word went round that the Kremlin was wide open, you could go where you liked, and see what you liked. I made a beeline for the Terem Palace because, like so much of the inner Kremlin, it was closed to the public and there were wonders there to behold. I had heard about fabulous sights so rarely seen: rooms used by the tsars in the seventeenth century, including the bedchamber and throne room, where they met the Boyars and the ambassadors, all low and vaulted, with ornate decorations and murals and tiled stoves. But that night, I never saw those rooms, because there was music coming from the St George Hall. There they were again, the men who ran the Soviet Union, gathered in a small circle in the middle of the enormous hall – it is nearly two-hundred feet long and sixty feet wide – roaring with laughter. Voroshilov had joined them. Now he, then aged eighty-two, senile and befuddled by drink, had lost his last, figurehead job as president and been replaced by another apparent blockhead, Leonid Brezhnev. Although he had been named a year or two earlier as being responsible during Stalin's time for crimes against the people, Voroshilov was back, drinking with the boys in the Kremlin and enjoying himself.

And then something unforgettable happened, and for anyone who knew a thing or two about Soviet history and Stalin's funny little ways, it literally took ones breath away.

The orchestra was playing something or other that I can't recall – perhaps a polka or a *russkaya* – but nobody was dancing, which didn't please Khrushchev. He cackled: 'Somebody must start the dancing. We have to get the dancing going. This is the New Year.' But there were only a few people in the huge hall, and hardly any women. So he suddenly barked at Voroshilov: 'You start the dancing Kliment Yefremovich. Come on, get on with it.'

'Yes,' the gang shouted. 'Dance, you Old Fool! Dance!'

And he did, lifting his legs like a performing bear, but not moving from the spot, and waving his arms in time with the music. He was trying hard but it wasn't good enough. 'Faster,' shouted Khrushchev, 'dance faster!' They all joined in, clapping their hands in unison. Voroshilov did his best, but old age and drink had taken its toil and he couldn't move much faster. After several minutes the music stopped and Voroshilov looked as though he was about to collapse. But his old colleagues applauded him, clapped him on the back and gave him a glass of vodka. He downed it in one gulp like the cavalry officer he had once been, albeit forty years earlier. He probably didn't have the energy left to hurl it at the wall – as some of those tsarist officers with their names on it in gold would have done.

I was stunned by what happened. Here was history repeating itself. For Khrushchev himself hated dancing. He once said that it was because his sister had tried to teach him when he was a boy – 'but my legs wouldn't move properly'. And he had once revealed that Stalin knew of his dislike for dancing, and at Kremlin parties insisted he danced the difficult Ukrainian gopak, taunting him and humiliating him for his clumsiness. Now it was Voroshilov's turn to play the court jester.

Then I noted that watching the scene next to me and with his back to one of the pilasters was a middle-aged man with bushey eyebrows; it was the chairman of the USSR Supreme Soviet. President Leonid Brezhnev had held the largely ceremonial job for three years. And, as the Russians say, the goat had been let into the kitchen garden. Within a year through scheming, intrigue and backstabbing, he was to get the job he had set his heart on – Khrushchev's. Right then, perhaps he was already thinking that when he became Communist Party boss, he would make Khrushchev dance to his tune.

It was my one and only conversation with Brezhnev, and it was not momentous. 'Wonderful evening,' I said. He agreed. 'I'm John Miller of Reuters,' I said. 'Are you enjoying yourself?' he asked. He may not have spoken to a Western journalist before, and I don't think he cared very much whether I was having fun or not.

'Oh yes. Wonderful evening,' I repeated. ' Great party.' But he had drifted away, preferring not to chat with a bourgeois, anti-Soviet slanderer.

It was time to go home.

7 - Two Men Named Boris and a Yuri

As a young reporter in Norfolk, I stood outside many a church in the wind and the rain taking the names of mourners and attending the service, in case the vicar said something significant about the deceased. I went to a few funerals in Moscow too and learned something about Russia and the Russians' unusually close relationship with death, which borders on a preoccupation.

Seeing Boris Pasternak's face in an open coffin was something of a shock – his was the first funeral I attended in the Soviet Union. Pasternak was Russia's most revered poet, who had become the centre of an international furore over his novel *Dr Zhivago*. In an act of defiance then unprecedented, but subsequently repeated many times by much lesser authors and dissidents, Pasternak sent the novel to the West, thinking that in the liberal atmosphere, following de-Stalinization, it could be published there and he could get away with it back home. It was, but he didn't. It was a blockbuster, albeit a political one. And when he won the Nobel Prize for Literature, a veritable whirlwind raged about his head. The blustering bullies in the Kremlin went for him. Listen to the crude language of the hacks of the time: the newspaper *Literary Gazette* labelled Pasternak a 'Judas' a 'rabid individualist', a 'malicious literary snob'. *Pravda* called him an 'internal *émigré*' and his book, a 'literary weed'.

Vladimir Semichastny, head of the Komsomol, the Young Communist movement, who appropriately went on to run the KGB, made a speech of unparalleled violence and vulgarity which included the passage: 'If we compare Pasternak with a pig, then we have to say that a pig will never do what he has done. Pasternak has fouled the spot where he ate and messed on those by whose labour he lives and breathes.'

Much later Khrushchev, in retirement, bemoaned the fact that he had not bothered to read the book before he approved the vicious campaign against a mild-mannered, cultured and decent man. He insisted that 'those bastards' – his Kremlin colleagues – had fooled him by telling him that *Dr Zhivago* was anti-Soviet. In retrospect he said he would have handled it differently – by cutting 'a few lines' out of the work, and then it could have been published.

I was determined to interview Pasternak but he had decided not to talk to any British correspondents – he had been badly let down by an unscrupulous *Daily Mail* journalist to whom he had misguidedly given a poem as a souvenir of their meeting. This was published and got him in further trouble. Something similar happened a few years later when I went to Malta to replace a *Daily Telegraph* colleague, whose parting front-page shot was to describe Malta's leader, Dom Mintoff, as a 'Mickey Mouse character'. I was not made welcome.

But when it became known Pasternak was ill, I went out to lovely Peredelkino, some twelve miles from Moscow, hoping he would answer the door and that we could talk. I arrived and rang the bell at the gate. A man came out of the dacha and walked down towards me waiting at the gate. I thought I was going to get a story, but it was his brother Alexander, who closely resembled him. Yes, the author was ill. But there was no question of talking to him.

I went away and a few days later Pasternak died. Tipped off at a party, Bob Elphick, the Reuters Bureau chief, drove to Peredelkino with some colleagues after midnight and had the misfortune to have a drunken Army officer stagger into the road in front of his car, a common hazard in Russia to this day. Badly shaken by the incident and nervous about the consequences – you could run over who you like, provided they were not connected with the Communist Party, the Army and the KGB – Bob decided to keep a low profile until the matter was sorted out. So I went to Peredelkino for Pasternak's funeral.

Because he was very much of a non-person, the death of Russia's premier poet was not reported in the Soviet press until the morning of the day of his burial. There was nothing about the time and place of the funeral, except for a few handwritten notices which suddenly appeared on the walls of Moscow's Kiev railway station, and near the ticket office for the *elektrichka*, the electric train, which stopped at Peredelkino. Some were removed by party people to whom Pasternak remained a 'scabby sheep'.

But the oft-tested bush telegraph put out the news of the funeral. Many thousands made their way to Peredelkino that morning and the KGB was called out, fearing that the occasion would be used for some kind of political demonstration.

It was the first time I saw them in action with their ill-fitting suits and open-necked shirts, and absurd attempts to listen in on conversations. They also resorted to taking photographs of mourners at random as though to make a point – 'we know all about you dissidents and troublemakers. We are going to get you blacklisted at your work place if we can'.

It was a remarkable event on a beautiful summer's day. A queue had formed in front of the wooden verandah of Pasternak's dacha, its doors having been thrown wide open. His apple and lilac trees were a mass of blossom. Curiously it was the first Russian home I had been in, and here, in a large, darkened room, I saw the open coffin, almost buried in wreaths and flowers. Pasternak, who was 70, looked younger, with a face carved in marble. He was dressed in the dark grey suit that had belonged to his father. It was the first time I had seen a dead person like this.

Sitting on chairs placed around the room were the family and some artists making drawings of him. Those outside were speaking in hushed voices, but in the room there was silence, broken only by the sound of tinkling music coming from a side room, where the greatest of all living Russian pianists, Svyatoslav Richter, was playing the Bechstein grand piano.

We waited in the garden for the coffin to be brought out. The pallbearers were members of Moscow's liberal intelligentsia and two of them, Andrei Sinyavsky and Yuli Daniel, a few years later stood trial and went to prison for their 'anti-Soviet activity'. In the light of what was to come, it was a breath-taking gesture.

The coffin should have been put on the back of a rather battered bus – it was either that or a lorry. But those carrying it went on down the lane and past the cornfield in the fierce sun and hot wind, for the half mile to the tiny cemetery on the side of a hill. Perhaps as many as 6,000 people followed the coffin – the KGB must have used a lot of film – and there was a crush to get near the grave at the foot of three tall pine trees, which Pasternak was able to see and admire from his window across the valley.

At the graveside, the coffin was placed on baskets of flowers and then came a succession of moving, short speeches which grace Russian funerals. I wasn't close enough to hear every word, but I

81

could see that a journalist, Edmund Stevens, then working for *Life* magazine, was tape-recording the service, so I marked him out as a good source for some quotes. As it turned out, I was wrong: he was brought up in a hard school of journalism and refused to share them with a news agency. But I heard enough: such as the young anguished voice which read 'Hamlet', the first from the cycle of poems from the novel *Dr Zhivago*, with the memorable line, 'to live your life is not as simple as crossing a field'; such as, someone deciding that the ceremony had to be brought to an end, and shouting 'no more speeches, close the coffin'...; such as a worker preventing the lid from being put on, saying 'Sleep peacefully, Boris Leonardovich. We do not know all your works now, but the day will come when we shall'...; such as another young voice, shouting, 'Glory to Pasternak'.

The words were taken up by some in the crowd: 'Glory! Glory!' People near me were weeping, and suddenly – a coincidence? – the bells of the nearby Church of the Transfiguration, its domes bluer than the bluest blue, whiter than the whitest white, began to peal. And somebody became nervous and blurted out: 'This... er... demonstration is not a good thing. Close the coffin.'

And they did. But not before Pasternak's domestic help placed a prayer for the dead on his forehead. The coffin was lowered into the grave. Lumps of earth thuded down on it. And the crowd shouted 'Glory to Pasternak. Goodbye to the greatest. Hosanna!' The sky had been darkening. Suddenly there was a crash of thunder and the heavens opened. It was somehow a fitting end to a funeral which had been so authentic – an expression of what people felt, and characteristic of a country which had so often stoned its prophets and did its poets to death.

I have been back to Peredelkino many times since that June day...: in the summer to picnic and in winter to ski through the pine woods, to visit the Louis family in their dacha nearby and to visit Boris Pasternak's grave.

Now there are many other graves on the side of the hill and, even when using the tallest pine tree as a marker, it is no longer easy to find the poet's last resting place. There are tall bushes and the area which was open to the sun is now dark, even gloomy, surrounded by a shoulder-high iron fence with a hinged gate. The white headstone

8. Some 6,000 people flocked to Peredelkino outside Moscow for the funeral of Boris Pasternak despite an official blackout of his death: they followed the open coffin to the hillside grave.

has Pasternak's profile. It is engraved Boris Leonardovich Pasternak with just the date of birth and death. There are always fresh flowers on the grave, a few sweets and apples. In the depths of winter after a snowfall, it is not long before there are foot tracks to the plot. People come to recite his poetry, and they always will…

⚜

There were other funerals, but none of them as moving as was Pasternak's that hot June day in the country. Impressive and sad, however, was the official state funeral for Yuri Gagarin, the fresh-faced carpenter's son who became a national hero in April 1961, after a pioneer orbital flight of the earth lasting 108 minutes – in other words, the world's first spaceman. This was a dramatic story and it was the first time I heard Radio Moscow suddenly go silent, to be followed by the Kremlin chimes and then the dramatic and measured tones of Yuri Levantin announce 'Govorit i pokazyvaet Moskva' – 'Moscow is on the air, and on TV' – and usher in the era of manned space travel.

Gagarin, a genuinely modest and likable man, became a fine Soviet ambassador and was fêted by the world for his feat; he had tea with the Queen – however unremarkable it appears today, with men spending months in space instead of just over an hour and three quarters. But only seven years after his triumph, he was killed flying an obsolete MiG-15 jet trainer with another member of the Soviet space team.

His death was the only occasion I threatened to resign from the Daily Telegraph because it gave so much prominence to an absurd story that Gagarin had been killed flying a top secret, high-flying stratoplane. The source was a Czechoslovak defector and science writer who had heard it in a telephone conversation with a friend in Moscow!

All sorts of stories circulated about the death of Gagarin, who had become a high priest of the space age. Typically Russian was the fact that many doubted that a man who had travelled to space had crashed in an ordinary plane. Some said he had been murdered, had gone mad, crashed while flying to see a mistress, or simply defected to the West. I always believed that Gagarin and his mate were returning to Moscow from Tula where they had been celebrating with some air-force friends. They shouldn't have been allowed to take off because

84

they were both drunk. Gagarin was heard to say on his radio that he was about to try an old fashioned loop-the-loop, to prove that he could still do it. The MiG's engine cut out and the plane went straight into the ground. The official version now was that a careless fighter pilot flew so close that Gagarin's trainer flipped upside down and the cosmonaut couldn't right it.

Gagarin was a popular man, and the state funeral was the most emotional since that of Stalin's in 1953. After all, he was a sort of Soviet 'Columbus', and, as it turned out, it was the last great Russian achievement. More than half a million Russians, many crying unrestrainedly, watched the cortège wind through the streets to Red Square. Gagarin's ashes were drawn on a gun-carriage, with air force officers carrying his medals, each one on a red cushion. The most poignant moment came when the ashes were placed in niches in the Kremlin Wall, as artillery salvos boomed across the city. The two widows were weeping uncontrollably. They dropped to their knees and kissed the portraits below the niches, before collapsing. I saw several Red Square funerals, but Gagarin's was the only one that moved me.

It was a good deal – three bottles of vodka for cleaning the office car once a week. Boris was the man for the job. He was one of a small team of Russian workmen entrusted with the task of servicing the Western ghetto we lived in, and his particular task was looking after the radiators and ensuring the temperature was correct. There was a splendid carpenter, Ivan, and another young man who was in charge of the dustbins. He later blotted his copybook with the Western community by appearing at the trial of an American journalist accused of spying, and having to say he had found in the journalist's dustbin scraps of the notepaper which, according to the KGB, had written on it 'anti-Soviet and intelligence material'.

Like the entire Soviet work-force, Boris would never turn down a job on the side and was much more interested in being paid with booze, than with useless roubles. So it was vodka, and later, whisky, and later still, cognac, which would fetch very high prices on the black market.

On a particularly cold, February day, Boris cleaned my car, and one or two others, before disappearing into the basement of the block where there was a warm, snug room. He got stuck into a bottle, before collapsing, and dying – due to a blood clot on the brain. He was forty-two with a wife and a small child.

I organized a collection in the yard, and those who had their cars cleaned by him gave generously, in roubles not in bottles, of course. There would have been an insignificant pension from his employers, UPDK, the organization looking after foreigners, and death insurance didn't exist. We collected two hundred roubles – two months' wages – and Bob Evans and I were invited to the funeral.

It was so cold on the day, that when we got into the car our breath froze on the inside windows. In fact it was twenty-seven degrees of frost and there was a wind too, coming from Siberia and cutting through you like a knife.

Boris lived at Skhodny, outside Moscow, and it was hard to find. Not only were the frozen roads treacherous and un-sanded as soon as you left the capital, but the village turned out to be beyond the forty-kilometre limit imposed on foreigners. Surprisingly, our car with its clearly identifiable foreign number plate – which not only indicated I was a journalist, but also my nationality – was not stopped at police check points and turned back. Did they know? Was it too cold for them to care?

When we found the cemetery, it was deserted. It was so cold there wasn't even a little old lady tidying the graves, so nobody was able to tell us which was the one for Boris, or even if we were in the right cemetery. But we did manage to find a freshly-dug hole. Back on the road, we met an old man with icicles on his grey beard and eyebrows, who wheezed where Boris lived.

We were still gasping from the cold, and every now and again the wind came as a razor slash across the chin. We had lowered the flaps of our fur hats as a protection against frostbite and warmed our noses and stinging cheeks with our gloves.

Boris had lived in a single-storey wooden dacha on the edge of the village. The open country was an icy white expanse of desolation. His drinking mates were there and had already been at the vodka; you couldn't blame them.

Outside, the air gnawed at our cheeks; in the dacha it was stifling. There was a sudden blast of accumulated breath of the mourners, smoke from the stove, the smell of heavy clothing, cabbage and cats. And as we walked into the fug, the first thing that happened was that our glasses misted over, completely. Blinded, I removed mine and tried demisting them with a handkerchief. The first thing I saw was Boris's face, as he lay in the coffin. Sitting on chairs on three sides of the room was the family and they were looking at us with the curiosity of Russians who have never seen a foreigner before. It was clearly expected that we kiss Boris or make some other gesture of the final parting. 'I suggest a minute's silence,' I said to Bob, and we bowed our heads.

They must have been waiting for us because, as we moved into the next room, the coffin was carried out of the house and down the path towards the road. Boris's wife and other near relatives followed it and there was a strange wailing cry which was taken up by other women, unlike any sounds you would hear at a funeral in Norfolk.

We followed at a respectable distance. The winter light was fast fading and the cold was attacking our feet despite fur-lined boots. Tears of cold were freezing on my face – I should have remembered the old Russian trick of dabbing vodka on the cheeks to stop it happening. We didn't follow the coffin that long mile down the road to the cemetery, where one more decent Russian went to a cold grave.

8 – Comrade Blue Pencil

Apart from the bugs – either blood-sucking or listening to your conversation – cockroaches, inexpensive booze, the cold and the garlicky, stale smell of communal flats, there was also censorship to remind you that you were working in Moscow in the early 1960s. It was the dominating factor in our lives, a daily worry that sorely tried our nerves. And although those enforcing censorship were too thick to appreciate the fact, the system was counter-productive – it contributed to our critical attitude toward Soviet reality, making us more bloody-minded than we might have been.

For why? I once got a cracking good story out of talking to Nikita Khrushchev at an embassy reception. There was a row going on between the Russians and the Americans over the Black Sea – the Pentagon had said it intended to send some destroyers into the area on an exercise. The Soviet Union considered the Black Sea to be its private lake, and indeed there were treaties to that effect. The Kremlin was cranking up a propaganda campaign against Washington over the issue and I asked Khrushchev about it. He blew a gasket, warning the United States that if its destroyers did sail into the Black Sea, there would be trouble.

'What sort of trouble, Mr Khrushchev?'

'Big trouble,' said he. 'Such an act will have very serious consequences for peace in the region, and the United States must think carefully about what they are doing. The USSR will not stand for it.' And so on... Nikita was getting it off his chest. All blather and bluster and propaganda bullshit. But... a STORY.

I got myself to the Moscow Central Telegraph Office that night, as fast as Grisha could drive the lovely old, maroon Humber – it was the sort of car British ministers might use and was one of the few touches of class Reuters allowed us.

The international section of the Central Telegraph, just a ten-minute walk up Gorky Street from the Kremlin, had a side door – Entrance number 12. You walked up a flight of stairs into a large, plain office, complete with tables and sofas. There were two rows of cubicles, each with a telephone, but you couldn't dial from them.

Effectively, this part of the huge post and telephone complex had been taken over by the small band of foreign correspondents, perhaps no more than a couple of dozen, from Britain, the United States, West Germany, France and Italy. In those days there were no television networks and no Japanese, and those representing Western communist newspapers had special facilities of their own.

No Russians came to this area of the Central Telegraph to send cables or telephone abroad – they would have been too frightened by the sight and the sound of an extraordinary gang of professional, bourgeois, anti-Soviet hacks, thrashing away at their typewriters (there were no telexes or teleprinters either), shouting, drinking, swearing, sometimes even fighting as agency correspondents punched and kicked each other, in order to get the first telephone line out of Moscow.

And sometimes even weeping. Because Soviet censorship created a massive physical and mental barrier to getting your story to London, or wherever. You were having to deal with a faceless, machine-like apparatus, against whose decisions there was no right or method of appeal. And because officially, censorship didn't exist – we were being looked after by Glavlit, a Government department which was there to perform only a literary function – to improve and perfect our style. As it happened, Glavlit dealt in the suppression of everything from pornography to works of 'religious fanaticism'. The only thing it did not do was to correct factual errors.

Hence the shouts of rage and of frustration that could be heard coming from tough, veteran journalists, seeing action not only in the front line of the Cold War, but also behind enemy lines. It was part of the 'Moscow madness' syndrome to do with frayed nerves and sleepless nights. And usually the tears flowed right there at a long counter, where sat not the censors, but often pretty girl clerks, the conduit to the secret office and desk of the hated censors.

These nice, friendly Russian ladies would disappear through a – now legendary – glass door, covered by an ugly green curtain, clutching your typed story, or rather three copies of it – one for Glavlit, one for transmission and one to be returned to the correspondent after censorship. You kept the fourth page of the 'book' – the one you had made with carbon paper.

And then you waited… For there was no point in trying to telephone London; if you had booked a call and it came through and you began dictating the story without it having cleared the censor, the line would be cut, and you would go to the bottom of the queue. It was a torture they had refined over the years.

So you waited… Some piece of rubbish – an item from *Pravda* reproduced without critical comment – would be in and out without much delay. Sometimes you could wait for hours. It fact, it could be days before the story came back bearing the Glavlit imprimatur, a tiny, jagged-shafted arrow enclosed in a circle… even years: there are said to be some ancient correspondents still waiting for the return of their reports concerning Khrushchev's sensational Secret speech of 1956!

Once – in the old days before these old days – correspondents knew the censors who were working for the press department of the Soviet Foreign Ministry. They could talk to them, even bargain with them to try and find a compromise formula – which, of course, was a pretty shocking thing to do, since it had the effect of blurring the message. It was possible, after hours, to go to the censors' homes and get them out of bed to look at a story – but, of course, these were men and women who quickly disappeared once the Great Purge got underway.

The system I knew was introduced in 1946. Glavlit – the Main Administration for Literary Affairs – took over the job of tightening up surveillance and making censorship harsher from the Ministry of Foreign Affairs.

There was no more arguing the toss or negotiating over a few phrases or a lead. Censorship was going to be carried out in total secrecy and anonymity.

Only one correspondent, as far as I knew, tested the system. A splendid, humourous Italian, Vero Roberti, learned that there were two censors for the Italian language: one of them a little old lady; the other a nasty young man who hated him. Roberti got hold of some priceless tickets for an Italian film week and, after memorizing the numbers, got one of the clerks to take the tickets, which were for every film at the festival, to his 'dear friends', the censors. She was to hand them over with his compliments. Night after night Roberti sat in his seat hoping that one or other of his censors, or both, would turn up, so he could see what they looked like. They never did. Who can blame them? Accepting a bribe, albeit a cinema seat, from a foreign correspondent was surely a heinous crime.

See them or talk to them? We never did. But we quickly learned their mentality – how they showed extreme caution or gave the thumbs down to anything that deviated from the line; that contained personal criticism of leading Soviet figures; that suggested instablity in the regime or rifts in the top leadership or portrayed the Soviet Union in a bad light.

That a story or phrase was true did not matter, Heaven forbid! You couldn't write, for example, about an English school choir performing just off Red Square within a 'stone's throw of the Lenin Mausoleum'. The censor spotted that one – nobody was going to be allowed to throw stones at Lenin under any circumstances. That phrase was out.

There is the story of a French journalist who commented on what he saw as a physical resemblance between Khrushchev and Marlon Brando. He waited ages until a clerk called him over and said that Glavlit wanted to know who was 'Marlon Brando'.

Told that he was a very famous American film star, she disappeared behind the green door. He continued waiting until she finally reappeared with another question.

'Is he a serious actor, or does he play comic roles?'

'Serious,' the Frenchman replied. There was further delay and when the copy was returned all references to both Khrushchev and Brando had been deleted. The censor took no chances.

Censorship was effected by the removal of words, usually with a black pencil – if they were feeling angry, offending passages were cut out with scissors – and it was this technique which could distort a story. You could knock out a story on the lines of: *PRAVDA* TODAY SAID STEEL PRODUCTION HAD INCREASED BY TEN PER CENT OVER LAST YEAR STOP ACTUAL FIGURE WAS NOT GIVEN BUT THIS ESTIMATED TO BE 100 MILLION TONS STOP DEMAND FOR STEEL MEANWHILE IS FALLING IN MOST WESTERN COUNTRIES WHICH SWITCHING TO PLASTIC STOP INCREASE HOWEVER PROBABLY MEANS MORE IF WEIGHTIER CONSUMER GOODS END.

This sort of cable was easy meat for the censor's grinder. It would emerge as: *PRAVDA* TODAY SAID STEEL PRODUCTION HAD INCREASED BY TEN PER CENT STOP INCREASE MEANS MORE CONSUMER GOODS END

It has to be said that even the last sentence may not have got through. A cynical censor may have grasped that there was a suggestion here that the Soviet people did not already have all the washing machines and refrigerators that they would have had, if the Soviet Union had not been turning its steel into tanks and guns.

This was bad enough, but often, against the rules, the censored copy would be sent to London as you were waiting to collect the blue-pencilled carbon showing what had been done to it. By that time it was too late to 'pull it' and some green sub-editor in London would be puzzling over your story, wondering whether you had written it while drunk, or whether you were simply incompetent.

My Khrushchev story turned up in London several hours after I had written it. It had badly worried the censor who rightly suspected it was a Khrushchevian off-the-cuff remark – he was the bane of their lives with his foolery and his boasting. So the censors held back any such cables until they had asked, and received, the authority of superiors to release them. I often wonder if Khrushchev knew of this, and talked to us to revenge himself for our impertinence or cynicism. Anyway, the version they got in London read: SOVIET LEADER NIKITA KHRUSHCHEV SAID QUOTE UNQUOTE END.

What censors were especially quick to jump on was anything, even a triviality, that could be construed as critical. I once wrote about seeing a police colonel queuing for some oranges, buying five kilogrammes and walking off with a pleased smile on his face. It all got cut, probably because the phrase carried, however remotely, a suggestion he was hoarding; but in any case, it might have tarnished the image of police officers to suggest they actually did shopping.

More difficult to understand was when I used the phrase 'a line of patient peasant women'. Out went the word 'patient' which, if nothing else, can certainly be said to apply to Russian women.

But Comrade Glavlit could be outwitted, and at the same time he could be a useful political sounding board. Every now again, we buried the essentials of the story in the body of the copy – hoping that the censor's attention would wander and fail to realize what we were up to. You relied on the man handling your story in London to have twigged what you were doing, pull out the important fact and make it the lead. But it seldom worked like that, because those in London were told to treat Moscow's copy carefully and not to mess about with it.

Just occasionally, we managed to stoop to a bit of slang or jargon, to convey a message, especially on the telephone. We always hoped to get away with something important on the principle that however well the censor understood English, he would be nonplussed by the odd Cockney or World War II phrase.

Once, an Austrian airliner, with some British and American air attachés aboard, crashed on its approach to Moscow. Tipped off about the crash, I spent the night wandering around the countryside before finding a farm where bodies had been taken. There was no doubt that Glavlit would block the story, so I rang London from my bedroom. You always knew someone was listening carefully to what you said on the telephone, recording it also, of course, for the KGB, just as you do when you are on a crossed line. I talked about there having been a major prang, that our Brylcreem boys-in-blue based here, who had been on holiday, had not had a good night; told them to get Vienna to pull their fingers out and do some homework and wished them goodnight. I sensed the censor trying to make head or tail of what I was saying, pretty certain I was trying to get across a story, but wanting to get the message before he cut me off. It worked. The full story of the Moscow aircrash, in which many people died, including the senior British air attaché, came out of Vienna.

Glavlit's tiresome and tireless subbing did have a use sometimes, by showing which way the wind was blowing. One of the big stories of the 1960s was the rift between Moscow and Peking. This created considerable tension and led to predictions that the two nuclear superstates were heading on a collision course to war. But at that time, the row was developing in an abstract way and between two phantom, ideological schools.

The Russians were revisionists; the Chinese were dogmatists. But *Pravda* and the rest of the Soviet press never said that the dogmatists numbered many hundreds of millions, lived in the Far East or that they had almond eyes and yellow skin.

Nor could you – not until one evening, just before the opening of the extraordinary gathering of all the world's Communist leaders when the forbidden word 'Chinese' was allowed to pass. A burst of cheering went up in the Central Telegraph and some of us took ourselves off to the champagne bar across Gorky Street to celebrate a significant victory. In actual fact, when the conference was over the Chinese again became dogmatists, but within a few months all censorship of comments about the Sino-Soviet schism was dropped. That rift, although not the one inside the Soviet leadership on how to deal with China, was out in the open.

There were not many victories over Glavlit, however, and I wasted many hundreds of hours hanging around in the Central Telegraph until the censors had done their dirty business. The one good thing about it was I was in the company of some warm, humorous and very fine journalists of several nationalities, some of whom knew a thing or two about the Soviet Union.

But censorship was exhausting, frustrating, nerve-racking. You knew that it tainted your copy because, if it hadn't existed, you would have said something else. And I have always thought it wrecked my style, preoccupied with writing to beat the censor, twisting and turning my copy so it passed through his needle. It certainly prevented the sort of balanced reporting about Khrushchev's Soviet Union that was badly needed at the time and on which Reuters had made its reputation.

It also led to all sorts of misunderstandings when journalists resorted, as they sometimes did in moments of acute frustration, to the use of codes. The story is told of the news agency reporter who suggested that if Stalin died, he would send a cable saying 'PLEASE SEND £50 FOR EXPENSES' and they should run the tyrant's obituary. When Stalin died, he sent the cable, expecting to be told he had achieved a world scoop. Nothing happened except that several weeks later he discovered that the £50 had been paid into his bank account.

And of course it was ineffective. Most of the important stories got out quickly – a day or two later – either taken by journalists in their pockets along with jars of caviar and worked up from abroad; by the thousands of tourists now coming in and out; or via the big diplomatic and military stories leaked out in other capital cities throughout the world.

Nor could it be taken seriously – by me, at least – after two hacks in the finest traditions of old Fleet Street, cut-throat rivalry, got carried away in the Central Telegraph, due to the old adage that facts should never be allowed to get in the way of a good story.

The occasion arose from the quite useless and rather wicked decision to send two little dogs, Byelka and Strelka, into orbit in a single space capsule. They were presented to us at a press conference, alive and barking, although it did occur to me at the time that these could be any old dogs – you could never really believe anything the Kremlin told you.

But it was clear that having progressed from the first sputnik, a kind of celestial ice-cream cart, the Soviet scientists were using the dogs as guinea pigs and manned space-flights were coming soon.

The *Daily Express* reporter pulled out of the news room for the story was decidedly tired and emotional from his Moscow experiences. The dog angle took second place and the whole of the Central Telegraph heard him shouting his story to London, which began: I DRANK CHAMPAGNE TODAY WITH SIX SOVIET COSMONAUTS ABOUT TO GO UP IN SPACE. And so on and so forth.

Those of us filing boring stories about the effect of weightlessness on Byelka and Strelka shook our heads in disbelief. But not the *Daily Mail* reporter, who was not going to be scooped by anybody. He wrote a story, cleared by the censor, which began: TOP-SECRET SOVIET PLANS TO SEND SIX COSMONAUTS INTO SPACE WERE SCRUBBED LAST NIGHT. Etc, etc.

They got away with it. We got callbacks from editors who wondered if it was just possible that we were too close to the story and too sceptical about Soviet space achievements to have missed something important.

To give him his due, Khrushchev knew censorship was silly, and he was a reformer. According to legend, Edmund Stevens, the veteran American journalist, sat down one day in his office and wrote a letter

96

to Khrushchev – as many journalists had also done over the years – suggesting he dismantled the ponderous stultifying censorship system. The letter from Stevens, however, dropped through the Kremlin letter box just at the right moment. Khrushchev desperately wanted the Soviet Union to be a 'normal' country and he wanted good publicity for its policies and its achievements, such as Yuri Gagarin's first space flight, which was about to take place.

So he got rid of it. For fifteen years the Central Telegraph had been a marketplace for the exchange of ideas, philosophy and gossip. There, some of the greatest post-war stories had been written and transmitted: the death of Stalin, the execution of Beria, Soviet possession of nuclear weapons, Khrushchev's de-Stalinization campaign, the Soviet crackdowns in Hungary and Poland, the launching of Sputniks...

Soon the door was to be padlocked. Glavlit, for us , although not for Russian newspaper editors, was abolished. Even then it was done in a typically Soviet – or Russian – manner. Correspondents were summoned to the Soviet Foreign Ministry where they were told, not that censorship was terminated – after all it had never officially existed – but that they could now telephone their copy to the West from their homes or offices. There was a rider, however. Lest we got carried away by our new found freedom, we were warned we would be found guilty for any 'incorrect rumours' we sent.

Soviet-style Alice in Wonderland, we thought, as we rushed back to our offices to file our first, uncensored dispatch.

Naturally, it was all about the end of censorship.

9 - Bugs and Buggers

Our first home in Moscow was in a bedbug-infested, foreigner-only ghetto on Prospekt Mira (Peace Street). Betty B lived in a flat above ours and she telephoned me: 'Come up and see me, Johnny,' she said. 'I've got something really interesting to show you. Come right now. And it's all right... he's working.'

She was referring to her husband, a first secretary at the British Embassy, a nice man who ended up with with a 'Call Me God' – a medal that came up with the rations for senior diplomats and meaning a Companion of the Order of St Michael and St George, and who was often embarrassed by his wife's behaviour. In those days she would have been described as being 'flighty'.

I took all the necessary precautions. Brenda was given instructions to telephone Betty B if I was gone longer than ten minutes and to say London wanted to talk to me urgently. Then I trotted up a couple of flights of stairs to see her.

In her flat a record of Tchaikovsky's *Nutcracker* was playing at full blast. She stuck her face close to mine and I caught a whiff of gin. 'Bugs', she mouthed. 'We've got the little buggers in the bedroom.'

They use to say that finding your first bugging device in Moscow was like having your first baby. Both events were of considerable importance and had a direct bearing on your entire future. You were a focus of attention. You had arrived. Additionally, it must be said it was possible to experience a peculiar horror and fear, a sensation of violation, like returning to your house and finding it had been broken into and burgled.

But from my very first day in Moscow, I had decided I wouldn't be bothered with all this nonsense. I had nothing to hide. So she had bugs. We all had bugs. Loudly, I said: 'They are coming up from the Ghanaian ambassador's flat in the basement. Listen, all you have to do is to keep your bed away from the wall. And stand the legs in tins of paraffin. That'll stop the little buggers from sucking your blood.'

She grimaced, took my hand and led me into the bedroom. She got down on her hands and knees and pulled up a piece of the floorboard. 'Look at that,' she said triumphantly. 'What's that? Scotch mist?'

I looked down a thin strip of electric cable. 'So what?' said I. 'That's what makes your lights go on.'

'Bloody isn't!' she said. 'That, Johnny Miller, is a bug.'

'That's not a bug. That isn't even half a bug. That is eighteen inches of electric wire. Mess about with that and you'll either electrocute yourself or fuse the place rotten.' She replaced the piece of floor board and we went into the living room. She put a blanket over the telephone - widely believed by us to be the major bugging device for either monitoring calls or listening to conversations in a room – and beckoned me to sit next to her on the sofa.

Again, I smelt the gin as she put her mouth close to my ear. 'I know what I am talking about. The Embassy has been round and defumigated us. The place was riddled with bugs.

'Even one in the toilet. God knows why. We never go there when we have something important to say. But I wanted you to see what sort of pressure we are under from you-know-who. Them.'

Seeing I wasn't impressed, she said: 'All right, what about a quickie to give them something to listen to...'

She was joking of course. Nevertheless, in the time-honoured tradition of a *News of the World* reporter, I made my excuses and left.

Two weeks later, I met her in the yard at Prospekt Mira.

'How's your bugs?' I asked, solicitously. She told me a story about how she decided that the bugs in the bedroom were putting her off her love-making. So she got her husband to arrange another sweep targeted at the bedroom. As he pulled on the wire under the floorboards, somebody, assuredly the KGB, was pulling on the wire at the other end. So he stopped what he was doing, so as not to 'provoke' them.

This story of a tug-of-war between the KGB and British intelligence over a strip of wire and fought out in a flat in Moscow was as daft anything I had ever heard in the espionage war of the 1960s.

'It seems to me that the only thing being pulled here is my leg,' I said, and that was the last time she ever called me up to come and have a look at her KGB 'etchings.'

Yet it was perfectly possible to become paranoid about the KGB buggers and their bugs and, if anything, tourists were worse than journalists, not to mention diplomats and their wives. For some reason, visitors to the USSR never seemed to be able to enjoy their stay unless they felt they were being bugged or tailed – that was why one went to the country and put up with the rotten food, rats in the bedroom and cockroaches in the bath. The thought that the KGB was giving one special attention, spending hundreds of man hours and roubles on keeping their eye on you was exciting, and made all the hardships of a visit to the land of Socialism worthwhile.

Many times have I heard variations of the story about getting things done by 'talking to microphones' in the ceiling, walls, telephone, even the ashtrays or flower vases! The most common one was about there being no soap in the hotel bathroom. So very loudly and slowly, in case the eavesdroppers' English is not up to much you say something like: 'The Soviet Union may have lots of rockets, Comrade, but it seems short on the soap. Who would want to live in a country without soap?"

Almost immediately the woman in charge of the floor, sitting at the end of the corridor – also KGB of course – and looking the spitting image of Rosa Khleb, knocks on your door and without a word of explanation hands you a bar of soap, albeit carbolic. She smiles, flashing a mouthful of silver teeth, says nothing and is gone.

Back at home, you tell the story to dinner guests to gasps of amazement and laughter. 'How exciting. I say, Darling, what a funny old place Soviet Russia is. We really must visit it ourselves next year.'

Visiting journalists, especially those with large egos, would come up with similar tales. One told me in all seriousness that his spacious room in the Hotel National – in those days my favorite Moscow hotel – was bugged-up to the eyeballs. When I asked him if he had actually seen any bugs, he said he hadn't. But he knew where they were. There was only one lamp working in the chandelier hanging from the ceiling of his living room. The five empty sockets were filled by tiny microphones for recording all his conversations. Or so he insisted.

A formidable journalist of my acquaintance sent from London to cover the visit of a US Secretary of State, also once came up with a remarkably silly tale of KGB bugging techniques. After the visit, she claimed, she had walked along a corridor in the hotel Intourist on the then Gorky Street where a party of American journalists had stayed and in nearly every room she saw microphones hanging from the ceiling to await their removal by KGB engineers.

But some stories about the skills of the boffins of the KGB's Technical Operations Directorate were true. Once, the West Germans sent a technician in counter-audio and debugging to cleanse the Moscow embassy. During his sweep he discovered numerous microphones, and whenever he found one he fed a high voltage charge into it, apparently giving KGB listeners a nasty shock.

They didn't like that one bit, but they were even more annoyed when he discovered a new electronic toy which they had carefully installed in a key room in the embassy. This gadget managed to pick up messages as they were typed for automatic ciphering, but before they were ciphered, enabling the KGB to read messages being sent to Bonn.

The KGB hit back. When the West German visited the Zagorsk monastery outside Moscow, they tailed him and struck. He was jabbed in the bum with nitrogen mustard gas. Fortunately, doctors at the American Embassy recognized the symptoms and after a long and extremely painful treatment, he survived.

When the Australians moved into a lovely old building used for many years by the Chinese mission, they found no fewer than thirty-three bugs which the KGB had installed to keep an eye on their erstwhile Chinese comrades. The only story which came out at the time was about the long and expensive redecoration of the building – a necessity brought about by the Chinese, who had smashed it up, and the staff who had apparently had the habit of urinating in some of the fireplaces.

There was the amazing, but true, story of the wooden plaque the Russians presented to the American ambassador in Moscow, referring to the old, wartime alliance, who had it put in his office. There was tiny bug in it. One day British technicians attempting to monitor Soviet government communications from the embassy across the road from the Kremlin were astonished to pick up the voice of the American ambassador dictating a letter to his secretary. The rest is history. The plaque and its bug were shown by the Americans at a meeting of the United Nations as an example of Soviet beastliness.

But for some reason or another, I missed out on finding bugs in any of several flats I lived in. The nearest I got to one was seeing a grubby hand-print high on the wall of one of the rooms which hadn't been there when we returned to England for a holiday. Perhaps this had something to do with a bugging device being repaired or replaced.

And I only saw one. Lunching with a British diplomat in his flat, I noticed he had a print on the wall of Tretchikoff's *Chinese Lady*. Having known Tretchikoff in Cape Town, I observed that although the artist claimed it was his most famous and most widely-sold print, I thought it was naff.

'So it is. So it is,' said the diplomat. 'But it is not my choice. It is supplied by the Ministry of Works. And it has a use. As I will demonstrate.'

He took down the print which covered over a large hole in the wall. In the hollow there was a pipe and on the pipe a small metal gadget – a bugging device.

I asked him why it was left there. 'No point. No sense in it,' he said. 'If they know we have removed it, they will replace it somewhere else. One of our maids could do for them when we are out. And it will be more cleverly concealed. So we will have to fumigate the place again and it simply aint worth the trouble. Also, they might start using long-range bugging techniques which we would certainly not know about. Not, of course, that I am going to say anything in this flat of any value to them. Nor, come to that, to bloody journalists either!'

It was the only bug I saw in more than thirty years of dealing with the Soviet Union – which is one of the reasons why I never believed half the stories I have been told. For example, a colleague said he had suspected there was a bug concealed in an electric point in the wall. One day he found the point was hanging off the wall and there was screwdriver lying near it. He said he thought he must have caught the KGB at work in his flat. But he consumed vast quantities of 'Stoli' and' under the influence' he could easily have attacked the point himself.

All the NATO embassies, however, were obsessed with the supposedly miracle powers of the KGB at picking up conversations, briefings and consultations. In several rooms of the British Embassy there were loudspeakers strategically placed to thwart the bugs. At a press of a button, music or garbled speech would drown out anything being said.

Then a team of engineers and building workers arrived from London with their own 'clean' bricks, cement, wood and other items. I counted them getting out of a minibus one day at the Embassy, with picks and shovels, and I nicknamed them the Seven Dwarfs. The result of their labours was the creation of a secret bug-proof chamber, known as 'the Tank', at the end of a gloomy, guarded corridor and which looked like a combination of a 'portakabin' toilet, bank vault and boardroom.

Effectively, this was a sound-proofed room, literally suspended within another room, which was itself sound-proofed. Its door was like a strong-room door and when it was locked, a green light said 'safe'. There were also warning lights to detect unknown electronic transmissions from inside the room in case, for example, the KGB had somehow managed to hide a bug in a diplomat's shoe, or up his arse...

Once, I managed to get inside the 'Tank.' And I was to be officially reprimanded over a story I had written which touched on KGB bugging activities. The diary item was about the mystery of some bones found in the Embassy's large, compound garden. One rumour said they were the remains of a Bolshoi Ballet company choreographer who, during the War, had had an affair with the wife of the British Ambassador. The Ambassador had lured him to the embassy and shot him dead. The body was buried in the garden.

I had a shrewd idea that the real truth was a lot more mundane and that these were the remains of someone working at the Embassy, perhaps not a Briton who died during the War from some illness or another and being without next of kin, his body was dispensed with in the garden.

Shortly after the item appeared, I was summoned to the 'Tank.' True, bones had been found in the garden, but it was made clear I should not have written the piece because... well... er... it's like this, John... bit sensitive... you know how it is, one of our chaps found a cable and traced it into the garden where it went underground. So the Ambassador's vegetable patch was dug up and some bones were found.

Those KGB rascals didn't miss a trick. One of them in the Soviet Embassy read the piece and – tongue in cheek no doubt – the Soviet Ambassador raised the matter of the bones with the Foreign Office. What bones? asked the F.O. Ah yes, those bones. Of course, they were not human bones, but the bones of guard dogs. And everyone should now let sleeping dogs lie.

Reputedly, the buggers worked from a former monastery a mile or so from the Communist Party Central Committee, and it certainly looked a funny place. But what really did go on there? I envisaged a huge area, like a telephone exchange, where KGB linguists listened to miles of tapes or were plugged in directly to the bedroom or living room of the targeted foreign residences.

Imagine the scene if you will. Rows of men, some in cubicles with headphones, smoking, drinking glasses of tea, yawning, scratching their armpits, dictating to each other or writing a report of their shift.

'British journalist Bloggs and wife returned to flat block at 02.47 am – militia post phoned in. They were drunk and arguing. He swore at her and called her a silly cow. Couple had several drinks, abused Soviet hospitality and criticized Soviet workmanship and peace-loving foreign policy. Wife said British diplomat Long was dirty old man, who had put his hand on her knee under the dinner table. Bloggs said Long's wife was a *prostitutka* (prostitute) who rubbed herself against him in the kitchen. They went to bed at 03.30 and made love but nothing near as noisy as on previous nights when the volume control was turned down. He snored. She swore at him. He got out of bed, turned on BBC which broadcast usual anti-Soviet lies and slander. No incoming calls from dissident traitor Ivanov. Suggested action: British diplomat Long should be targeted for swallow trap. Intensify telephone taps to see if his wife is having affairs.' And so on, and so forth...

By and large Russian friends professed little interest in KGB bugging techniques. It was simply not a subject they wanted to discuss – they either had bugs or they didn't. There was nothing they could do about it. But English-speakers with a sense of humour used codewords for the KGB and what it meant: they would talk about 'Galina Borisovna', a euphemism for the (K)GB. They would swear at the behaviour of 'Sofia Vasilievna' – she was *sovyetskaya vlast*, or Soviet power. Nervous Russians would use sign language such as flicking at the top of the shoulder with the hand to indicate that the person they were talking about had epaulettes, a security policeman.

A frequent visitor to our flat was Natasha, whose concern about KGB bugging was exceptional and taken to almost absurd (to us) lengths. But then she was a terribly sad case. During the grim war years in Moscow she was one of those lovely Russian girls who made life far from grim for a few young Britons working at the embassy. Some of these girls may have had to report to the NKVD, the forerunner of the KGB, but most of them did not, and persisted in their love affairs with a fatalistic recklessness that is purely Russian.

Natasha married her Briton in a ceremony at the Embassy. When he had to return home and the Soviet authorities refused to give her an exit visa, he decided to smuggle her out. As she was about to board a British ship in Leningrad harbour, dressed as a man, she was caught and sentenced to a term in a labour camp. She served three and a half years and was twice beaten up and raped by her guards.

Stalin died and she was released along with millions of others and she foolishly thought she would be able to be reunited with her husband. Life had moved on. Thinking he would never see her again he had married and had children. With the help of the British Embassy, her case came before a judge in London who, like Solomon, was asked to rule on the validity of the second, English marriage. She lost. And the Soviet authorities were never going to give her a visa to leave the country.

Natasha refused to give up her British connection. She befriended wives of diplomats and journalists, including us. Time and time again she told us her tragic story – blaming, of course, the British government for all her troubles.

We had a name for her – Goodie Two-shoes because we bought her shoes, clothes and other items she wanted from the West in exchange for bits and pieces she would discover in Commission shops (Russian second-hand stores) that sold Russian antiques and art works.

But her visits to our flat – any foreigner's flat – were fraught. Fearing the KGB and its microphones, she believed she was still a target and that they were interested in what she was saying.

She always brought with her two heavy bags of belongings – she dared not leave them in her single room in a communal flat, in case they were stolen – and as soon as she sat down she would take out an exercise book.

Virtually everything was written down – that she had for the umpteenth time applied for a visa, been to seen somebody at the embassy who had sent off her visa application to London. 'Ah! that's good news,' you would say in order to move the conversation on a bit quicker. 'So you still think...'

She would interrupt, pointing to the ceiling and shaking her head. 'No, no. No speak'– and she would hand you her exercise book and a pencil.

The conversation, such as it was, often lasted an hour. The exercise book would be filled with scribbling, adding up to nothing. Nobody can help her, except the Soviet authorities. They were never going to give her an exit visa because she had thrown in her lot with foreigners, preferring them to her own kind. They would not have even wanted to eavesdrop on her conversations.

I do not know what happened to her. She suddenly stopped visiting the Embassy and made no contact with the British wives, who would sit down with her and go over and over her story. Perhaps the KGB decided that she would not be allowed to live in Moscow any more and she was exiled. Perhaps she died. One thing is certain: she never got to see England...

After the collapse of Communism, the buggers could no longer do what they liked. A few facts emerged about their techniques. Conversations were recorded slowly on a moving steel wire, considered to be more reliable than recordings on magnetic tape. Bugged phones were connected to a voice-activated disconnect system, so that if Russians said anything nasty about the Soviet system and its rulers the telephone was automatically disconnected – which made life hard for dissidents and those Westerners who were heading for a nervous breakdown.

It also become clear that the attention Western diplomats and journalists were getting, or believed they were getting, from the KGB was nothing compared to the bugging of top Russian politicians. After the abortive *coup* against Mikhail Gorbachev, it was revealed that the KGB employed 1,500 agents to bug and follow him and his family. Mrs Gorbachev's hairdresser was also bugged, as was Boris Yeltsin's tennis coach.

And the buggers got a new identity with a name - FAPSI, or the Federal Electronic Surveillance Agency. More than that, several of its top officials were jailed for fraud and corruption, involving millions of dollars.

It couldn't have happened in the good-old bad days.

10 – Lies Have Short Legs

So censorship was abolished. Now we could write what we liked, when we liked, how we liked. Well, up to a point, Lord Copper. There was still the little matter of Stalin-era regulations – interviews from anyone, from Ivan Ivanovitch Ivanov to Nikita Sergeyevich Khrushchev, were supposed to be arranged through official channels – the Soviet Foreign Minister, the Society for Cultural Relations, and other dreary, bureaucratic organizations.

And, to be fair to the Soviet government, those who formulated the rules had a certain sense of humour: there were exceptions, and these were set out in Article 6. For example, you did not need to inform the Foreign Ministry if you were going to a restaurant or a cinema or buying a newspaper or calling the fire brigade! But the 1947 regulation existed for one reason and that was to to guarantee that getting to talk to anyone with the Foreign Ministry's help would be a frustrating, cumbersome and lengthy procedure.

Take the Press Department of the Foreign Minister. For many years a lady by name Tamara Mikhailovna Gorbacheva – was she related to that nice Mr Gorbachev, I now find myself wondering – was supposed to look after every need and whim of the small British *corps*. I recall my first conversation with her years ago, as though it took place yesterday.

Khrushchev was off on his travels and there were rumours he might make a stop in Peking to talk to the Chinese leaders over the increasingly bitter row. So I asked, politely, like an English gentleman, not a comrade: 'Madame Gorbacheva, can you tell me please, will Mr Khrushchev be flying non-stop to the Far East?'

There was a distinct pause. 'Ah, Mr Miller, it seems to me, yes,' said she at last.

'Thank you, Madam Gorbacheva,' I said. 'But does that formulation mean that you know? Or is it really just your opinion?'

'Mr Miller,' she said, so very sweetly: 'It means it is just my opinion. Because if I knew for sure, I would say "maybe".'

There were many such conversations, full of Soviet mumbo-jumbo. For we were regarded by Soviet officialdom, quite rightly in my opinion, with suspicion. After all, we had let them down on so many occasions and they had tried hard to be nice and helpful.

To get to know you better, they would invite you to call on them in their offices at the Ministry of Foreign Affairs, one of Stalin's wedding-cake palaces on the Ring Road. It was a daunting experience to ride to the seventeenth floor in a lift, rubbing shoulders with Soviet diplomats, privy to all sorts of secrets.

The chat would take place in the office of a deputy chief, and I had two or three over the years; they were unfailingly the same, conducted as if according to a script.

First the handshake, then the offer of a chair and, if you were lucky or they were thirsty, you might get a glass of tea, if not genuine sympathy, because they could be pretty cynical themselves about their role. And what they said was always eminently reasonable.

One of my chats was with a certain Yevgeni Kuznetsov, who as good as told me a few years later when he was very drunk that – surprise, surprise! – he was KGB. He looked Soviet, complete with dandruff on his jacket collar and a mouthful of silver teeth, and he was badly out of shape. When he was sober he told me proudly that during his career he had held press attaché jobs in Soviet embassies in Africa. When pressed to say where, he admitted that he only worked in one country, the Congo, an experience which would have made anybody reach for the bottle. Sipping his tea from a spoon and between slurps, he read the Department's riot act: 'Welcome to the USSR, Mr John Miller... slurp... We are here to help you in any way we can... slurp... But, Mr Miller, we have to ask something of you. In exchange for our help, perhaps you will help us... slurp... We would ask you that when you make your report about our country and our Soviet way of life, please, please be honestly objective in your approach. By doing so, you will help create a better understanding between our peoples... slurp... because, Mr Miller, that is what we are all trying to do. Aren't we?'

'Of course we are,' I would agree, and slurp a little tea myself. But, as the Russians say, I was a sparrow that had been shot at. I knew the score and the harsh reality behind the superficial geniality of the welcome. And that Mr Kuznetsov was watching me, and whenever I sought to lift the dust covers off anything especially sensitive and asked for his help, I wouldn't get it.

I don't think anybody from the Press Department at anytime ever told me anything I did not know, except, perhaps, the time of a press conference that wasn't worth attending. Meanwhile, the vast majority of requests for interviews would be filed and forgotten. One of the very few that was arranged for me with the Soviet long-jumper and then Olympic champion, Igor Ter-Ovanisyan, illustrated the sort of game the Press Department played. A KGB car with two officers followed me for miles across Moscow to Igor's flat, waited until the interview was over, and followed me back to my office.

In fact, the Kremlin beat from the time of Stalin right up to Gorbachev very much resembled a detective assignment, except that you rarely had the chance to interview the prime suspect. You would work painstakingly on stories or cases, talking to third-hand sources of varying reliability. And at the end of the day, you would discover that you were the accused.

Because much of what you wrote was scrutinized by the Foreign Ministry or the KGB, or both – hardly surprising, given that – ACC – it was revealed that of the 3,900 staff at the Foreign Ministry, 2200 were also on the payroll of the KGB. Upset the wrong people and you would know about it. You wouldn't get invitations to important events. Your permission to travel would be curtailed even further – 'No, Mr Miller, you cannot go to Omsk, Tomsk or Novosibirsk because there are no flights/no hotel rooms/all bridges to those cities are under water/all officials are on holiday.'

You could be attacked in the Soviet press, or called to the Ministry for a reprimand or a warning. Not that I suffered unduly. Being identified by a newspaper as a bourgeois hack was like being mentioned in dispatches. Being called in and reprimanded by the Ministry of Foreign Affairs was the equivalent of the Military Cross. If you were kicked out, you had won a Victoria Cross. Although I went over the top on many occasions and had a moderately good war, I didn't manage to finish up with any worthwhile gongs, in fact only with a few mentions. Perhaps I wasn't brave enough.

TASS, Moscow Radio and *Izvestia* all had a go at me at one time or another. The TASS report appeared in several newspapers over my favourite Soviet newspaper headline: *Lies have Short Legs* – a guffaw, if only from me. Virtually a cliché, it was snappier than a similar line about how 'Lies walk on a cockroach's legs', i.e. they are brittle and collapse.

So what item of disgraceful and sensational reporting upset the Soviet government and warranted bringing to the attention of millions of Soviet citizens the *Daily Telegraph* – most of whom had never had the chance to see the paper or, come to that, any other British newspaper other than, perhaps, the *Morning Star*?

It was a story about the year's harvest figure – or rather, the absence of it – that upset TASS. The figure was not given at a meeting of the Supreme Soviet, the pseudo-parliament, because it was so bad; the lowest for many years, despite a huge investment in agriculture. Instead, to disguise the Kremlin's disappointment and alarm, the minister involved came up with a coy formula, a little classic in gobbledeegook – that over the Five-Year Plan the average harvest of grain exceeded by eight per cent the level reached in the previous Five-Year Plan from 1966-70. It was a good try and it would have confounded deputies, who wouldn't have had the grain figures to hand. But I wasn't having any of it and wrote about how the grim truth of the disastrous harvest had been hidden from the people.

TASS reprimanded me with some classical 'Sovspeak'. The tone of my story was 'hysterical'. I had juggled with words, trying to create the impression that the Soviet economy was on the brink of failure. TASS went on to say I had quoted from a CIA estimate on the harvest, not concealing the sources of my information and those who inspired me. And to what aim?

'Soviet people cannot but feel indignation at the attempts by certain circles in Western countries to use concoctions about the Soviet Union as a means of diverting the attention of public opinion at home from the very real and tangible difficulties in the socio-economic field, and precisely such an attempt was made by John Miller.'

Moscow Radio, in one of its English-language broadcasts, took umbridge at a story I had stumbled on about the Kremlin suddenly becoming genuinely concerned about the possibilities of a nuclear war – as distinct from pretending to be for propaganda reasons – and its consequences. Victor Louis was the source of the story and it turned out later to be accurate. It was a complex account, but essentially about a KGB officer in Washington who had written a report for the

Lubyanka to the effect that the Pentagon was cranking up a nuclear strike against some Soviet targets, which, of course, it wasn't. I suspected Victor had got the story from someone in the Foreign Ministry and, because it was serious stuff, even passed up the opportunity to trot out the old Armenian Radio joke – Question: 'What do you do in the case of a Western nuclear attack?' Answer: 'Wrap yourself up in a white sheet and proceed slowly to the nearest cemetery, so as not to cause panic.'

This time it emerged that I was being paid to write such stories in order to keep up the circulation of the *Daily Telegraph*, but Moscow Radio couldn't understand why I was doing this 'with the help of brazen lies'. It was a sensational report, it said, that would not win more readers and concluded with a Doomsday scenario: 'Lies about nuclear war may finally lead to a situation when there will be no one to read the paper and, incidentally, not only the *Daily Telegraph*.'

This was pretty tame compared to what was dished out to some British journalists. One in particular was David Bonavia, who was *The Times* correspondent in Moscow in the 1970s and came to wish he hadn't been. Almost from the day he set foot in the Soviet Union he was the target of press attacks, which got increasingly nasty. Once, he wrote an amusing piece about a talent competition on Soviet television, observing that one of its chief failings was a shortage of microphones. 'The mike is passed from speaker to speaker with much grabbing and fumbling, and you keep expecting the wire to get tangled up in someone's ankles.' I chortled when I read the article, having witnessed many occasions when the big spider – the overhead mike – suddenly appeared at the top of the screen, during what purported to be a chat show or a play, and wandered about from side to side.

The Times was attacked for 'slandering the Soviet state since its inception' and Bonavia was accused of 'unusual lightness of thought' – a quotation from Gogol – with the head of Soviet television saying that the station had '1109 microphones'. So, he thundered, it was outrageous to suggest there was a shortage. Bonavia did an unusual thing – he wrote to the newspaper complaining he had been misquoted – which he had. The response was another attack, such as the charge that Bonavia's fingers had 'grown thin from him continually sucking out of them anti-Soviet stories'.

Next Bonavia was accused of 'anti-Sovietism' for writing about dissidents and Jewish *refuzniks*, and then, to the envy of some of his colleagues, he was called a 'Twaddling Bleater', apparently a reference to a character in Dickens. But the matter became serious when a whole page of readers letters was devoted to him in a newspaper, under the headline 'How much Longer?'

What a charade! Several Soviet citizens, some living in obscure places like Dzerzhinsk (a town named after the first secret-police chief), wrote in as though they were regular readers of *The Times*; they couldn't have been, since only a few dozen copies were allowed into the USSR in those days.

A plumber from Minsk kicked off his letter with the familiar cliché about Bonavia sucking stories from his fingertips; a teacher said his scribblings were not worthy of the *The Times*; a scientist said he was surprised Bonavia had not suggested that Soviet television's microphones had all been sold to buy vodka (which may well have been the case!) and a teacher of English expressed concern that Bonavia was only contributing to a deterioration in Anglo-Soviet relations. This was particularly ironic because only a few months earlier, Britain had expelled more than a hundred Russians working in London as KGB officers. And a pensioner whinged on about Bonavia and asked: 'How long can *The Times* hold up *détente* in Europe?'

All this nonsense was setting the scene for Bonavia's expulsion. And that was what finally happened. He was told his activities were 'incompatible with those of a foreign correspondent'.

That was how things were done. When a journalist was marked down for expulsion, he had better beware. The means at the authorities' disposal were many and varied. The Soviet press did what it was told: newspapers could libel you without any fear of a comeback and take your articles apart, misquoting or taking them out of context, and you could do nothing about it. You didn't even have to 'tease the geese', as the Russians say, to get expelled.

But did Peter Johnson provoke them? Here was a Reuters journalist of the old school – fast, accurate and with impeccable shorthand. And absolutely honest, completely free of so much as an iota of cynicism, and in love with Mother Russia. He had desperately wanted to work in the Soviet Union and had taught himself the

9. Peter Johnson and John Miller discussing Reuters scoops on Red Square and away from the KGB microphones before having a long lunch.

language. He was never going to speak it as fluently as he spoke German, but he did his best.

His integrity inevitably led him into trouble. The longer he worked in Moscow, the larger grew his file at the the Press Department of the Foreign Ministry.

But his first and extremely serious run-in with the Russians came, not in the USSR, but in Yugoslavia, where he had gone to cover a visit by Khrushchev. This was a major turning point in relations between Moscow and Belgrade because the Soviet leader was effectively apologising to Marshal Tito and the Yugoslavs for what had happened during the schism of 1948.

Enraged by Tito's drive for independence from Moscow, Stalin threatened to shorten him by a head. He failed, and relations between the two countries had been tense ever since. Khrushchev knew that he would not get Yugoslavia back into the Communist camp, but he was banking on putting relations on a better footing. The visit indeed went well. And at the end of it, Khrushchev held a press conference on the island of Bironi and said how much he had enjoyed visiting Yugoslavia, how well he and Tito understood each other now, and how harmony had been restored between their two countries. Peter Johnson, however, asked one of the most undiplomatic questions of all time: 'Would Mr Khrushchev tell us whether he thinks there is a higher standard of living in Yugoslavia than in the Soviet Union?' Such a question, of course, is on similar lines to the one about when you last stopped beating your wife. And Khrushchev was caught, as he might himself had said, between the hammer and the anvil. Unable to give an honest answer to the question without upsetting either the Yugoslavs or the Russians, he resorted to abusing the questioner. First he suggested that Johnson was a West German journalist – which, given his background and brilliant command of the language, was not so wide of the mark – and a 'revanchist' (or revenge-seeker) which he certainly wasn't. Then he uttered a Khrushchevism, about which there is still a dispute. Some of those present who had good Russian said that the Soviet leader muttered that Johnson was a rear part of a cow, and not its arsehole. Others insist that Khrushchev referred not to a cow but a goat. Johnson himself, recollecting the incident ascribes to Khrushchev the comment that if 'people went and put their snout to the rear part of a goat, they will get a nasty smell.' Whatever he meant, he was implying that Johnson was a prat. And it stopped the press conference in its tracks. Khrushchev left in a huff, and Johnson's name went in some Soviet official's notebook. After I had left Moscow for New York, Johnson finally got his marching orders. Certain subjects anti-Semitism, questions of racisim and African students, or Soviet minorities were well-known invititations to trouble, and later the list was to be extended to dissidents and dissidence.

Whether he had ever looked at covering news stories from that angle, I doubt, but he walked head-first into trouble when a Ghanaian student travelling with a Russian girl on a train in southern Russia was murdered. This was almost certainly a racist killing. Then, as today, Russians were notorious racists – they don't like blacks, and they detest the swarthy people from the Caucasus who sell them their fruit and vegetables in the markets. It is not uncommon for even well-educated Russians to say bluntly that they don't like blacks because of the colour of their skin, and openly to call them 'monkeys'. Their resentment was compounded in those days by Khrushchev, anxious to show his anti-colonial credentials by opening the doors to thousands of African, Arab and South-East Asian students.

They flocked to Moscow to attend the Patrice Lumumba People's Friendship University, the Marxist-Leninist seat of learning for future leaders of under-developed countries. And they found themselves victims of slurs and physical attacks as Russians' deep-seated racism boiled over. Giving blacks free education was one thing, but Soviet hospitality demanded they were given preferential treatment in all things. Thus, they were taken to the head of all the queues for train tickets, theatres, even for food, and they were allowed to get away with drunken behaviour, crime and black marketeering. No wonder they met public hostility, especially when they were seen in the company of white, i.e. Russian, girls.

The murder and the Soviet authorities' inability to arrest those responsible enraged Ghanaian students, who decided to hold a demonstration on Red Square. I had got to know some of the students before I left for New York and they telephoned Reuters about the demonstration. So the next day Johnson was on Red Square when the students tried to hold their demonstration – the KGB, who also knew all about what was going to happen, soon put a stop to the protest and dealt toughly with the students. Johnson had a scoop, and that was his trouble. It was one he didn't want. Or that he should have quickly passed around, so other news agencies could also put it out. He didn't, so Reuters had the story all to themselves for hours, giving the Russians the chance to accuse him of being involved in cooking up a sensation, trying to poison relations between the USSR and Ghana, etc.

They got out his file and there were other 'offences' to be taken into account. They called him in and gave him five days to leave the country. He had really been soft on Russia and he took it badly – they're the ones who always did...

Others were more blasé and it is worth remembering that, during more than the last forty years, dozens of journalists have been expelled from the Soviet Union. The American press *corps* was often in the wars, but it was sometimes a case not of what they had written, but if their publications or networks had stepped out of line. And of course, it did not matter if what had been written was true. The *Time* correspondent, Israel Shenker, was chucked out for an article about Lenin, which referred to the *menage-à-trois* relationship with his wife, Nadezhda Krupskaya, and Inessa Armand. He was accused of 'touching with dirty fingers the memory of the founder of the Soviet state'. We now know that all the time the Soviet state archives had evidence: Lenin's letters and notes to the lady, couched in very familiar language of hanky-panky, if not, a leg-over situation.

Khrushchev got rid of censorship for a while and there was a dramatic change in the status of foreign correspondents working in the Soviet Union. But the pressure and the harassment and the surveillance and the expulsions continued. Moreover, for a decade from 1966, the beginning of a period of turmoil and convulsion that gave rise to the dissident movement, the Soviet authorities were, if anything, nastier than before. But we were not going to let the bastards get us down...

11 - Stalin's Englishmen

By inclination, I am not vengeful about political wrongheadedness. After all, there was a time when I was young and idealistic and did some silly and irresponsible things. But I had little compassion for Kim Philby, Donald Maclean, George Blake and other unrepentant Communist spies because I hold that they prolonged the Cold War by propping up the Soviet Union's military power with their espionage. Without their help – the most wicked crime of two or three of them was to provide the Kremlin with bits and pieces of atomic weapon intelligence – the appalling regime in Russia would not have survived for long after the War, let alone become a world super-power. For this they deserve a special circle in hell.

Philby was the traitor I wanted to interview more than any other. He gave one or two interviews at the behest of the KGB, his spymasters and for whom he still worked, and to favoured British journalists in the sixties, but such meetings took place in hotels. We never found out where he lived.

I met him just once, by accident. I was having lunch in the Baku restaurant on Gorky Street with Dev Muraka, an Indian journalist who has lived in the Soviet Union for years, when he said: 'You won't believe this, but I really do think that Kim Philby is sitting across the room.' So he was, and with two ladies. And one of them was Mrs Maclean.

My blinis and caviar could wait. I went over to Philby's table and looked down at him as he spooned his borsch. He knew many hacks in Fleet Street and from his days in the Middle East, but we didn't know each other.

I asked the question we have always wanted to ask; 'Kim Philby I presume?'

'Fuck off,' said the Soviet master spy.

'I was rather hoping you might invite me to sit down and give me an interview.'

'I'm not.'

'Are you well, then?' was all I thought of saying.

He said: 'Yes. Now fuck off.' Once more he used that word in front of two ladies. And it was said he was a gentleman and a charmer.

I turned to Mrs Maclean. There was strong gossip that she had left poor Donald and was having an affair with Philby. I suspected that the other woman at the table was Philby's wife, Eleanor, who put up with the cold and the discomfort and the loneliness of Moscow, as well as with Philby's drinking, before twigging that she had joined the long list of those he had betrayed.

'I think we have met. You are Mrs Maclean?'

She said nothing.

'We met at the funeral of Guy Burgess,' I persisted. She stared at me.

Philby stood up. He offered me his hand.

'That's it,' he said. 'You have your lunch and we'll have ours.'

I ignored the hand and went back to my table. There was not really a story here. But wasn't every picture worth a thousand words? With rat-like cunning, I continued to eat and talk before getting up like a man in search of a toilet – I was making for the public telephone in the restaurant entrance.

I called an old friend, Gilbert Lewthwaite of the *Daily Mail*, and suggested he came to the Baku as quickly as possible, and with a camera. There were photos to be had of Philby and his ladies, I said.

Gilbert did move himself. But, sad to relate, missed the really interesting picture. When Philby emerged from the Baku with his wife and Mrs Maclean (Headline?: '*Red Menage-à-trois*') he failed to recognize the group until they broke up at a nearby underground pedestrian way and Philby went off alone.

Only then did he catch on to what was happening. He followed Philby down Gorky Street, madly snapping the master spy until, eventually, Philby stopped, and glaring at him menacingly, said: 'Haven't you got enough?'

Gilbert did not want to lose a precious role of film at this stage and fearing Philby might call a policeman, said: 'Thank you very much, Mr Philby, for being so patient.'

An hour later I met up with Gilbert. 'I think I've got some great pictures,' he said and he certainly had a roll of film. Mission

10.   Kim Philby (behind). Gorky Street, Moscow, April 1969.
Got him at last!

accomplished! But we had to get the film developed and the pictures printed so as to divide them and send them to our different, rival, newspapers in London.

Anywhere else in the world, this would not have been a problem. But this was Moscow. We could have handed the film to the two rival American news agencies who had darkrooms, but they almost certainly would have wanted a picture for themselves. And in any case, only the Soviet news and photo agency TASS could move the pictures to London on its photowire.

It was a huge gamble, giving the film to TASS. But they developed and printed it that very same day, for a few dollars. So, after the share-out of exclusive pictures of a cold-blooded, ruthless and murderous spy and traitor walking the streets of Moscow, we went to the Central post Office and handed them in for wiring to London with captions such as 'A tourist in Gorky Street'. Then we telephoned our offices and told them to expect some photos of Philby. Exclusive and very good.

We should have known it was not going to be as easy as that. Nothing was received in London for five days. When the fruits of our cunning labours did turn up, Gilbert's paper used a picture of Philby striding down Gorky Street, passing shoppers and wearing a Keir Hardie cloth cap – a picture that has since been widely syndicated. But not my paper. Peter Eastwood, the Managing Editor, rejected the picture saying: 'We don't need to give that bloody traitor any more publicity.'

So Philby eluded me again. I never gave up and discovered that he had mail box 505 in the Kirov Street Post Office. Whenever I was passing that way, I would pop in and hang about, hoping that one day he would come and collect his mail, including an air mail edition of *The Times*, and we could have that chat. He never did, but I learned one or two items about the Soviet way of life, such as the dealing in new issues of postage stamps. Groups of men stood around in the Post Office buying and selling stamps and I sometimes got dirty looks, as though they thought I was working for the police, or worse.

I wrote two letters to Philby, using his postbox number and suggesting that we talked, but he never replied and I never had a call from one of his KGB minders setting up a meeting. What sort of a gentleman is it who doesn't reply to another gentleman's letters?

But of course, he spent his time playing out his 'Honourable Englishman' role, whingeing about the British Post Office delaying his copies of *The Times* and insisting that he was always a man of the highest integrity and ideals.

The KGB gave him a medal or two and a general's rank, and he gave their spy-school lectures on how to outwit the stupid English police and MI5, but it is known he was treated rather like a sad old pensioner, whose bedpan needed constant changing. The KGB's PR department tipped off the British press in Moscow about the funeral and were rewarded by a good turn-out of hacks who, predictably, played the story as if it were one of the most momentous events since the end of the War.

After he died, Philby's fourth and final wife, a Russian woman, Rufina by name, talked about their seventeen years of marriage and of the alcoholism which nearly destroyed him and 'turned the cleverest of men into a fool'. She described his 'nightmare' drinking binges and said that helping him to cut back to a few drinks in the evening was the only thing in her life that she could be proud of. Philby must have been drinking some to disturb a Russian woman! Living in the Soviet Union destroyed Burgess, but with Philby I suspect it was simply a guilty conscience – the result of his long life of deceit and betrayal. After all, he betrayed everybody and everything – his country, his service, his family, his friends and, I suppose, his class.

But in the end, he did alright by Rufina. All his KGB medals, souvenirs and jumble from his Soviet life were auctioned by capitalist Sotheby's, raising more than £150,000 and securing a comfortable old age for his widow.

He must have been laughing in his KGB grave.

Nor did I manage to track down the equally disgusting George Blake, who spied for Moscow for years, betraying hundreds of Western agents. He was jailed for forty-two years but with the help of some scumbags – including a London clergymen and the KGB – he escaped from Wormwood Scrubs in 1966 hidden in a van and made it safely behind the Iron Curtain. The collapse of Communism should have been bad news for Blake – but he has survived it and has more or less cheerfully given interviews to anyone who will pay him.

Gilbert Lewthwaite and I nearly got him once and we were really pushing our luck with the KGB. The *Daily Mail* somehow or other got an address for Blake. We found the street, but not the block, suggesting we only had half an address. We knocked on the door of a couple of flats but were given short shrift by the owners. And we didn't have Blake's Russian name. Later, it transpired that the flats we visited were owned by the KGB, for whom Blake was lecturing on the wicked ways of British intelligence.

Burgess, Maclean, Philby and Blake were a special breed of defector because all were traitors, and if you go back into their lives, it was nothing but deceit and betrayal. They handed over to the Kremlin every secret they could get their grubby fingers on, doing great harm to freedom and reason on both sides of the political divide, contributing to the arms race and the chances of an East-West nuclear conflagration.

There were others who chose to live under Communism and with the odd exception, were also unable to admit they had got it hopelessly wrong. But there were also reasons of love and sex, as well as ideology or bitterness, that led them to live out their days in the twilight zone of the expatriate community in Moscow.

There were half a dozen of these grey-men, who had gone over in the harshest days of the Cold War, when Stalin was still alive. After he died, they began putting themselves about a bit and you could find yourself invited to their homes to meet their Soviet wives.

There was Archie Johnstone, who had been Editor of *British Ally* a magazine started in the honeymoon period at the end of the War, but which was finally forced to cease publication. Johnstone chose freedom, Soviet-style, and tore up his British passport. Russians seemed to treat him with thinly-veiled condescension, bordering on contempt.

Another of the shadowy, guilt-ridden figures inhabiting the no man's land between the Western ghettos and the Soviet lines was Robert Dagleish, who had abandoned his diplomatic career at the British Embassy to marry a stunningly lovely Russian girl, a switchboard operator at the Embassy. Dagleish also had to turn out propaganda glorifying the Ruritanian shambles that was the Soviet Union, and only partially redeemed himself by editing a fine English-Russian dictionary.

Another turncoat was Ralph Parker, a big suspicious red-nosed man, who had been a *Times* correspondent in Eastern Europe before the War. In the first German air attack on Belgrade, his wife, a Czech Communist, and son were killed, and he nearly lost his own life. He came to Russia for *The Times* on one of the dangerous convoys to Murmansk and met up with Valentina, a vivid Russian woman, the daughter of a general, who became his translator. At one time she was also in the Red Army as a woman sniper and once boasted of taking part in operations against tribesmen in the far corners of Siberia. She was certainly a tough lady and, before Parker, she had been wed to an American negro who went to the Soviet Union at the time of the Depression.

Parker was once a Tory, he told me, but he had a fatal infatuation with Valentina and ultimately the system, and after the War, stayed on as the *Daily Worker* correspondent. In 1949, he wanted to return to England to see his mother, but his comrades refused him that magic exit visa. He was hooked and the price of the visa was a vicious, shoddy little book exposing the machinations of the British Embassy and some of its diplomats, with whom he had had close and friendly relations. Having burnt his boats with a vengeance, he went on to cover the Stalin purges and the show-trials in Eastern Europe, which he must have known were macabre farces.

Only under Khrushchev could he afford to relax and in his last years, before he died of a heart attack while cruising on the Volga, be became a critic – gentle, rather than bitter – writing for the *New Statesman* aspects of the Soviet way of life. He still had to watch what he wrote.

Just once he stuck his neck out. The publication of Alexander Solzhenitsyn's *One Day in the Life of Ivan Denisovich* in the journal *Novy mir* in 1962, was a political and literary sensation. Parker saw it was worth translating into English, and that he might pick up some hard currency to pay for his imported scotch and trout from Helsinki.

He went to work at breakneck speed and phoned me: 'I've got a problem with Solzhenitsyn,' he said. 'How's your swearing?'

Not having lived in Britain in twenty years, he wanted help to translate Solzhenitsyn's labour-camp slang into idiomatic English, and from time to time he would telephone me to discuss the best way to translate Russian oaths and crude insults.

All serious swearing in Russian is based on the ancient *yob tvoyu mat*, or 'fuck your mother' formula. Not that anyone's real mother is involved. But the worker and peasant use the expression if it starts to rain or if the sun is too hot, and have some really obscene and blasphemous variations for serious occasions. In fact, my Russian swearing at that time was confined to crude Ukrainian expressions I had learned from Poles living at a Polish resettlement camp just outside Brandon, in Suffolk, where I was the local reporter.

Much of the swearing in Parker's long-forgotten version for Gollancz comes out rather mild. But it was rushed, and he didn't want too many 'mothers' involved. My contribution is not acknowledged, which I'm pleased about, since Solzhenitsyn later wrote that *Ivan Denisovich* was 'mauled into English in Moscow by the pot-boiling parasite, R. Parker.'

Parker may have made a few hundred pounds from the translation, but it was hardly worth it – shortly after Khrushchev was done down by Brezhnev and other comrades, Solzhenitsyn got into trouble. With the exception of a couple of fairly uncontroversial short stories, he was not published again until ACC. Parker told me that some comrades had told him he had been a naughty boy by rushing to get Solzhenitsyn into print in England and thus encouraging the anti-Sovieteers in the West to blacken the name of the Soviet Union. At least he laughed sardonically as he was telling me. Soon after he died, they had his wife out of the rather comfortable flat they had shared for many years and she was moved to the outskirts of Moscow to a one-roomed flat. One Saturday afternoon, I decided to track her down; it took me two hours to find her. Saturday afternoon in a suburb of Moscow among high-rise flats was a Hogarthian scene transferred to Russia. There were dozens of men lying dead-drunk on the grass and paths between the blocks of flats. It was a terrible place for her to spend the last years of her life, but she accepted what had happened to her with a shrug of the shoulders.

She gave me a book of his essays which had been published in Moscow in Russian to mark his death. Not one of them can stand the test of time because a majority were on themes, such as: 'The Soviet Union – an example for all the world' (and he wasn't being ironic) or 'The Way to Mutual Understanding'. There was a glowing foreword about his character, him being a good friend of the Soviet people, and his writings, but, predictably, nothing about *One Day*.

Another capable of producing clever, pro-Soviet propaganda for consumption in the West was Wilfred Burchett. A formidable journalist and author and a nice man, Burchett came to the Soviet Union after Stalin's death and never quite fitted in to the twilight land of the grey men.

I first heard of Burchett during the Korean War, which he covered from the side of the enemy, North Korea and China. It has been said that he and a Hungarian journalist cooked up the allegations that the United States carried out germ warfare against the North Koreans, which they didn't; but the most damaging charge levelled at Burchett was that he tried to persuade British soldiers in PoW camps to change sides, or at least, make anti-West and anti-War statements.

Burchett launched one libel action after another during the next twenty years, usually in Australia, to try and live down the suggestion he had done any such thing or had ever worked for the KGB. But although he got his Australian citizenship back in the end and returned there, he never managed to shrug off evidence that he had collaborated with Australia's, and Britain's, enemies. When I first met him in Moscow in 1960, his name for me was a dirty word, but he quickly disarmed me with his charm and friendliness. We had lunch at the lively Uzbekistan Restaurant and he told me that he saw himself as a 'progressive' journalist, whose views about the West, and particularly the United States, had been coloured by being one of the first journalists into Hiroshima, after the dropping of the A-Bomb.

Between generous spoonfuls of caviar, he told me what a wonderful country the Soviet Union was and how lucky I was to be working there. He also had a great deal to say about the virtues of the Russian people. And while Burchett was lecturing me about meaning of true comradeship, which apparently only existed in the USSR, a man stood up at the next table and brought a vodka bottle crashing down on his companion's head. Two *druzhiniki*, or volunteer policemen, appeared as if from nowhere and started beating up the comrade-assailant with small truncheons, before dragging both of them, bleeding, along the floor and out of the restaurant.

Neither Burchett or anyone else in the Uzbekistan, me apart, seemed to think anything untoward had taken place. Spreading caviar on a piece of toast he said: 'They were drunk, of course. Russians do like a drop now and again. But tomorrow morning, they will be the best of comrades.'

Perhaps he was right, but he did have a habit of looking at Soviet life through rose-coloured spectacles. One book he wrote *Come East, Young Man* is about Siberia. The GULAG and its consequences for Siberia is not mentioned once. The Great Terror, Stalin, Soviet foreign and domestic policy, and anything remotely political were matters he declined to discuss.

Burchett, like Parker, was at his most gullible, or simply, dishonest, covering the show trials staged throughout Eastern Europe after the War. He eventually admitted having been shaken by them, but it took him nearly thirty years to do so. But in his memoirs, he is not entirely convinced they were the result of Stalin's paranoid terror, clinging to the absurd notion they were somehow instigated by the CIA and John Forster Dulles.

Burchett lived in a skyscraper block built for top people on Stalin's orders. This was, and is, a magnificent example of heritage kitch, one of several staggering monuments remaining in Moscow to a heroic age of Soviet Communism that never really existed beyond the façade of Stalin's taste in architecture.

Galina Ulanova, the most famous of all Soviet ballerinas, lived there – Stalin had personally decided who were to be the first occupants of the building. She was still exciting audiences at the Bolshoi, including, me although over fifty years of age, and caused my head to turn on one occasion when as she got out of her chauffeur-driven car to go into her palatial flat.

One day, during lunch in Burchett's apartment, I brought up the subject of the deteriorating relations between China and the Soviet Union. Burchett knew something about what was going on but he didn't dare write about it for the *Financial Times*, for whom he was the

Moscow stringer. By and large, he stuck to stories about Soviet steel production or the introduction of a new washing-machine.

I floated a tale in his direction – that there were rumours the Russians had protested to the Chinese about an incident involving shooting along the 6000-mile border. Lowering his voice to a whisper, he said, sourly: 'Well, they would, wouldn't they? They've always behaved badly to the Chinese comrades.' I was astonished. This was a criticism of the Soviet Union. Although I did not know it then, Burchett, a good comrade who had written tens of thousands of words of support for the Soviet Union's 'peace-loving policies', had become disillusioned.

His sympathies were with the Chinese Communists, revolutionary movements in Asia, and men like North Korean's disgusting Kim Il Sung. He admits this in his memoirs, while saying he became fed up with living and working in Moscow after eight years because of the almost totally negative attitude and lack of respect towards foreign journalists.

He tells the story of a Khrushchev press conference when a Soviet journalist came up to him before it started and persuaded him to ask a planted question. This was an example of disrespect for journalistic integrity which rankled with him for the rest of his time in Russia.

I thought he lost his integrity when he crossed the line from objective reportage to unquestioning support for Communism and for men like Stalin and Kim Il Sung.

Burchett was allowed to leave the Soviet Union when he wanted, if only on a tattered and stained North Korean travel document, having had his British passport cancelled. But he was never really able to get much further than North Vietnam, where he covered the war cycling into attack with the Vietcong. He was at least courageous, if not foolhardy.

For some years, this freedom to travel far outside Moscow and away from a life of unrelieved drabness was refused to Len Wincott, a man who made several mistakes in his life in the cause of Communism and the Party. One of the worst was to allow his British passport to expire and to take out Soviet citizenship on the advice – so he always insisted – of Harry Pollitt, the British Communist party leader.

Wincott's story is a remarkable one. He achieved notoriety as one of the ringleaders of the Invergordon Mutiny of 1931, (although a recent television programme about the event failed to mention him) when 12,000 ratings from fifteen ships in the Atlantic Fleet mutinied in protest at new pay rates, which left some of them with only twenty-five shillings a week. Wincott, an able seaman, organized meetings which prevented the cruiser *Norfolk* from sailing for two days. The men's protests were doomed to fail. Dismissed from the Royal Navy, he joined the Communist Party and was sent to the Soviet Union as a symbol of the British working class, fighting for their rights.

There, he was given the status of a hero and received VIP treatment. He toured the country delivering propaganda speeches and was given all the vodka and women he could manage. 'I had a wonderful time,' he told me on many occasions in his Staffordshire burr. 'They loved me when I stood up on platforms telling them about the British worker struggling for his rights and a bit of bread. They treated me like a little foreign god. But I bloody paid for it, and in blood.'

Having become a citizen of the USSR – he claimed Pollitt told him that it was only a question of time before there would be a Communist world and he was lucky to have got ahead of the queue – Len was put in charge of a seamans' club in Leningrad. His job was to indoctrinate the crews of British ships into the virtues of Communism, when they visited the club on shore leave.

The end of the good times for Len came with the 900-day Siege of Leningrad, when more than a million people died, mostly from starvation, cold and disease. He was there throughout the time and had difficulty in talking about the horror, sacrifice, the terror and the mistakes.

Wincott was always worrying about bugs in the ceiling and was a confirmed whisperer when it came to anything remotely political or critical. It was agony, because he suffered terribly from halitosis and insisted on whispering close to your face. Backed into a corner, you were doomed to suffer, while having to listen to a tale you had heard many times before.

His main contention was that it had all gone wrong when Stalin had Sergei Kirov, the then Leningrad party boss, murdered in 1934

– jealous of his popularity. His own troubles began in 1946, when he was working in a factory and was suddenly arrested by the NKVD as a British spy. When he addressed the president of the *troika*, the three-man military tribunal, as 'Comrade', he was told to shut up – his only comrades were the forest wolves. They sentenced him to a long term in a labour camp in god-forsaken Vorkuta, the mining region almost within the Arctic circle. It was the *troika's* stock answer to those who had devoted their lives to Communist cause and had been caught up in a purge.

He was among a million prisoners sent to mine a rich coal seam, of whom a third died. Today, you can still see the relics of the camps: ramshackle wooden barracks, now family homes, abandoned watchtowers, strands of rusty barbed wire. But no graves – the whole town is built on them.

Somehow, he survived ten years in the GULAG. At one time, he was in the same labour camp as Victor Louis and he is the source of the story that Louis was a *tolkach* or 'informer'; but it may have been Len talking from bitterness.

Indeed, he was a bitter man. Having given the best years of his life to the 'cause', he finished up in a labour camp where, he would say, spitting out the words, he was 'treated worse than shit'. Freed in 1956 along with millions of others equally innocent of any crime, Len was rehabilitated by another *troika*. But this time, he was addressed as 'Comrade', received an apology, and told he had been the victim of a judicial error. Donald Maclean heard of his plight and gave him 500 roubles – in those days about £150 – to help him make a new start. Len became a translator and also wrote occasional articles for the Anglo-Soviet Friendship Society magazine, omitting, of course, any suggestion he hated the Soviet Communist Party, the KGB and all the *svolochi* – bastards – he blamed for ruining his life. But the comrades back home had a pretty good idea of how he felt and their leader, Harry Pollitt, founding member of the British Communist Party, ensured that Len was not let out to visit the old country. Pollitt, who had a portrait of Stalin prominently displayed in the living room of his suburban semi, rightly suspected that Len would be a nuisance once he arrived in London, kissed the ground, and then started saying nasty things about the Socialist Motherland and his treatment.

Assailed by homesickness, he often called on British correspondents to relieve them of their old London newspapers and catch up with the football news. Once, he asked me to bring him back a matchbox full of English soil, and on another occasion, a gross of British condoms because, he said, 'Soviet ones are like bicycle inner-tubes'.

He wrote the story of his life in the GULAG, but didn't want it published in order to protect his Russian wife, some twenty years younger than him – a woman of grace and serenity. He did visit Britain shortly before he died. And she was allowed to leave Russia with his ashes, which were scattered off the English coastline, at his request.

Like Burgess and Maclean, he had come home.

12 – The Green Snake

Two Russian drunks are staggering along a railway line. One says: 'Shit! These fucking stairs! They go on for ever and no banisters!' 'Don't worry,' says the other drunk. 'I think I can hear the whoring lift coming.'

There are many other jokes about the Russian drunk, but that vast country's deeply-ingrained alcoholism is no laughing matter. As elsewhere, alcoholism is the major cause of crime, divorce, absenteeism, and accidents.

For more than seventy years, however, it was a social issue clothed in socialist myth – drunkenness was a primitive vestige of a capitalist past, a bad hangover that would disappear as the country travelled the path toward socialism. Nonsense, of course!

Russians drink to get stinking drunk, to obliterate themselves, to ward off the cold. Vodka is known as the 'little ray of sunshine in the stomach' and, from the colour of the label on bottles of Moskovskaya, 'the green snake'.

It is a comfort in long, dark, cold winters, a release from the tedium of life. But the fact remains that a people who have always enjoyed strong drink in large quantities have been pushed to desperate and depressed drinking by a regime that robbed them of humanity by the grey dreary life under Communism.

St Vladimir (965-1015), the first Russian Christian, is quoted as saying: 'It is Russia's joy to drink. We cannot do without it.' The Tsars positively encouraged drinking and would own a drinking tavern in each town to make money for themselves or courtier friends.

Two Englishmen who visited Russia in the sixteenth century both commented on the amount of drinking they witnessed:

Anthony Jenkinson wrote: 'I heard of men and women that drank away their children and all their goods at the tsar's tavern and, not being able to pay, having pawned himself, the taverner bringeth him out to the highway, and beats him upon the legs; then they that pass by, knowing the cause and peradventure, having compassion upon him, giveth the money so he is ransomed.'

George Turberville versified to friends in London in 1568: 'Folke fit to be of Bacchus train, so quaffing is their kinde, Drinke is their sole desire, the pit is all their pride. The sob'rest head doth once a day stand needful of a guide, and if he go into his neighbour as a guest, he cares for little meat, if so his drinke be of the best.'

Vodka has indeed played a strong part in the life of Russia. The word *pianii*, meaning 'drunk' or 'smashed', is named after the Pyana river where two armies fought in 1377. Neither side won – all the soldiers who took part in the fighting were drunk and they wiped each other out.

Lenin and his heirs conspicuously failed to stop the rot, although priggish young Communist, zealots bidding to clean up society, shut down most of the beer houses in the 1920s and 1930s. But 400 years after Turberville sent his eyewitness account from Moscow, it is an established fact that the country's per capita consumption of hard liquor is probably the highest in the world. And one clear reason is that the state has mixed feelings about drinking – as does the Treasury in Britain about smoking.

For vodka has been a state monopoly since before World War I, when alcohol provided one-quarter of all income. Sales of vodka, beer and wine since then have been colossal, totalling billions of roubles a year, playing a big part in balancing the former Soviet Union's budget, making possible the creation of the huge military-industrial establishment. It has been a matter of guns and vodka.

It is a puzzle to me that having witnessed drinking and its effects in Russia over thirty years, I have not turned to orange juice. In the last years of Khrushchev's rule it was not unusual to see drunks lying in crumpled heaps, face down and slate-blue with cold on the snow-covered ground. They were sometimes stiff as boards and passersby stepped over or around them, taking no notice whatsoever.

Some stood up, arms clasped around drainpipes or lampposts, heads resting against them, as if in an embrace. Others, not yet dead drunk, staggered through the streets bent nearly double, arms flailing, falling to the ground, dragging themselves to their feet to stumble homewards.

In the restaurants tables were covered with empty bottles of vodka, Armenian cognac, champagne or wine. I have seen men so drunk their heads have fallen into their plates. They could have drowned in their soup or ice-cream for all their wives and girlfriends seemed to care. How they got the men home was a mystery, unlike the question of where the money came from. That was simple. With few consumer goods available, Russians spent their money on booze, as if there was no tomorrow.

This was about the time when the Soviet Union was beginning to open up to tourism and the authorities rightly decided that such sights would reflect adversely on the country's image. Khrushchev, who liked a drop or two himself, nevertheless launched a campaign against alcoholism and police were given the hopeless task of getting the drunks off the streets.

In those days, Moscow police were equipped with motor cycle sidecars. They drove around the streets, picking up drunks like litter, strapping them in the sidecars and taking them off to the nearest 'sobering-up station'. These appalling places had existed even under Stalin, but they were revealed only during the Khrushchev era and only then as an awful warning to drunks about what would befall them if they made a public nuisance of themselves in front of foreigners.

The Soviet equivalent of Dante's Inferno, they were run by people who had to be cruel to be kind. Inmates were stripped, hosed down, forcibly put to bed and then strapped to them. When they had recovered they were fined a few roubles for board and lodging and told not to come back. This was how Communism treated alcoholism.

When I heard about the sobering-up stations, I asked permission to visit them but was turned down, as my request was not felt to be 'serious enough'. A Western correspondent became a guest at one, however, and how it happened is a reflection of the time. For she was the victim of a dirty scheme hatched by the KGB in close collaboration with Alexei Adzhubei, then editor of the Soviet government newspaper *Izvestia*, and Khrushchev's son-in-law.

At a diplomatic cocktail party, Adzhubei was harried by Aline Mosby, a terrier of an American reporter. A bully and a prodigious drinker, he cut up nasty. Not used to being badgered by Western journalists, he picked up a napkin from the table, rubbed it around her mouth, called her a *prostitutka* and told her to get out of his sight. She was distressed enough then, but could not have imagined there was worse to come.

A few weeks after the incident she was having dinner with a young Russian friend in a restaurant when a 'Micky Finn' was slipped into her drink. She became ill, managed to get up from the table and to stagger into the street where a KGB photographer was conveniently waiting. There was also an ambulance which whisked her off to a sobering-up station with a waiting bed. The story was apparently worthy of half a page in Adzhubei's official government newspaper, complete with a photograph of her in bed with another woman drunk. The point of the story? Here was a typical Western correspondent who also dabbled in currency and ikon speculation and was not a fit, i.e. decent, honest and sober person to report accurately about the wonders and the policies of the USSR. Aline Mosby was taken to a sobering-up station against her will.

I asked to visit the biggest vodka factory in the Soviet Union and should have known what I had let myself in for. The Krystal factory, built before World War I, was huge. It made four different kinds of vodka: Moskovskaya, favourite, cheapest tipple of the workers with a green label which gave rise to the 'green snake'; Stolichnaya, which I came to love best of all when drunk neat and very cold; Okhotnichya or Hunter's vodka, and a very rough Ukrainian pepper vodka known as Gorilka. A few more brands are now produced, all much better than anything offered by the West. One Siberian vodka is magnificent when poured straight from a bottle, long chilled in a freezer, and accompanied by blinis and Sevruga caviar. It should be taken in strong, uncompromising bolts, not timidly diluted with various tonics.

Having been told to put on a white coat, I was taken round the factory and from time to time offered a taster of vodka kept in huge steel vats. All the workers were women – they even loaded dozen-bottle crates of vodka onto the back of lorries – so it was clear they were thought to be trusted. Men were liable to steal the odd crate and knock off a bottle or two in the toilet.

Apart from vodka, the factory also made other alcoholic drinks, among them *rhum*, *benidiktin*, *kvontro*, and *kremdermant*. After a couple of hours my translator and I were ready to go home.

But no! 'Not possible,' said the Chief Engineer. 'You are an honoured guest. Now we have lunch.'

136

It was going to be the best, or worst, kind of Russian hospitality. For around the plate were a dozen little glasses – four for vodka and seven for the likes of *rhum* and *benediktin*.

Seated round the table were nearly as many factory officials. The Comrade Director, his No. 2, the Communist Party cell secretary, the sales and distribution manager, his deputy, the trade union leader, the young man who ran the factory Komsomol, a plug-ugly man who had the look of the KGB about him, and a couple of male workers who had over-fulfilled their working norm, although for what, it was never made clear. All of them looked like men who were waiting for the bar to open.

The meal was modest. Sausage, slices of cheese, pickled gherkins, brown and white bread. I have never particularly liked Russian sausage but I wolfed down a slice or two to try to create a base for the drinking that was surely to come. All the glasses had already been filled, including those for the nasty French and Jamaican imitations.

We worked through them. I started off sipping the national firewater but was soon caught out.

'Oh, no,' said Comrade Director. 'No, no, no. You must drink bottoms up. You should know very well, Mr Miller, that you do not drink the toast in sincerity unless you drink bottoms up.'

He was right. I did know, but it wasn't fair – I had already sunk a glass or two in my travels around his factory. So we continued, a toast and a chat, a toast and a chat… There was a lot to toast in those days. Peace. Friendship. Peace and Friendship. *Détente*. The visit. Wives. Our children. Peace, or rather, No More War. Friendship during the Great Patriotic War – the one that took place after the Pact between Stalin and Hitler, and Britain had stood alone with its back against the wall, fighting off the Fascist hordes.

But I saw the game that was being played. The guest put them back, bottoms up, but not all of the comrades round the table were doing the same. Some of them were sipping sneakily. Deciding to do the best I could, I thought of Charles Laughton as Henry VIII where, sighing at the rear view of another of his wives, he commented: 'The things I do for England.'

To slow down the drinking, I threw out questions while endeavouring not to get any refills of the nasty greens and dark browns.

How much were the workers paid? Very well indeed. How long was their working day? Not too long. Did the workers think they were exploited? Helpless laughter. Did they have any complaints? No, not one. What were the costs of production? Looks of astonishment. Comrade Factory Director says he is not too sure because it doesn't matter – which is something he wouldn't get away with today.

What was the vodka output of the factory in litres and how can the drive to meet work norms and fulfil and over fulfil the Plan be reconciled with the current campaign against alcoholism? This was rather a good question but the director, who had become transformed into a jolly, friendly, red-faced comrade did not have the figures with him on the yearly output in litres, nor come to that, the number of bottles produced. Therefore, he did not know if output was up or was down, and whether or not the Plan had been fulfilled, let alone over-fulfilled.

But he leaned across the table confidentially. He could tell me, one man to another, that the factory was 100 per cent, no, 110 per cent, behind the Government and the Party in its campaign against alcoholism. And, wait for it, if he was told to cut production he would do so, and the trade union and the workers would support him.

I tried again. But if production was cut, didn't that mean less money for the government to spend on subsidising cheap bread, fares, rent, and – tricky this – building up the Soviet Union's military might, such as its giant rockets? And they wouldn't want to do that, would they?

The Party secretary spoke. I got an earful of the peace-loving policy of the Soviet Union. There was an attack on the aggressive polices of some Western governments. Communism would triumph, it had already. And now, with a smile, it was their turn.

Did I like the Soviet Union? Did I want peace? Why were British workers exploited? Were British whisky factories any better equipped than their factory? And so on and so forth with the most peculiar and unlikely question of all coming from the Young Komsomol leader, who persistently asked me about what I thought of Randolph Churchill, son of Winston. I tried to draw a parallel between the lives of the sons of Churchill and Stalin, for both of them became alcoholics and died early and suffered the hell of having extraordinary fathers. We nearly got into a discussion about Stalin, but the young comrade's legs were kicked under the table.

They brought in The Book to be signed, a fate that befell all visitors to Soviet factories, workplaces and collective farms. The Book was for writing in nice happy thoughts which were good for morale and helpful to the director's career.

I concentrated hard on writing in a straight line – every bit as important as saying how much I had enjoyed the visit and been overwhelmed by the generosity. Hands were shaken and Randolph Churchill's friend helped me into a taxi. I thought at one point he was going to whisper something in my ear, but it didn't happen.

I fell through my front door when it was opened. Put to bed, I failed to function for a day and a half...

Russian hospitality is all about getting your visitor, or new acquaintance, drunk – Russians only feel really comfortable with a man if they have got smashed together. In private homes it is expected that the bottle of vodka bottle which appears on the table is emptied. Once, when a Soviet journalist came to my flat for lunch and I removed the litre bottle of Stoli from the table after filling glasses, he tut-tutted that what I had done was 'uncultured'.

Official entertaining, and with it generous helpings of hard liquor, is seen as an excellent way of making friends and influencing people. But in Russia, there is more to it than that. For vodka can also be useful for numbing the foreigner's critical faculties. It can disguise badly-cooked food. And it can also demonstrate the Russian prowess in being able to drink most foreigners under the table.

Such entertaining, however, can also be counterproductive to its giver, as was demonstrated during a trip to the Donbass, the huge coal-mining basin, organized by the Soviet Foreign Ministry.

The capital of the region was Donetsk, known until 1924 as Yuzovka, after John Hughes, a Welshman, who built a metallurgical plant among ragged fields and developed the huge deposits of coal, iron ore and manganese. Hughes also built hundreds of red-brick terrace houses, very like those of the Rhondda Valley, complete with outside privy, charging his workers four roubles a year for rent. A few still exist and are recognizable for what they were, although the

English church now belongs to the Russian Orthodox Church with half a dozen golden domes perched on the top and ikons inside.

We were taken 2,000 feet underground and after crawling on our hands to the coal-face, stood next to miners working with hand-drills and other tools. It was hot and unpleasant, and, frankly, scary. An official told me that the Abukov show mine which the French had owned before the Revolution, had a one hundred per cent safety record – but you wondered if this was going to be the time when its luck ran out.

As it happened, a bigger danger lurked at the pit head and in its canteen, because the mine bosses were not going to allow a group of Western journalists to leave without them experiencing some good old-fashioned Ukrainian hospitality.

The lunch was borsch, 'miners' cutlets, which were tough, fatty pork chops, cold chips and Gorilka, the pepper vodka which, fortunately, had the colour of the soft drink they were surprisingly also offering us.

Greater demands were made on us than eating pork chops. Each of us was required to bring fraternal greetings to the Donbass miners from the miners of the countries to which we belonged. There were a great many toasts and a great many glasses emptied at a gulp. And that was before we got down to toasting peace and friendship.

Even the Swedes, who have the reputation of being considerable drinkers, were literally looking green by the time we were eating ice-cream. Tucked away at the end of the table, I took it carefully, using the soft drink for toasts as often as possible, without being noticed.

Lunch over, we were ready to return to our hotel for a sleep and a bath before the obligatory evening's visit to the ballet. No such luck. The programme called for a visit to the local Palace of Culture. I protested to the minder from the Foreign Ministry.

'This is not a good idea,' I said. 'Some of my colleagues are unwell. They need to go to their hotels for a rest before the evening programme.'

Indeed, the Swedes had disappeared and were vomiting up their lunch in the canteen toilet. The Germans and the French were still sitting in their seats, unable to speak. Terrified East Germans, Poles and other East European lickspittles were glumly silent for different

140

reasons. They too had had enough, but didn't want any trouble with Big Brother.

So we went to the Palace of Culture. Formerly, it had been named after Nikita Khrushchev, who had worked at a nearby coal mine as an air-blower – he once told me he had played left-half in the mine's football team against the British mine managers and engineers.

When he fell from grace, it became a plain old Palace, but they had tarted it up for us. There were banners of welcome and hosts of flags. There were hundreds of children lined up to greet us and a brass band.

When the bus drew up in front of the building, the children cheered and the band crashed out the Soviet anthem. For our part, we stumbled and staggered out of the bus. A Swede threw up on the grass. A German relieved himself in a hedge. Two of the East Europeans fell over and had trouble getting up. Others supported each other as they passed between the line of children and into the Palace of Culture.

Some of those children may never have seen a Westerner before. But they may not necessarily have been shocked – the chances being that they had seen their fathers acting in a similar fashion. But they must have thought that, however smartly dressed some of us may have looked, we were a strange bunch.

It was not a performance of which we were proud. The Ministry minder pressed on, however, introducing us to the Director and staff of the Palace of Culture, who in turn showed us the cinema, and the sports hall, and the Communist Party lecture room, and finally the library. Here, it became known that a concert had been laid on for us, and I felt it was time to fight back.

I asked the librarian, proudly telling us about the thousands of books available, if she had anything by the local boy, N.S. Khrushchev. She blushed when she said she hadn't.

The Swedes were the quickest off the mark. 'Why not?' they asked in chorus. 'Didn't he work in the mine down the road? And didn't he rise to become the General Secretary of the Communist Party of the Soviet Union?'

'Well,' said the wretched librarian. 'Comrade Khrushchev made some mistakes.'

'What mistakes?' said the Swedes, enjoying baiting the woman. 'Tell us about them. Tell us why he was sacked.'

Now I felt sorry for her having to handle such a hot political potato, to explain to a large group of lurching, excitable Western hacks why Khrushchev had been brought down in a Kremlin *coup* and cast, like his speeches, into the dustbin of history.

The Man from the Ministry knew what had to be done.

'We are leaving now for the bus,' said he, by now a very unhappy man. In a flash we were outside, in the bus, and roaring off to Donetsk, the concert forgotten, the Swedes singing dirty songs, the East Europeans snoring loudly and the rest of us looking slack-jawed and glassy-eyed out of the window at the bleak landscape.

⁂

Shortly after he came to power Mikhail Gorbachev decided to do something about the alcohol problem. His father was an alcoholic and he was appalled by the statistics: one in ten citizens had a severe drinking problem; each year twelve to fifteen per cent of the population were processed through the sobering-up stations; at least one third of fatal traffic accidents, three quarters of murders, and an overwhelming majority of lost production hours were alcohol related. As a moderate drinker himself – he was happy to share a bottle of cognac with four other people – he cut the production of vodka and reduced the number of hours that liquor was available in shops and restaurants. There was a propaganda campaign with 'Lemonade Joe' Gorbachev personally exhorting his people to give up the demon drink.

Pravda, a newspaper with more than its fair share of drunks on its staff, did its bit. One story it carried was breathtaking for its sheer effrontery. It reported the country's first 'milk' wedding. The reception was totally without any alcohol and the couples' health was toasted in glasses of milk. The reception lasted six hours and, according to *Pravda*, no one had complained about having to swig milk the whole time. And, it said, the idea was catching on.

Pravda, of course, means 'truth' but as everyone knew, that was a commodity that particular newspaper has always been short of. It was careful not to name the (happy?) couple or reveal whence they came, presumably in case they were the subject of ridicule and worse, had pig-shit sent them through the post.

Izvestia, which means 'news', which it also conspicuously lacked over the years as the Soviet government newspaper – nowadays, it is a campaigning liberal newspaper – referred to problems connected with wedding receptions at a time of a government crackdown on booze.

Two sisters living in a village near Odessa were enterprising enough to start up a cottage industry. They distilled a drink called 'knockout hooch' a kind of home-made vodka, which they guaranteed would make wedding receptions and other anniversary parties go with a swing. Police had got wind of a special consignment being made for a reception of a relative and raided the place, seizing twenty-seven four-gallon drums of the knockout hooch, and 130 gallons of fermenting beer. *Izvestia* revealed that 'at a rough guide', it was necessary to provide a pint of vodka for every person at a Russian wedding, in addition, of course, to the champagne and beer.

ACC, the good old days of constant inebriation returned to Russia, and in the mid-1990s Russians had overtaken the French as the world's leading drinkers. Boris Yeltsin, a tippler himself, lifted the state monopoly on vodka, allowing the free sale of alcohol in kiosks, springing up under his market reforms. Russia now consumes fifty per cent of the world's hard liquor with the average Russian male consuming ninety litres of vodka a year. Unsurprisingly male life expectancy is fifty-eight years.

Russians can see the funny side of their drinking. At one time there was a Gorbachev vodka said to make those who drink it talk uncontrollably about glasnost and perestroika. Yeltsin has admitted to drinking a glass or two at home on a Sunday evening and has impressed Russians with his unsteady public appearances. And after his extraordinary behaviour at Shannon Airport a few years ago he has been accused of being in a 'permanent state of a visit to Ireland'.

And there is a another joke that, for some reason, Russians find hilarious. A boy asks his father: 'Dad, now that the price of vodka has increased, does that mean you will drink less?'

'It certainly doesn't, Son,' says the father. 'All it means is that you will eat less.'

13 – The Soul of Russia

Novodevichy was, is, will always be one of my very favourite places in Russia. It should be a must on every tourist's list. For this cemetery is the soul of Russia, with its cruel history and its truly terrible secrets. Nothing better symbolizes how Russia – whether ruled by tsars or by general secretaries or by democratically elected presidents – remains Russia.

Novodevichy (New Maidens) ranks second to the Kremlin Wall in the pecking order of final resting places. Beneath its birches and pines, among plots overgrown with grass and weeds, are writers like Chekhov and Mayakovsky, composers like Rimsky-Korsakov and the man who wrote one of the first songs my children knew – *Let there always be sunshine, let there always be sky, let there always be Mama, let there always be me* – marshals, scientists, diplomats and, of course, Communist politicians.

Here, graves are examples of remarkable funerary art, Soviet-style. There is an impressive bust of a man on the telephone – he was a marshal of communications – raising all sorts of questions, such as was he talking to God, was it a transfer charge, or what?

There is a ten-foot long T-34 tank on a tank-general's grave, and a famous obstetrician is holding a newborn child. The gravestone of the man who wrote *Let there always be sunshine* has a few bars of the tune. A broadcaster has a microphone and there is a large stone aircraft for the man who designed the real thing.

The necessary qualification for top politicians to have a place in Novodevichy was not to die in office. Thus, someone of the stature of Nikita Khrushchev finished up in Novodevichy and not in the Kremlin Wall which, at the time, he would almost certainly have preferred and deserved. He was denied his rightful place of burial by his old comrades, Leonid Brezhnev and Mikhail Suslov, who were mean-minded and jealous of his reputation in history, determined that he should pass from this world as inconspicuously as possible. So, having ruled the Soviet Union for a decade, his reward was an obituary comprising one sentence in a Soviet newspaper. No party or government official attended the funeral, although several hundred police and KGB surrounded the cemetery in case of pro-Khrushchev demonstrations – which, of course, there weren't. No sane person would have stuck his neck out for Nikita.

Khrushchev's son, Sergei, spoke a few words over the grave on a grey drizzly day. It was up to history to judge his father, he said. But he had left no one indifferent.

'There are people who love him and people who hate him, but no one can pass him by without turning to look. A man has gone from us who had the right to be called a man.' I agree wholeheartedly.

Wherever he is, Khrushchev need not be bitter about the way he has been treated by his own kind. The cemetery is an honourable resting place, by the side of a sixteenth-century monastery, one of Russia's loveliest architectural monuments with a couple of working churches and walls built by the same Italians who completed those of the Kremlin.

The area, Maiden's Field, was the locality of a market at which Tartars in old times purchased Muscovite girls for the harems in Constantinople and Isfahan. Nuns lived in the convent from 1525 until the Bolshevik Revolution.

The cemetery is also something special, albeit the apotheosis of bad taste, accurately reflecting the spiritual essence of those who liked to think themselves as being members of the Soviet élite. The Communist-controlled Moscow City Council had a secret list of people in the prime of their lives who qualified for burial in Novodevichy, and in its annex of Kuntsevo. A telephone call from the relatives of the deceased would immediately establish the position.

For the most part, leading artists and intellectuals are buried in the older part of the cemetery, among them Chekhov, Gogol and Prokofiev, all in modest and simple graves. So is Stalin's wife, Nadezhda, who shot herself, after cruelly being told over the telephone by one of Stalin's bodyguards that his boss was in bed with the beautiful young wife of a senior army officer. There is a lot more to this story than the one about her taking her life, because she realized her husband was a nasty bastard about to unleash the Great Purge. Buried in the Alliluyeva family plot, her white marble head has been more than once vandalised and her nose was once broken off, perhaps as pathetic revenge for Stalin's monstrous crimes. It is now protected by unbreakable glass.

For years, Russians flocked to Novodevichy enjoying it as a museum of famous names, admiring the different and often imaginative styles of headstones. Because of the way they regard death, Russians have been known to join in graveside burials, to kiss the forehead of the dead person, even to weep over the stranger.

Sometimes I visited the cemetery to meet Anatoly Krasnov-Levitin, a remarkable writer and teacher who described himself as a Christian Socialist. He had had several spells in different labour camps for 'anti-Soviet agitation' but he was still prepared, albeit somewhat furtively, to lay his head on the block again. He would walk me round and round the cemetary, even in the depths of winter, beating my ear about the scandals and infighting in the hierarchy of the Russian Orthodox Church, but mostly about how the church establishment had allowed itself to become a tool of the atheist state which had, moreover, sold out to the KGB. As it proved, he was dead right. But then it was like attending an open-air sermon and not at all easy to remember the list of priests who had got in trouble with the authorities, their parishes and the names of the bishops who had gone over to the Communist Party side. It was even harder to sell the story to the paper. But I got to know my way around Novodevichy.

Khrushchev's grave has a large, cheerful-looking bust, but it was not easy for his family to secure a decent headstone of the country's former leader.

It was the old story – the Russia of dams and space-rockets had no funeral industry, apart from the manufacturer of simple wooden coffins. To get a tombstone meant paying someone in a factory, producing marble or stone slabs for the building industry, to drop a piece off the back of a lorry. Another bribe was necessary for the craftsman to chisel out the details. There were cases of comrades visiting the West on official business, who would purchase marble slabs in antique shops or funeral parlours, and take them back to Moscow... and be damned to excess baggage.

Khrushchev's erstwhile colleagues were still giving him a bad time even when he was dead, and they wilfully obstructed the family when it commissioned a memorial to him by Ernst Neizvestny. A talented and decent modernist sculptor, Neizvestny – who I would visit in his old, lumbered but colourful studio in the pre-tsarist red-

147

light district off Tsvetnoi Boulevard – was wounded several times, fighting at the front in the War. A great Russian patriot, he clashed with Khrushchev at a famous exhibition of works by young artists.

'This is shit,' Khrushchev said of one of the sculptor's pieces. Of a modernist painting, he demonstrated how much of a boring old fart he could be by commenting that it must have been painted with a brush tied to a donkey's tail. Later, at a meeting of artists and writers, he came out with a chilling Stalinist phrase to describe what he thought of someone who indulged in modern art: 'Oh, well,' he exclaimed, 'I suppose only the grave will correct a hunchback.'

This prompted Yevgeny Yevtushenko, a poet whom we had dubbed Russia's 'Angry Young Man', to comment, somewhat courageously, that he thought the days when that sort of thing happened were over.

For many years after clashing with the Soviet leader, Neizvestny received no official commissions. But when Khrushchev, too, became a non-person and began thinking of writing his memoirs, he realized how badly he had behaved. He invited the sculptor to his dacha, apologized, and a curious friendship grew up between them. After Khrushchev died, the family asked Neizvestny, who was more and more thinking of emigrating, to do the headstone and tomb. Then followed an extraordinary three-year battle between Neizvestny and 'them,' the bureaucrats, terrified to approve plans which might be considered ideologically incorrect.

Neizvestny sought to express his idea of Khrushchev as a dualistic figure of the time, with two intertwined black-and-white stone blocks, surrounding a realistic head of the former leader. The two stones suggested the struggle between good and evil, which the bureaucrats spotted at once. They wanted the monument in grey. Then they wanted just a pedestal with a bust. Then they urged the family not to have a bust at all, just a pedestal with an inscription. Finally, they asked there should not be a pedestal at all, just a simple slab with Khrushchev's name on it, lying flat on the ground. Neizvestny was visited by officials, who made it clear that by pursuing his commission from the Khrushchev family, he would lose others, much more valuable. They even tried to start a quarrel between him and the family.

Such games were often played during the Brezhnev era, although it must be said that when Neizvestny approached Alexei Kosygin, the then Soviet Prime Minister, about the issue, he was told he could do anything he liked. The bureaucrats were delighted that someone higher had lifted the burden from their shoulders, and work went ahead. Eventually, Neizvestny was allowed to go to the United States where he became a world-famous sculptor and – ACC – an honorary member of the Russian Academy of Arts.

The result was that more and more ordinary Russians flocked to Novodevichy than ever before. Some of those who respected Khrushchev simply for unleashing the campaign of de-Stalinization, and for freeing millions from the GULAG, came to lay flowers on his grave. Crowds would stand around the grave, discussing his rule, and whenever I was there, I never heard a bad word said about Nikita Sergeyevich.

'They' didn't like it – ordinary people standing around in a public place saying nice things about a leader they had removed in a dirty Kremlin manoeuvre, making pilgrimages to Khrushchev's grave. They knew what to do: they shut down Novodevichy to all who had no business there, i.e. no dead to visit. Novodevichy effectively joined the long list of other establishments in the Soviet Union to be 'closed' – places, such as meetings of the Communist Party élite, shops for the top people, dacha communities for the *nomenklatura*, not forgetting libraries and archives for the party priests.

One day, however, I learned that Western correspondents could visit Novodevichy, but they would need permission from the Soviet Ministry of Foreign Affairs. You wrote to them, stating the day and time you wanted to go and whose grave you wanted to look at. The request was passed to Moscow City Council, which was responsible for the cemetery. I tried it out, nominating Chekhov, and it worked.

On the day I visited Novodevichy with my wife, we were followed wherever we went by two men, presumably from the cemetery's KGB section. They tailed us from a distance of some one hundred yards, laughably trying to hide behind grave stones and taking notes of the graves in which we showed interest.

I served them up a mixed bag of plots. Vyacheslav Molotov – he of the cocktail hurled at tanks, and the Cold War's 'Mr Nyet', reflecting the Soviet Union's attitude to negotiating with the West but, historically, more important as the man who signed the Non-

Aggression pact with Nazi Germany in 1939. On being told by the German ambassador in Moscow that Germany and the Soviet Union were at war, he came out with one of the most pathetic quotes in modern history: 'What did we do to deserve this?' Though long dead, he has never had a bust, having to make do with a large, sepia portrait, complete with pince-nez.

We visited the grave of Anastas Mikoyan, another scoundrel and a great survivor – he managed to remain in the front row of the Soviet leadership for more than fifty years – whose claim to fame was introducing American automobiles and ice-cream to Russia. He has a bust four metres high, the effect of which is spoilt by encrusted bird shit on his head. Mikoyan was pathologically anti-British and blamed us, wrongly, for the execution of his brother, along with other commissars in Baku in the early days of the revolution in the Caucasus. We argued about it in the British Embassy and he became quite irate.

Another, among the famous and infamous interred at Novodevichy, is Andrei 'Grim Grom' Gromyko, the veteran Soviet Foreign Minister. He is someone who should have got Red Square, too, for his services to Soviet diplomacy, but who, in retrospect, must take some blame for keeping the Cold War going. He had something in common with so many Soviet *apparatchiks* and this was that after he was in his early twenties, and had a foot firmly on the ladder of the *nomenklatura*, he never again travelled on a bus, walked in a street or went in a shop.

There was also Marshal Nikolai Bulganin, spitting image of the Kentucky fried chicken colonel, a former sidekick of Khrushchev's when he was a prime minister. And there are many, many more. We saved Nikita for last. For our KGB spooks, it must have been an education in their country's history.

Gorbachev stopped all the nonsense about having Novodevichy closed. Now there are guided tours and no attempt is made to ignore or gloss over the fact that here lie, some of the country's monsters who didn't manage to find a more 'honoured' place on Red Square. Such as Lazar Kaganovich, Stalin's great slave-driver, who died peacefully in his bed, aged ninety-seven, the last surviving actor of the Great Purge. There is a plot for the Kaganovich family, including a place for his brother, hounded to suicide in 1941, after slanderous charges of collaboration with the Nazis, and whom he did nothing to help, preferring to save his own skin. I doubt if there will be many flowers laid on Kaganovich's grave, or, for that matter, morsels of food left there or women keeping vigil.

14 – The Sword and The Shield

As every schoolboy, cinema-buff and spy-writer knows, the KGB or *Komitet Gosudarstvennoi Bezopastnosti*, the Soviet Union's Committee for State Security, was an all-pervasive, sophisticated organization which, at the height of the Cold War, employed tens of thousands of spooks, goons and general 'nasties'.

In Soviet jargon, the KGB motto: – The Sword and the Shield – was known as 'the organs' or the 'competent organs'. One of the few Soviet jokes I heard about the KGB involved a gynaecologist who, for some reason or another, was embarrassed about telling people what he did for a living. When asked, he replied: 'Well, as it happens, I work in the organs.' That stopped people asking him any more nosy questions.

The KGB made loads of money for authors of the espionage genre, and jolly good luck to them. But I spent much of my working life on the front line, rubbing shoulders, sometimes almost literally, with the KGB, certainly living, as it were, under the organization's shadow.

I managed not to get paranoid about what the KGB did or did not do. During the Cold War, this monstrous organization spent a great deal of time and effort keeping a close eye on people like me – we were 'spies, diversionists and anti-Soviet Cold War warriors' – and it was not surprising that you soon knew all about it.

Because, of course, every now and again, they wanted you to know you were being watched, tailed and bugged. It was the KGB's way of warning you that if you contemplated doing something naughty, you would quickly be caught out and, if that happened, you would be in trouble.

Shortly after I got to Moscow I met Ruari Chisholm. He introduced himself as the Foreign Office's visa officer in the USSR and laughed, as he often did, about things Soviet.

'Can't say I'm overworked,' he said. 'In fact the job's a doddle. I'll tell you something: the other day I approved the 2,000th visa given to a Soviet citizen since the end of the War, sixteen years ago. I'm lucky if I get half-a-dozen applications a month from Sovs to visit our lovely country. One freedom the Russians certainly haven't got is the one to leave the country and go where they like. The stuff about there being no hard currency for them to take is just an excuse. There's plenty of it available for the sort of bugger we should be keeping out, because the peace and friendship delegations are packed with KGB officers. A little trip to London is one of their perks. And my job is to rumble them.'

'But surely they are not all after doing some crafty spying?' I asked. 'There can't be anything secret about the Tower of London.'

'Nothing like that,' he said. 'They come off the plane and head straight for Marks and Spencer to stock up with underwear for their bosses, mistresses and wives – in that order. They make an obligatory visit to Highgate Cemetery to see the other Marx – Karl, and then it's off home. All I do is keep a check on the names, tip off MI5 and chuck out the visa applications of buggers who have given us trouble in the past.'

I didn't know then that Ruari was the Moscow Station Chief for the Secret Intelligence Service, also known as MI6. Our spy in Moscow. The representative of 'the Friends' in the USSR. But I soon saw give-away signs that he was not one of your actual, regular diplomats.

He liked to drink with hacks. He poked fun at the ambassador and other senior members of the embassy. On one occasion, when we couldn't get a table at the popular Praga restaurant, he hammered on the plate-glass door until it was opened by an angry doorman, who asked: 'Who are you to behave in such a rude, uncultured way?'

To which Ruari, in a loud, commanding voice, said: 'I, Comrade Doorman, I am the King of Laos.' We were immediately led to the best table in the restaurant, while the real King of Laos, on a state visit, dined in the Kremlin.

Ruari was bitterly and openly critical of the Soviet Union and its system – something which most diplomats preferred not to be in public for fear they were overheard, upset the Soviet Government and got thrown out of the country. They were paranoid about the KGB.

Ruari was not only Control for the greatest espionage *coup* since the end of the War, but also at the time he was attempting to bug the Kremlin across the river from his office in a wing of the embassy. Later, that part of the embassy was to catch fire, giving rise to suggestions that the electricity circuit had been overloaded by eaves-dropping equipment. Much of the wing was destroyed – Soviet firemen had to be kept out of the embassy compound and well clear of the building, in case the KGB officers among them started looking around.

I soon twigged Ruari was up to a great deal of good when he gave me a lift home one night from the club in the embassy that opened two or three times a week for a film or bingo or some other social event. Driving along a virtually deserted Ring Road after midnight, he said: 'Your friends are busy.'

'My friends?' I asked. 'Who are we – you – talking about?'

'The nasties,' – it was his way of referring to the KGB.

I turned to look out of the rear window. It was easier to spot a tail-car when you were driving because you could see it in the rear mirror. Not that it mattered. Driving a foreign car, you were far too conspicuous to shake off the KGB by taking the kind of counter-surveillance measures that would work in Western cities.

'You don't need to turn round to look,' he said. 'There's quite a show being put on for us tonight. I've spotted two, possibly, three cars. And there seem to be two in front of us, keeping our speed.'

'Perhaps it's a training exercise,' I suggested. 'Any vehicle with a foreign diplomats' number plate will do. Scare the shit out of them. Show them who is running the country.'

'Could be,' he said, picking up speed. 'In that case we will give them something to do.'

As an afterthought, I asked: 'So… is it you or is it me? Just who is the target, a humble visa clerk or an ideological Trojan Horse?'

'Both of us,' he snorted, but he didn't mean it. He knew very well who was the KGB's target. And he did what you were not supposed to do – provoke them. He pulled into the side of the road and watched, engine running, as two cars in front and one behind, did the same. Then violating traffic rules he drove fast up the Ring Road and did a U-turn, only not where it was allowed. He had reduced working in Moscow to essentials and one of them was that if the Soviet government was going to throw you out, it didn't need an excuse, such as a traffic offence. The change of direction caught out the KGB cars in front of us. But the car behind stuck with us; it wasn't a difficult thing to do. We raced back down the Ring Road until all three KGB cars were back in position and Ruari got fed up with the game. Pleased with ourselves, we went home.

'So what was that all about?' I asked him, standing in the yard in 'Sad Sam', and not expecting an answer.

'One day,' he said, 'one day, my son, all will be revealed. Watch this space.'

It took many months before I understood.

Even as we were showing off to the KGB, and more especially its Second Chief Directorate, responsible for controlling foreigners inside the Soviet Union, an extraordinarily brave, foolish and suicidal Russian, Oleg Penkovsky, had become the West's most important secret source of information. Code-named 'Yoga' by British intelligence – the CIA appropriately called him 'Hero' – and a senior colonel in the GRU, Soviet Military Intelligence, he was betraying his country like no other Soviet citizen before or since. Regularly getting into the Soviet military's most secret archives, he was photographing hundreds of documents, such as discussion papers about the development of armaments and tactics, material denied to the West since the shooting down of the U-2. Arguably, as far as the West was concerned, it was the most extraordinary intelligence feat of the twentieth century and I had a ringside seat at it. There is probably little or nothing that is not now known about Penkovsky's sixteen or so glorious months of spying which embraced 1962, the year of prolonged crisis in Berlin; the Soviet introduction of long-range missiles into Cuba and the confrontation between Moscow and Washington.

I met him on one occasion at a party given for Western businessmen held at the National Hotel. I recall nothing of what we said, but I still see him in my mind's eye as though it was yesterday – a short, square, serious Russian with little to say for himself. And rare for a Russian, he had reddish hair. I shook his hand – not many Britons can say they shook hands with a man later executed for tipping the balance of terror away from nuclear war. During his trial, he was presented as a frivolous, drunken playboy who habitually mixed with tarts and liked to drink champagne from their shoes. This was meant to blacken him, but he went up in my estimation. When he was socializing with Westerners, he posed as a scientific officer, working

156

11. The American film star Kim Novak came to Moscow in 1962 for the Moscow Film Festival when her career appeared to be on the slide. But as snow flakes fell on Red Square she charmed Miller.

for a Soviet committee on technology and who was clearly given permission to have such contacts.

I talked several times to Greville Wynne, the English businessman who became embroiled in the affair by agreeing to work for SIS and link up with Penkovsky. I found him a typical English businessman, boasting about how well he knew the Soviet Union and of his Soviet friends in high places. In fact, he performed bravely in Moscow.

But my friendship with Ruari would have been the basis of the file on me that the KGB undoubtedly built up over the years. For there is little doubt that he was 'blown' from the day he arrived in Moscow – at about the same time I got there – having been on the lists of British agents given to the KGB by George Blake, for one.

It would never have occurred to me to have avoided Britain's chief spy in Moscow because he was a dangerous man, and some of the danger may have rubbed off on me. He was running the West's greatest spy ring since the end of the War, and it wasn't easy. The logistics of arranging secret meetings in Moscow, relieving Penkovsky of his intelligence loot and giving him new targets, was an awesome task.

In fact, towards the end, Ruari's wife Janet became the Moscow cut-out. She met Penkovsky in Svetnoi Boulevard near 'Sad Sam' and elsewhere on some twelve occasions. Sometimes he would give the Chisholm children a box of *drazhes*, a rather nasty chocolate-covered sweet, in what was called a 'brush contact'. And some of the sweets would contain exposed Minox microfilm, prompting at the time of the trial, a cartoon by Giles of the *Daily Express* on the theme of 'Don't forget the fruit gums, Mum.'

Inevitably, it all went wrong. No spy ring can last for ever. He was, as the Russians have it, as active as a squirrel in a wheel, and the strain of leading a double life began to tell on Penkovsky. Wynne was not as clever and as crafty as he thought he was – the KGB was not staffed by village idiots and they had had a lot of practice in counter-espionage. The KGB spotted Penkovsky meeting Wynne and they ultimately got on the track of his meetings with Janet Chisholm – there are KGB photos of them leaving a 'dead-drop' off the Arbat. After all, even in those days, Russians were not supposed to talk to foreigners.

Penkovsky was arrested in Moscow. Wynne was snatched by the KGB in Budapest. With the spy ring collapsing, the Chisholms got out fast, and nobody could blame them. I was in no way involved so the KGB left me alone. I stayed to cover the trial with Peter Johnson. Moving many thousands of words a day to London on a clapped out World-War-II Lease-Lend telex was a formidable operation, but Reuters did really well. In flowed the 'hero-grams', and we deserved them. For by putting out every important word said at the trial, we provided a fascinating record of that extraordinary era of espionage and the human agent. This was before computer and satellite-technology took over, allowing the Americans to eavesdrop on the car-phone conversations of a Soviet leader with one of his marshals, or the Soviets to read the insignia on the uniforms of a US airman strolling around a US air base in East Anglia.

But what a sweaty, messy, confused, nonsensical and even bloody business spying was shown to be! It was fashionable to laugh at the tricks the KGB got up in their espionage operations in Britain, such as chasing all over the country to find 'dead letter boxes' where their pathetic British agents could leave secrets.

British intelligence and the CIA did much the same in Moscow. Penkovsky had several such hiding places, including one in a cemetery, and when he had deposited anything he would mark a cross on a certain lamp-post. The mark would be noticed and the cache cleared. When he went to the British Embassy for a reception, he went to the toilet. There, he swapped a special tin of Harpic lavatory cleanser, with space for rolls of his exposed Minox microfilms, for a new one placed there earlier.

And the ring got too big. Penkovsky was being looked after not just by Ruari and later his replacement, but several American and British attachés and CIA officers.

'The Americans screwed it up,' Ruari told me later.

'Originally they turned down Penkovsky, thinking he was too good to be true. Then they sent in some clown to work him who made a balls of it. So we took him up and got things moving. They offered to bankroll the operation, so we shared everything we got. At first, they couldn't believe there were so many golden nuggets. Then they milked him for all he was worth. But he was demonic, possessed.

He couldn't stop spying. We should have tried to slow him down, but we didn't. And it got complicated. There were too many people in the know and the Americans had their traitors too, and in the National Security Agency, which was getting Penkovsky's stuff.'

And Ruari told me: 'When Penkovsky came to London a couple of times, we used to work him really hard – we had him all to ourselves for nearly 150 hours – and he was terrific. Once we said to him: 'Look, Oleg, you don't have to go back there. You've done a lot for us, for the West. And we are grateful. Now you can stay. And we will look after you.' But no. He wouldn't have it. He said his work wasn't yet done and so he went back. Back to the *rodina*, the lovely old Motherland.'

Back, of course, to receive a death sentence for spying on behalf of Britain and the United States, a verdict which, when read out, was greeted by those in the courtroom with applause and cheers. They clapped like mad when they heard he was going to be killed, just like they did at Stalin's show trials before the War.

There are two versions as to how they killed him – one official version and the other, a macabre tale, whispered to me by Ernst Neizvestny, the sculptor, in his workshop just before he emigrated to the Unites States. The official version is that he was shot in the back of the head by the executioner of the Ministry of Internal Affairs at the Butyrka Prison.

Neizvestny's version is straight out of Edgar Alan Poe or Beckett, and he says he was told it by a worker at the Donskoi Crematorium, where he was making a bas relief for a client, albeit while they were drinking vodka.

A few days after the verdict, Penkovsky was brought to the crematorium at night by a squad of KGB men and strapped to a stretcher. He was wheeled into the chamber and when the doors of the furnace were opened the stretcher was pushed far enough in for the soles of his feet to burn. But then over his terrible screaming came a loud speaker announcement that that slot was for another body, and Penkovsky was pulled back. The body appeared and was put into the furnace. After a while came another announcement that it was now the turn of Penkovsky, Oleg Vladimirovich, traitor to the Motherland, and while still alive he was shoved into the furnace. *Pour encourager les autres*, perhaps.

160

True or not, Wynne, by comparison, didn't do too badly. He got eight years, five in a labour camp, after quite rightly asking for mercy. Let's face it, he had only been a pawn in a 'dirty game' played by British and American intelligence against the nice, peace-loving, honest Russian people. His misery was compounded when he met his wife at the end of the trial and had to answer one of those idiotic questions British journalists asked, when unable to think of anything more original but needing to show they were on the story. This was: 'How are you, Mr Wynne?'

'Fine, thank you,' said he, but he wasn't at all. Shortly after the trial he was moved from the Lubyanka to a prison in Vladimir, and that was rough. He never got to the labour camp which would almost certainly have been more comfortable, because eleven months later, he was swapped for Gordon Lonsdale, the KGB 'illegal' arrested in London along with other members of the Portland Spy Ring.

Wynne never recovered from his experiences, which was not really surprising. Her Majesty's Government paid him £15,000 for his Moscow endeavours, a sum not to be sneezed at in the 1960s. The CIA was more generous. It gave him a 'resettlement allowance' of $200,000, which again was a useful sum to help recover from the trauma of a Soviet prison and, indeed, it bought him a rose garden in Malta and a lot of booze. He became a thorough pest to his old spy masters, shed his wife and became an alcoholic. Right up to the day he died, he was exceedingly litigious, especially if anyone suggested he made up some of the stories about his life as a courageous dare-devil spy.

Harried by the hacks to say what he thought of the trial, the best Ruari could manage was:

'It is the finale in a three-act farce. As far as I am concerned, the whole trial was a joke.' He got a commendation from President Kennedy for his work in Moscow and thanks from MI6 – after all, it was all in a day's work. A few years later we met again in South Africa, where he was the Southern Africa Station chief. There, because I was returning to Moscow, he propositioned me. Straightaway I said 'No.' I was patriotic and anti-Communist, all right. I stood up and stood to attention for 'The Queen'. I laughed and cried when they sang 'Land of Hope and Glory' at the Last Night of the Proms. I knew by heart 'I vow to thee my country' from Holst's Planets. And a regular, if small, retainer from HMG would have helped feed our pussy cats. But I wanted as uncomplicated a life as possible, preferring my kind of spying – uncovering stories about the Soviet Union and writing them for the paper – in my way and in my time. And if MI6 and the CIA learned anything from what I wrote, then all well and good. More than that, of course, was my knowledge of what happened to those like Wynne who got caught and did not have diplomatic immunity. I very much wanted to see the inside of the Lubyanka, but not as a long-stay prisoner with a pining wife and hungry children.

'We won't ask you again, Old Son,' he said. 'You know how it is. We would have liked you to come aboard, what with your knowledge of the Sovs and you going back there for the *Daily Telegraph*. But… it's your life.'

It was. And I never became a spy…

Philby wrote in his memoirs: 'One does not look twice at an offer of enrolment in an élite force.' Apparently he despised journalists and businessmen who volunteered to undertake occasional jobs for the British or any other intelligence service, passing on tit-bits that came their way, usually valueless gossip. But he was trying to justify his treachery and, in any case, he was full of crap.

Ruari never said he was disappointed in me and never mentioned the attempt to recruit me again. I liked him very much and was saddened by his death – suddenly and stupidly, from a particular malignant form of malaria caught in Tanzania, after he had left the SIS to become a military historian. He was fifty-four.

One curious and ironic aspect of his life was that his East Sussex home backed on to Seacoxs, the Soviet Embassy's country retreat. From the end of his garden you could sometimes see the KGB burning their shredded secret-files on a bonfire. We once sneaked into the back garden and kicked over the ashes for a disappointing reward – the only thing readable was a list of items on a BBC news broadcast. I doubt if MI5 monitor Russian bonfires these days.

Later, the Penkovsky affair was to be worked over – inevitably there were those who insisted he was never executed but went on to live the life of Riley – not Sidney Reilly, the British agent during Lenin's time, who was also executed – in a nice little dacha in the country. Because, Peter Wright and other such potty conspiracy-theorists argued, Penkovsky had been run willingly or unconsciously all along as a double agent. So, it was argued – and the odd Soviet defector was produced to back up the theory – he had been merely a conduit for disinformation; that the West had been conned by the Kremlin… et cetera… et cetera… The so-called wilderness of mirrors – where defectors are false, lies are truth and truth lies. It becomes all very confusing.

I must say that I was stunned by how much material Penkovsy handed over – some 5,000 frames of film of subjects well outside his sphere of responsibility – and found it difficult to believe that Soviet security could be so lax. But Ruari swore blind that Penkovsky had been the real McCoy, and that is good enough for me.

Of course, the British were no sluggards when it came to spying. And the Sixties were a heyday for spies and spies as heroes. *From Russia with Love* is a line I have been trotting out since 1963, when the second, and for me, the best, James Bond film hit the screen.

Suddenly, everyone learned what I had known for years: that every Russian worked for SMERSH – the special secret police-unit with an acronym meaning 'Death to Spies'. If they were not heavy men with mouthfuls of silver teeth and ill-fitting suits and baggy trousers, they were pretending to be English, exposing themselves by ordering red wine with fish. Or, if they were Russian women spies, they looked like the rear end of an Egyptian bus and had knives that sprang out of the end of their boots. Or, alternatively, were gorgeous bits of crackling that dropped their knickers to turn you on with the sole aim of 'turning you', i.e. joining their ranks.

ACC, the KGB set about improving its image and had a Miss KGB contest. The winner, Natalya Maiyorovo, was five feet seven inches with green eyes – matching her epaulettes – high cheekbones, fine teeth and good skin, indicating she was a member of a well-fed élite, and there was nothing secret about her vital statistics: 36.24.35. But, although she wore her bullet-proof vest 'like a Pierre Cardin model', she was apparently capable of stunning an opponent with a karate kick to the head. Not Rosa Khleb, perhaps, but obviously a lady not to be trifled with.

As it happens, I cannot think of a single occasion when I was the target of a 'swallow' operation – the KGB term for using a girl, or girls, to tempt foreigners into trouble. It was one of their biggest weapons during the Cold War in attempts to recruit diplomats, journalists and businessmen as Soviet agents. The fact that they never tried me suggests either that they knew I was incorruptible and resistant to seduction and simply wasn't worth the trouble. Or that I suffered from BO, halitosis, or both. All I do know is that you should never make a date to meet a Russian girl. Because Tamara never comes.

There is the story of the Swedish businessman in Moscow to conclude a big deal with the Russians, who was seduced by a 'swallow'. Next morning, before the negotiations began, he was ushered into a room and shown photographs of him in a compromising situation with a lady.

'So,' said the KGB Colonel, 'what we would like is for you to be sensible and reasonable about this deal.'

'And if I'm not?' asked the Swede.

'Well,' said the colonel, 'we guarantee we will send copies of these pictures to your boss, your wife and your government.'

The Swede thought for a moment. Then he said: 'You should know I am my own boss. And what do you think my wife is up to while I am away. As for my government, they will be grateful to me for spreading an aspect of Swedish national culture abroad. And finally, can you run off several more copies of my best positions to give them away to my friends, when I get home.'

The KGB officers I knew in London and Moscow wouldn't have come down to that sort of mucky blackmail and, by and large, they came across as fairly straight-forward sort of chaps. One was Yuri Zemskov, a first secretary at the Soviet Embassy, whom I took out to lunch on a regular basis.

Lunching Soviets was always a delight. They ate as though they hadn't eaten for days, all the while giving you an earful about what a lying, rotten, anti-Soviet newspaper you worked for; how wicked was Britain's foreign policy; and how badly-off was the British working class. Zemskov was no exception, and once he complained that we always ate at the same table in Fleet Street's El Vinos, and was it possible that it was bugged? 'Ho-ho. Only by a rival newspaper',

I said. Later, he became the second-ranking Soviet diplomat in Australia and he featured in an article in the *Readers Digest*. This spoke of there being an ultra-secret service within the KGB called 'Special Reserve', and that Zemskov was one of their stars – 'he never attempts to bribe, recruit or induce anyone to do anything wrong.' Instead, he endeavoured to persuade Australia to adopt policies that would rupture its military alliance with the United States and join New Zealand in a plan to create a 'nuclear-free zone' in the South Pacific, and so on and so forth. Big deal!

Two other KGB chaps, with whom I was acquainted, also did well for themselves. One was Yuri Loginov, who was briefly my 'minder' working for the State Committee for Cultural Relations with Foreign Countries. He accompanied us on visits laid on by the Committee, until one day he disappeared. Gone to America, they said, to work in the Embassy in Washington. And then, sometime later when I asked about him, I was told he had been killed in a car crash. 'How sad', said I.

In fact he was alive and well and preparing to become an 'illegal', so as to live abroad in disguise and blend inconspicuously into the society he was sent to work in.

It turned out to be South Africa, and when I was there. Van Der Merve was not known for being especially sharp at catching Soviet illegals, unless they had black faces, but, by all accounts, they soon rumbled Loginov who was wandering around Johannesburg, taking pictures of police stations and army barracks. He was never brought to trial, but spent months in Pretoria Prison. One day, I happened to interview the head of the security police and asked him what was going to happen to Yuri. 'Well, he has sung like a red (sic) canary, every day he has been enjoying our good South African hospitality,' said General Van den Bergh, 'and I don't think he is any use to us now. I am offering to swap him for one of the West's spies, but nobody is interested. So, I am very seriously thinking, Mr Miller, of taking him myself to Berlin and... well... tossing him over the wall.' Which is what happened.

Right up to the hardline *coup* against Mikhail Gorbachev in August 1991, Moscow Centre was the last refuge of Cold War conspiracy theory. The barking head of the KGB warned of a bizarre

Western plot to poison Soviet grain imports, and one of his deputies disclosed another CIA project designed to destabilize the rouble (which in fact happened, but not as the result of a plot hatched by the wicked West). And abroad the KGB's motto was still 'Carry on Spying.'

Nobody can be sure how many Russians, Americans, Britons, West Germans, Chinese – not forgetting the Israelis – to name just a few nationalities, were involved in espionage worldwide at the height of the Cold War; but some estimates have suggested a total of about 1.5 million people.

Nor do we know how much it has cost – perhaps £10 billion annually, perhaps more, and with the Americans and the Russians, who could ill afford it, having the biggest budgets.

Just what value all this expensive spying has really been is not known and, you can be assured, will never be revealed. No files are going to be opened to tell us whether this or that stolen secret was really put to good use. Over the past three decades, in Britain several spies have been sent to prison for long terms of imprisonment for apparently 'irreparably damaging national security'. But did the stuff they flogged to the KGB really benefit the Soviet Union's military or economic capabilities? Did the infamous Portland Spy Ring of Britons and Soviet 'illegals' actually lead to an improvement in Soviet submarines or increase the Soviet arsenal for waging underwater warfare? Was all that spying really necessary? On balance, I tend think that it wasn't worth an empty eggshell, as the Russians say, although, while it lasted, it was a damn good story.

The Penkovsky case is the exception. It is hard to think of another spy in Penkovsky's class, who has had a greater impact on history. The stuff he shovelled to the West changed its perceptions of Soviet nuclear weapons. He helped President Kennedy outface Nikita Khrushchev in the Cuban Missile Crisis of 1962 by revealing that, despite their bluster, the Soviets were not strong enough in rocketry to start a war.

A quarter of a century after he was shot, I was visiting Moscow and decided to take a look at the entrance in Pushkin Street where he used a radiator in the hallway as a dead-letter drop. It was a cold Sunday morning, snow was falling, few people were about. Standing on the other side of the road, I took a photograph of the building and as I did, a man came up to me.

He pointed across the road and to my astonishment said: 'That's the Penkovsky House.'

'You are absolutely right,' I said. 'How did you know that?' I asked.' Are you KGB?'

He smiled. 'No, of course not,' he said. 'I'm a scene shifter at the Bolshoi.'

Another man appeared. 'Why are you taking a photograph of the Penkovsky House?' he asked pleasantly enough. 'You should know he was a traitor. He betrayed his Motherland. He was scum and died like a dog.'

'Yes,' I said. 'I know all that. But not to me. Not to the West. To us he was a soldier of freedom. A brave man. A great man, even. A spy who may have just possibly saved the world.'

But I could see they didn't understand what I was saying.

ACC, it was only a question of time before the KGB went the way of the Soviet Union. About the only people who regretted its passing were the tens of thousands of agents who got fired. The smartest, who knew a thing about Western ways, had read forbidden books and spoke passable English, promptly got into business...

The KGB became the FSB with a severely diminished role in the daily life of Russians. Spying has, of course continued – the Russians are still obsessed with it. (They even have a saying that it is better to fart openly than secretly like a spy!) But there are new targets, such as the mafia, weapons-smuggling and industrial espionage.

Dodik, my photographer son, was in Moscow on assignment when the mob marched on Lubyanka Square and began pulling down the statue of Felix Dzerzhinsky, founder of the Cheka and father of Soviet spying, on the traffic island in front of the Lubyanka. He told me that the crowd roared with delight as the statue crashed to the ground, while the police and the KGB looked on. It was a small wonder that every window in the Lubyanka was not smashed and that the building was not set on fire.

But that night signalled the end of the KGB. Or, certainly, of the KGB that I knew over some thirty-five years.

15 – The Great Leveller

They were telling jokes about the death of Leonid Brezhnev even before he died. And forecasting his successor: Brezhnev was addressing a Party meeting and reading from a piece of paper as he always did during his last ten years of senility and decrepitude: 'Today we are seeing off on his final journey a loyal son of our Party, (he reads more slowly) General Secretary of the Central Committee of the Communist Party of the Soviet Union, (still more slowly) Marshal of the Soviet Union, President of the Presidium of the Supreme Soviet of the Union of Soviet Socialist Republics, Leonid (pause) Illich (pause) Brezhnev!...' He looks at the paper tersely, then at his clothes. 'Sorry, Comrades,' he says, 'I've put on Comrade Andropov's jacket again.'

Another joke at the time also touched on the mechanism of succession, assuming that Brezhnev was mortal. A question to Radio Armenia: 'What were Brezhnev's last words?' Answer: 'Comrade Andropov, please stop fiddling with that life support machine...'

In the end, however, it was kindness, or what sometimes passes for it, that finished off Brezhnev after his long and boring innings as Soviet leader, now remembered, if at all, as the 'Era of Stagnation'. His comrades in the Politburo probably did not deliberately set out to shorten his life so that they could grab all the top jobs after a seemingly interminable wait for some eighteen years, but that was how it worked out.

A word or two about Brezhnev from a man who wrote tens, if not, hundreds of thousands of words about him. Ecclesiastes 9:11 comes to mind: 'The race is not to the swift, nor the battle to the strong, neither yet bread to the wise, nor yet riches to men of understanding, nor yet favour to men of skill: but time and chance happeneth to them all.' Brezhnev's career provides as good an illustration as any of this truth.

Brezhnev was lucky to have been at the right age, thirty-two, at the right time, 1938, and to have been sufficiently obedient and blank-minded to have been taken into the party apparatus, and advanced over the bodies of his seniors. He was clever and far-sighted enough to stick closely to Nikita Khrushchev so as to climb the greasy pole with him, until choosing the time to push him down and off it.

169

One of Brezhnev's outstanding features was that he never spoke a memorable sentence or initiated any new policy. Another was his love of baubles. He dished them out to himself as though there was no tomorrow – six Orders of Lenin, two Heroes of the Soviet Union, two Heroes of Soviet Labour; all told, more than 250 medals and awards, not to mention a Lenin Prize for Literature. Poorly-educated, he never read books – preferring to play dominoes with his bodyguards for money – and, as a result, everyone knew his ludicrous little book was ghosted. During the War he was a political commissar and there were hundreds like him – never saw a battle but just about got to be a Major-General. He made up for being awarded only a handful of minor medals and orders when he got to the top.

Then he showered himself with medals for 'bravery', including the exceptional, large and beautiful Order of Victory, of which only fourteen were issued after the War to a few famous Marshals like Georgy Zhukov. There was a joke about him having an operation to widen his rib-cage as there wasn't enough room on his uniform for his medals. He liked pigeons, dogs, shooting boar, watching ice-hockey, drinking and power. And it is just possible that after bloody Stalin and chaotic Khrushchev, the country needed a nonentity, a nobody. It got one.

At the end it seemed we were constantly speculating about his health because we suspected, rightly as it turned out, that he was slipping into senility. I had him suffering from all sorts of ailments ranging from cancer of the jaw, through mild heart attacks, to sclerosis. Such stories irritated Soviet officials and they would never confirm them.

Thanks to his doctor, Yevgeny Chazov, we now know that Brezhnev was a pill-head. For the last ten years of his life he was dependent on tranquillizers and sleeping pills given him by his colleagues, but largely by his nurse, who also provided him with other bodily comforts. She had such a strong hold over Lyonechka, that for years he brushed aside a plea by KGB chief Yuri Andropov to get rid of her. Brezhnev rewarded both the nurse and her husband, who rose quickly from KGB captain to general. Chazov says the diet of pills hastened the aging process and did irreparable harm to the leader. After taking strong sleeping pills he was like a zombie and

12. Nikita Khrushchev emerged briefly from forced retirement in 1967 to vote in the Soviet elections. Miller asked him for a comment. He replied: 'There should be peace'.

the bodyguards would dress him, set him on his feet and propel him forward as though he was a car that wouldn't start.

This was the head of the other superpower, and at a time when so many clever-dick Western hacks were ridiculing Ronald Reagan, who at least had most of his marbles, albeit at the end he suffered from Alzheimer's.

I was in Moscow for the last days of Brezhnev. He was only working an hour or two a day, spent mostly at his dacha. He had a holiday in the Crimea – it was a curious aspect of Soviet political power that members of the Politburo, come what may, took holidays of exactly twenty-eight days according to a rota – and when he returned to Moscow, someone suggested the Old Man put himself about a bit. Late in September, he flew to Baku, the capital of Soviet Azerbaijan, for three days of glad-handing the natives. It was unusual, he had not been out of Moscow on business for months, and what the Azeris had done to deserve him descending upon them will never be known.

Then, as now, Azerbaijan was heavily rural, impoverished and predominantly Moslem, and despite numerous campaigns and crackdowns, it won all the prizes for corruption. It was, and probably still is, also known for its *pokazukha*, which can loosely be translated as 'bullshit', or putting on a phoney show in order to impress those in high places.

Pokazukha has been around a long time in Russia too. We all know about the Potemkin villages, the fake buildings which Prince Potemkin is supposed to have built in 1787 for the benefit of Catherine the Great in order to impress her of his industry and organization. Yet this could be an anti-Potemkin calumny. There is not a vestige of evidence to suggest that the prince built such villages, with cardboard houses and paste palaces, or that he drove millions of unwilling slaves dressed up as farmers and their cattle to places were Catherine could see them, so as to create a false picture of prosperity.

All he actually did was to insist that buildings along his lover's route had a new lick of paint, were cleaned and tided up, and to have constructed a few new buildings for her use. But why spoil a good story with the facts...? In Azerbaijan, Brezhnev was fêted for three days, and flattered until his old head must have spun. The climax was a party and government rally which went on for hours and was mostly an orgy of obsequiousness, carefully orchestrated by Geidar Aliyev, then the local party secretary, smooth, clever and exceedingly ambitious. On television news, Brezhnev looked knackered, slurring his words and managing to confuse Afghanistan with Azerbaijan. It proved to be a long speech, too, because it was interrupted twenty-eight times with applause. *Pravda* faithfully recorded – as it used to do for Stalin – that there were twelve cases of continuous applause, three of stormy applause, and two of continuous and stormy applause. Stalin would have been jealous.

Aliyev dragged Brezhnev around the republic in the hot sun and through the dust, chalking up creep points and underlining what was widely known – that he was a *zhopolis* or 'arse-licker', par excellence. Brezhnev returned to Moscow worn out. It took him a month to recover, and then he was wheeled out again to deliver a major speech to the Armed Forces' top commanders and political commissars. It was an unusual event and it took a student of Soviet affairs to realize that it was held, twenty years to the day, that the Soviet Union had suffered a humiliating political defeat, bowing to President Kennedy's demand for Soviet missiles be removed from Cuba.

So Brezhnev's speech to a military, already fed up with him claiming to have won World War II, and giving himself all the best medals, was about the Soviet Union matching the United States rouble for dollar in the Arms Race. Of course it couldn't – certainly not in the long run – and he looked neither confident nor happy.

Came the traditional 7 November parade on Red Square. For the eighth or perhaps ninth time, I wrote about the crack troops swinging across Red Square, the 214 items of hardware on show, the noise and the clouds of acrid blue smoke emitted by the tanks; the solid wedge of marching men, women and children; the banners with their tired mechanical slogans and the familiar calls for peace and friendship, combined with threats. Brezhnev was atop the Lenin Mausoleum with his cronies on the stroke of 10 am – via an escalator built for him – and remained there for much of two hours, waving to the crowds.

This was a red-letter day in the Communist calendar. The Soviet tsar had to show himself to his subjects, who surely loved him. And it was a particularly lovely November day. The temperature was just below freezing, but the sun was so bright that Brezhnev wore sunglasses, as well as a fur hat and heavy overcoat. There was a reason for that extraordinary fine weather. The previous year it had been nasty, with some heavy snowfalls, and several times the Boss had nipped inside the Mausoleum to warm up and have a glass or two of cognac.

But not this year. The comrades apparently cared desperately about the welfare of Lenin's heir and turned to the wonders of science to deal with any threatened nasty weather. I reported how Soviet aircraft had taken to the skies to break up snow clouds heading for Moscow by sprinkling silver iodide crystals on them. And this had ensured a fine day for both Brezhnev and the people.

There were not a few colleagues who laughed at such a tale – 'fanciful' was one word used. Two months later it was official. Four aircraft sprayed the snow-clouds, preventing more than eight inches of snow falling on Moscow, thus saving millions of roubles in snow-clearing operations. But no Soviet newspaper mentioned that the project had had the effect of keeping poor old Brezhnev atop the Mausoleum for a full two hours, so that when he eventually went in for the Kremlin reception, even Western diplomats noted that he looked ill – eyes glazed, and walking with difficulty. Three days later, he was dead.

And of a heart attack at 8.30 am, while on the lavatory. Such is the degree of secrecy surrounding the private lives and deaths of the Soviet leadership that we knew little more, although the official bulletin said Brezhnev suffered from 'arteriosclerosis of the aorta with the development of aneurism of its abdominal part; stenosing arteriosclerosis of coronary arteries; ischemic heart disease with heart rhythm trouble and electrical changes of myocardium after he suffered infarctions'.

It would have been interesting to have known his last words. Stalin's final menacing and incomprehensible gesture was to lift his left hand, as though he was trying to bring down a curse on those who were watching him die after a cerebral haemorrhage. Within minutes of Stalin being pronounced dead, his colleagues rushed for the door. Most of them were torn with sorrow and relief – Beria was probably the exception. But there are still people alive in Russia who believe that Stalin was murdered, or somehow speeded on his way, by his 'devoted' comrades, especially Beria. There was the providential timing of his passing, as another great purge was signalled following the 'Doctors' Plot'. Some of these comrades, among them Molotov, Mikoyan and even Voroshilov, were fearful that they were about to go the same way as the Old Bolsheviks – to Lubyanka and the grave. Also, of course, nobody of any importance in the Kremlin had died a natural death for years and years. There was also the still unexplained disappearance shortly before Stalin's death of two of his most faithful and trusted retainers. Were they got out of the way? If so, by whom? Perhaps one day we will be told.

It seems inconceivable that anybody would have tried to get rid of Brezhnev – those at the top did rather well out of his rule; he was no Stalin and was not feared. In his case, the news of his passing was quietly telephoned to the inner Cabinet, the Moscow-based members of the Politburo, who met quickly to take decisions on the funeral arrangements and decide who was going to run the country.

It is history that the Central Committee of the Soviet Communist Party met and elected Yuri Andropov, for fifteen years the KGB boss, to succeed Brezhnev. These comrades merely rubber-stamped the Politburo's decision on succession, taken within a few hours of Brezhnev's death. There was no debate. Andropov's KGB background clinched the job for him. He knew more about his colleagues – especially their peccadillos – than they knew about themselves. He had the sort of power-base that could not be ignored.

But on the day Brezhnev died, the news of it was limited to only a few hundred people at the most. Even TASS, the Soviet news agency, was not told – as he was being taken to the Kremlin mortuary, it put out a story saying he was awarding medals to some factory workers. Nor, of course, were Western journalists, but they were a lot quicker on the uptake.

For that night, some strange things happened on Soviet television and radio which perfectly illustrated how the media worked and was controlled under Communism.

Suddenly television presenters are wearing dark suits and black ties, or black dresses, and inform viewers that programmes are being rescheduled. A variety concert to mark Soviet Police Day is replaced by a film about Lenin and reminiscences of the Great Patriotic War. On the other channel, much to the annoyance of millions of Russians crazy about ice-hockey, the showing of a big match is replaced by a recorded concert of Beethoven piano music. A radio station switched from its usual diet of pop music to classical music.

All this indicated that somebody very, very important was dead – certainly to perceptive Western journalists. John Osman of the BBC phoned: Did I know that Ed Stevens was going hard on Brezhnev being dead? As it happened, it didn't do Stevens any good. His Italian newspaper didn't use the story because the foreign editor didn't believe it – it wasn't on the News Agencies.

We are now locked into a familiar Moscow news song-and-dance act where nobody has any hard facts, and rumours and conjecture are being passed around at high speed, adding little to the sum of knowledge. Even Victor Louis, who had made his name with important news tip-offs that were never wrong, appears to know nothing of Brezhnev's death. But he says he will try and find out. It is now 1 am in Moscow; there is a three-hour time difference with London where they are getting anxious about having some sort of story in the early editions of the paper. I go to the office and put the light on in the kitchen where the telex is installed, crunching the odd cockroach underfoot, while dozens of others scuttle for their lives to get out of the light into the cracks in the wall, down the sink, back into the gas stove. There is a message from London telling me that Reuters put out a story about changes to television programmes and has no inkling why.

'Like yours,' they say, as they often do. I make another call to the Louis dacha – after all he has a good, if ghoulish, track record on being first with big deaths. Jennifer answers the telephone and she is cautious.

She says: 'It very easily might be the old man himself. On the other hand, it might not. The chances are that it is. But of course, it might not be.' I try very hard to get her to say 'Yes, Brezhnev is dead,' but tonight she won't. You can't blame her.

Now, at a moment of what seemed then to be high drama, it is a question of having to knock out some words. This is what I am paid to do. There is no censorship. I can write what I like. I can take a chance and have Brezhnev definitely dead, have a good run at it and tell the *Telegraph* to blow the dust off the Brezhnev obituary and shove it in.

Because this is a big story – it is the end of an era. It is a development that could have enormous consequences for East-West relations and the future course of the Soviet Union. But supposing Stevens, the Louis, and others had all got it wrong, been badly or mischievously informed, misunderstood what they been told or implied? After all, Brezhnev has been killed off several times, alarming stock markets and some governments fearing a period of instability in international relations. Perhaps he who appears to have died is another of the eight men out of thirteen in the Politburo who is over seventy. But the bottom line is that you simply cannot kill off the Soviet President and Communist Party General Secretary unless he is dead. Any self-respecting government would have considered the story over the top, not to say impermissible, and I would have been on my way home to London.

In the end it came down, as always, to 'how you write 'em'. Newspapers worth their salt don't like reporting rumours, but there is a case to be made for using the word rumour if the fact of it is a story. What is needed is a strong story to get the newspaper through the night and to keep it happy.

I punch straight onto the telex: 'Rumours shook Moscow late last night that President Leonid Brezhnev, the Soviet leader, had either died suddenly or was near death, bringing to an end eighteen years of rule.' I say there is absolutely no confirmation of the rumours. I decide to waste my time and telephone the Communist Party Central Committee building, just in case there was some action there.

The telephone is answered by a woman who sounds half asleep and is evidently the duty clerk. I ask her if her boss is dead. In turn she asks: 'Whereever did you hear such a dreadful thing?' and she slams down the phone. And true to form, there is no reply at all from any of the telephones at the Soviet Foreign Ministry, suggesting the duty officer there was either keeping his head down or was drunk, or both.

Back tickling the telex I quote an unnamed, long-time Moscow correspondent, who could have been Ed Stevens, or even myself, as saying he had heard Brezhnev was 'definitely dead', and it needed a day or two to prepare for the succession. The story included two red-herrings, reporting that Andrei Kirilenko and Arvid Pelshe had been ill, and that they might warrant being given the full treatment. It is the best I can do, and the *Telegraph* responds very quickly telling me I am hitting the story harder than the agencies. I leave the kitchen to the cockroaches and go to bed.

Brezhnev is dead reports sweep Moscow was the second lead in the *Telegraph*. There is a certain irony that the big story and lead in the paper was the thirty-five-year prison sentence handed out to a taxi-driver, Geoffrey Prime, who had spied for Brezhnev for fourteen years while working at the British government's top-secret code-cracking and communication centre in Cheltenham. A bigger irony, however, is, that contrary to trial evidence, Prime was almost certainly 'shopped' to MI5 by Oleg Gordievsky, Brezhnev's KGB boss at the Soviet Embassy in London.

The Kremlin eventually got around to announcing Brezhnev's death and it took some twenty-six hours. Predictably, he was a true maintainer of Lenin's great cause, an ardent champion of peace and Communism, who would live forever in the hearts of the Soviet people and all progressive mankind. Oh yes! But the news was greeted more with stunned silence than with grief. I only saw dry eyes.

The next day, the police and the KGB appeared in their thousands, sealing off the centre of Moscow for the lying-in-state at the House of Unions, the green and white former Club of the Nobility, as an army of workers swung into action across the country. Even we bourgeois, anti-Soviet slanderers had a black-bordered red flag stuck into the stanchion outside the living-room window in 'Sad Sam'.

Brezhnev's body was taken in the dead of night to the beautiful Hall of Columns, with its marble and vast wall-mirrors, and sixty crystal chandeliers which had bathed in light the dancing nobility, where Lenin and Stalin had both lain in state and where, memorably, I covered the U-2 spy plane trial. Also staged here were the show trials of the Old Bolsheviks, where, one after the other, they were told they were guilty, before being taken up the hill to the Lubyanka to be shot, or to disappear in the GULAG for ever.

This glittering legacy of the tsars had seen a thing or two, and now tens of thousands filed slowly past Brezhnev's body which lay on a bank of wreaths and flowers, his vast collection of medals on dozens of crimson cushions at one end, his portrait at the other.

There was music for the filing, blank-faced throng; unrelieved mournfulness of Chopin, haunting Tchaikovsky, some exultant Beethoven. Rarely was heard the conventional symbol of mourning, the sob.

We were not allowed to linger. 'Keep moving, Comrades,' urged the ushers. 'No photographs. Do not stop. Keep moving.'

When Lenin died in January 1924, millions flocked to Moscow for the lying-in-state and funeral. They clambered aboard trains and long processions of sleighs built up around the city. It provided an opportunity for the authorities to perfect crowd-control and show how a modern city could be sealed off.

After Stalin's death, security troops took over Moscow and used tanks and trucks to shut off the circulation of traffic and block streets. But such was the intensity of feeling, and tension, over the death of Joseph Vissarionovitch, ranging from grief to relief that the tyrant had gone at last, and the authorities' unconcern for human lives, that several dozen – or several hundred, it is still not clear – died, either by being crushed up against the sides of the tanks and the trucks, or simply being trampled to death. Nobody was blamed.

So Stalin died as he lived, in a sea of blood. Poor old Russia – remember the coronation of Tsar Nicholas II, when hundreds gathered to receive beer mugs and scarves in the Khodynka Field outside Moscow and were crushed to death? The terrible memory was to haunt him throughout his tragic reign.

They got it right for Brezhnev's last journey, and for several reasons. There was television to bring the funeral into the homes of millions throughout the USSR, and Brezhnev was no Stalin or Lenin, loved or feared enough to bring in the crowds. So Muscovites stayed at home as another impressive display of Soviet military pomp unfolded against the background of the haunting beauty of Red Square. On a mild morning his body was borne on a gun-carriage, draped in red and black, followed by his widow, other members of the family and a handful from the Politburo – the first time most of them had walked publicly any distance in a central Moscow street for years. In front of the Mausoleum the lid of the coffin was removed, and Brezhnev lay as if viewing events and listening to the funeral oration from those standing on the rostrum, where he had taken so

179

many May and November parades. Speeches were brief, unemotional, routine and clichéd up to, and including, Andropov, who has suddenly become one of the most powerful men on earth, attacking imperialists for trying to create hostility and military confrontation, and warning about dealing aggressors – i.e. the West – crushing blows. Nobody's voice so much as trembled with grief. No tears were to be seen. They came down from the Mausoleum and followed immediately behind the pallbearers, carrying the body towards the grave in the front of the Kremlin Wall.

This procedure had been followed at several Red Square funerals of top politicians and marshals, taking place during the last years of Brezhnev's reign. And it spawned jokes, such as at the funeral of Mikhail Suslov a senile Brezhnev keeps looking around anxiously, before turning to the other comrades as they all walk slowly together beside the coffin and asking: 'And where, Comrades, is our Comrade Suslov?'

There was just one moving moment. Brezhnev's widow bent over him, kissed his forehead, dabbed away her tears with a handkerchief. Her daughter kissed his face twice. This was the last ritual of the Russian Orthodox Church before the coffin was closed.

It was lowered – but so clumsily into the deeply-dug plot, that one end fell with a loud clump. At least, that was what we thought at the time. But years later, the undertaker, Georgy Kovalenko, flatly denied it. He said the loud noise was not Brezhnev hitting the bottom of the grave, but that of guns firing the salute, picked up by a television microphone. Kovalenko was a most interesting man and had it not been the collapse of Communism you would never have got to meet him. For he claimed to have buried four Communist Party leaders, a couple of dozen members of the Politburo, and scores of Soviet ministers and other dignitaries, as well as Roman Lopez – who killed Trotsky on Stalin's orders – and Kim Philby.

'We never dropped Brezhnev's coffin,' he said. 'Had anything like that happened, I would never have been trusted to bury Andropov and Chernenko.'

And about his work, he said: 'It is traditionally believed in Russia that if one works in a cemetery one must be a drunk and a beggar, the lowest class, a real down-and-out, a dead beat. I utterly disagree with

180

this. Why can't normal people work in a cemetery, dig graves and ensure a sumptuous funeral passes off in a smooth and business-like manner?'

He was right about one thing: there was an artillery salute, which scattered the grey-haired ravens nesting in the Kremlin spires. And the Kremlin clock chimed, and factory sirens sounded a five-minute work stoppage throughout the country.

There was more church ritual for the Communist of more than fifty years: relatives and comrades threw small handfuls of earth on the coffin. Troops from the Moscow garrison goose-stepped across the square. The General Secretary was dead, long live the General Secretary. One more ceremony that day underlined Andropov's emergence as a world leader. Statesmen and political leaders from more than 70 countries flew to Moscow and in the cool splendour of St George's Hall, they offered condolences to Andropov. The idea was that they shuffled along a red carpet laid in the magnificent hall, shook hands with the new tsar, moved on to bow their heads before a large portrait of the old one, and went home. The East Europeans, the disgusting old gang that Brezhnev was forever kissing, and Robert Maxwell wooing, knew their place and got the proceedings off to a good start by moving swiftly past Andropov, heads down. But inevitably there were those who for all sorts of reasons – vanity or politicizing – were not going to waste their visit to Moscow.

China's Foreign Minister, Huang Hua, showed what could be done by holding Andropov's hand and chatting with him for more than three minutes. What was discussed was never revealed but not only was the new Soviet leader visibly unimpressed, but the visiting VIPs waiting in line became agitated, and began muttering. Huang also spent an interminably long time before Brezhnev's portrait, as well as making a most obsequious bow – surprising given that 'revisionist' Brezhnev was a dirty word in Peking. Huang's reward for going over the top in Moscow was that on his return to Peking he was fired.

This international wake took well over an hour, during which time Andropov shook some 350 hands, an occasion enlivened only by the presence of two ladies, both remarkable in their own way. One was Mrs Gandhi wearing a black sari and managing to look bereaved. She wasted no time in small talk with Andropov and quickly moved on. The other was Mrs Emelda Marcos, who had left her husband at home and was looking like a high-class tart. Heavily made-up she was wearing a tight-fitting blue dress and, of all things, red high-heeled shoes – presumably carefully selected from the thousands of pairs she owned – but which at least made for a smashing pair of legs. Certainly she briefly cast a spell over Andropov and the other Politburo sobersides. They positively drooled over her hand, turned on the smarmiest of smiles. Again the line was held up.

I caught Mrs Gandhi looking across at what was going on and you could see what she was thinking – the shameless hussy!

Fifteen months later I went to another Red Square funeral, identical in every way except for the fact that it involved Andropov. His death did not surprise the Kremlin-watchers; his absences from work had become even more frequent than those of Brezhnev, one lasting nearly five months.

After he missed a Red Square parade, I telephoned the Kremlin spokesman Leonid Zamyatin, a propagandist I had sparred with for some twenty years, and asked him if his boss was seriously ill.

'This is rubbish. This is nonsense. Such a thing is a lie. Not only that, it is untrue,' said Zamyatin, who had a zero credibility rating. 'The President has a cold.'

Zamyatin was always worth baiting. 'A serious cold? I asked. 'An average cold? An occasional sneeze, perhaps? Or can we say a slight cough?'

He was very displeased. But I didn't care. Zamyatin was a lying, shifty careerist, the worst kind of *apparatchik*. Gorbachev's ambassador to London, he became unstuck, to the joy of a great many people, when he publicly backed the gang who mounted the *coup* against his boss. What was especially satisfying about his downfall was that it only really came about because he was waylaid by journalists outside the Foreign Office, and said the *coup* was 'constitutional' – which, of course, it was anything but.

When Andropov died, there was once again a sudden change in television and radio programmes, and the long wait until his cronies decided who was going to have his job. A medical bulletin told Russians the extent of his decrepitude: he suffered from fluctuations of blood pressure and diabetes, complicated by chronic kidney trouble requiring dialysis treatment for much of the time he had been running – or ruining – the country.

If it can be argued that trying to be nice to Brezhnev played a part in killing him off, it can also be said that it was the KGB which helped along Andropov's demise.

Consider: the symptoms of Andropov's ill health emerged during his long tenure as KGB chief. He was attended only by KGB doctors, and his illness would have been a state secret. So he soldiered on, and when he moved into the Secretariat he would still have been looked after by the KGB, still being their man at the centre of power, and his health was no business of the doctors who cared for other party and state leaders. This is not to say that the KGB did not have the very best equipment and could not get the best drugs, but it would not have sought outside advice on Andropov's special problems. The secrecy could not have helped him.

One of the most remarkable aspects of Andropov's brief reign was the tosh written about him in the West. This secret policeman was portrayed as a closet liberal who courteously courted the Soviet intelligentsia, spoke fluent English, listened to the BBC, collected American jazz records, read Western spy novels, especially those in which he appeared as a KGB chief, and played an energetic game of tennis – if he did, he would have been doing it from a wheelchair! In other words, rather a good egg, not like the Andropov who had cracked down on dissent, locked up several hundred mostly young, caring Soviet citizens, harassed the country's finest people, among them Andrei Sakharov, and conducted an espionage war against the West.

About the only thing Andropov did as leader was to launch yet another campaign against corrupt officials, dishonest policemen, layabouts and the drunk and inefficient workers. Like all such campaigns, it had a short life, but while it lasted policemen went looking for skivers in shops, cinemas and even in the public baths. Secretaries, who also happened to be housewives, were pretty annoyed when they were detained in big stores for doing their shopping in office hours – as you would do, if you were suddenly tipped off that some item or other in short supply had suddenly appeared. He couldn't stamp out corruption either, although the Soviet press was full of stories on the lines of Gogol's *Dead Souls*. Only after six decades of Communism, it was a question of 'dead factories' – factories that had never been completed, but where the management team drew salaries and claimed that their non-existent work staff were fulfilling the plan, and even deserved bonuses.

So Andropov succeeded Brezhnev, and Konstantin Chernenko, who at one time was Brezhnev's chauffeur, succeeded him. Now he *was* a disaster – taking over the Kremlin at the age of seventy-three, visibly sick and inadequate. In his last days he was roused from his sickbed to take part in brief, heavily-edited television appearances, stumbling, mumbling and nodding complacently, as another official waved and grinned at him as though he was a baby. The only person who seemed to care about him at his funeral was his wife, and the Soviet Union watched for one long minute as she kissed him, embraced him and stroked his forehead again and again before the lid was put on his coffin.

A Russian woman told me that two years after Brezhnev died, she had an inexplicable impulse to demonstrate her affection for him. She bought some carnations, took them to the block of flats where he had lived in Kutuzovsky Prospekt, and laid them on a shelf below a plaque bearing his portrait in bas-relief.

Then she realized that a man had been standing behind her and watching everything she did. She went to the curb and hailed a taxi. Instead of the cab, another official-looking car pulled up. The man approached her, stepped forward, opened the back door of the car and motioned to her to get in. He escorted her to her home, asking her questions all the time about herself.

'It became clear who he worked for,' she told me, 'and that he thought I was either a dissident or some kind of nut. Finally he asked me why I had brought those flowers and laid them on the shelf by Brezhnev's plaque.

I told him I had acted on impulse, but I thought that the former President deserved to be remembered by somebody.'

'Really?' said the man from the KGB. 'I'm surprised by all that. You seem to be an intelligent woman. Don't you know that nobody remembers our leaders after they are gone?'

16 - The Desperate, Daft and Dissident

The young Russian was shabbily-dressed and had a strange desperate look in his eyes. He walked purposefully along the embankment and as he came level with the gates of the British Embassy, nipped into the yard before the two Soviet *milimen* could stop him. '*Svoloch*' they shouted 'come back here, you little bastard'. They didn't dare go after him – there was no promotion for violating the Embassy's territorial integrity. Instead, they dashed into their sentry box to report a defection to KGB headquarters.

Inside the Embassy, the duty officer and then the senior diplomat he summoned were friendly and polite. The young man told them his name. Now he wanted political asylum and to live in Britain. They had heard it before. The diplomat, with a son at public school in England who was about the same age as the young Russian, listened sympathetically. Then he laid it on the line. 'First of all, Alexei, there was the… er… little matter of you getting an exit visa from the Soviet authorities. When you do, come and see us again. Then we can talk about getting you a British visa. And talk about your future then. Meanwhile, the best of British luck.'

They showed him the door, that was all they could do. And when he walked out into the sunshine, he saw there were more police standing at the gate. A police car and a van and men wearing black-leather jackets had also arrived. They were all looking through the gates towards the entrance of the Embassy, waiting.

Alexei knew what that meant. So he sat on the steps of the Embassy and took out a knife and slashed several times at his throat. A British doctor, Tom Austin, dashed across from his surgery and put clamps on the young man's throat to try and stop the bleeding. A *skoraia pomoshch* – an ambulance – was summoned to take him to hospital. The steps were scrubbed clean of blood. The Embassy was never told whether he lived or died. It may not have asked.

Sometimes, journalists provided the outlet for the desperate and the daft. 'Hello, hello,' says the voice urgently over the static that our telephones never managed to lose, and you wondered how the caller had got your number. The voice surges on: 'I want to meet you. We must talk. I have something important to tell you.'

So begins another furtive encounter which – BCC – were part of our routine. Several times a month the calls would come in from Soviet citizens with a tale to tell about official injustice, corruption, high-handedness. They were the victims. We apparently constituted a last hope for help. And their thinking was curious. They sought to plug into a kind of circuitous chain of communication. They wanted us to write about them. So the story was picked up by the BBC's Russian Service and played back to the USSR, where the offending official would hear about it and solve the problem. QED.

They were nervous – these people with their hard luck stories and they had cause to be. They rightly assumed they were also talking into KGB tape recorders and they may have known that they could be seized on the street by the KGB before I had arrived for the meeting.

Every encounter took place in an atmosphere of threat. For quite simply a provision in the Soviet criminal code on anti-Soviet agitation was broad enough to encompass whingeing to a British journalist about some aspect of the system. And they could finish up in a labour camp, lose their job or be summoned to the KGB headquarters for a warning as to future behaviour. Yet still they came with their stories of housing problems, rows with their factory bosses and, occasionally, their thoughts on Soviet foreign policy and the shortages of meat or sugar.

There were risks for some of us, too. Most of the callers were genuine, opening a window or two on a closed society. But we had become prudent, wary to the point of paranoia. And we would sniff the air to try and smell the difference between the honest innocent caller and those preparing to set a KGB trap, a *provokatsia*.

But, unless you were hard-boiled, cynical or a left-wing journalist – in which case you dismissed dissidents as being of no consequence – it was uncomfortable to accept that taking an interest in the problems of some of these people was a complete waste of time. You were not in Moscow to fight for Western ideals or enlist in the struggle for human rights in the USSR. You could do nothing for the people you met. Their stories were not news and they revealed little or nothing you did not already know about the country.

Typical of my encounters was one with a woman who telephoned me several times and implored me to meet her. She said she was desperate and needed my help. Finally I gave in and agreed to meet her across the road outside the Puppet Theatre. You could get there before the KGB got their act together, or so you thought, because after a while they had a man semi-permanently patrolling the area.

At three in the afternoon on a summer's day, I stand with the *babushkas* and a host of little kids and join in their delight, as a cock on the façade of the theatre crows three times, bells chime, a blue rabbit pops out from nowhere to nod, as the music plays the simple little repeating tune that drives us mad on hot nights in neighbouring 'Sad Sam'. As the crowd drifts away, a woman comes straight up to me. Aged about forty-five she is tall and wears a simple dress with a cheap printed-scarf on her head. She has no make-up on and has dark rings under her eyes.

We walk in an uneasy silence until we find an empty bench in the Red Army Park. From time to time, I turn to see if we are being followed, either because the KGB has taped the call, or because I am being set up by one of their 'ringers'. I wonder if there is a KGB photographer sitting in a car or in a room in a near-by block of flats with a long lens snapping frame after frame. A torrent of words now pours forth from the nervous, trembling, unfortunate woman's lips. It doesn't take me long to know that what she has to say is not worth a sentence in the paper. But I listen…

It is a story of a woman who lived in Zaprovozhye in the Ukraine and who has had a nervous breakdown. Her drunken husband beat her, their daughter was taken from her, and she herself was put in an asylum. As she describes the conditions there she begins to weep.

She talks about men and women sharing the same wards, and the same beds, of the fights and squalor, of poor food, and inmates being beaten and drugged. I believe it all. She produces a few pieces of yellowed, thumbed and folded paper, proof that she had been committed to a mental hospital, copies of letters she had sent to the authorities insisting she had been wrongly certified, cold brief replies from disinterested officials. She wants me to write a story about her case which would appear in the West so as to make the Soviet government admit it had made a mistake. A touching faith in the power of the British press. That's all, she says, that's all. It is an apology that she wants, now that she is out of the hospital and has her child back.

She tells me her story several times as we sit in the sun in the Red Army Park. I am thinking about the stories I should be writing for the newspaper that day. She repeats the names of those guilty of having her wrongly certified, and when, and where she has been to get justice. There is nothing particularly anti-Soviet about what she is saying.

She is weeping as I stand up to leave. I've got work to do. 'You will write about me,' she says. 'Promise me you will write about me. I am relying on you.' And then, finally, 'I will kill myself unless I get justice.'

Several times she telephoned me over the next fortnight to ask me if the article about her case had appeared in the newspaper. I told her the truth: it had not. I never said whether I had written her story.

Did she get what she wanted, I wonder...?

I believed every word of that woman's story and others I heard from doctors, engineers, scientists and musicians, who had lost their jobs after applying to emigrate or had fallen foul of the authorites for other reasons and were now being harassed. But they were commonplace and there was no point in writing them. And so you would try and avoid such encounters and give such callers the brush off.

Occasionally you would get interested. One day a caller asked me to meet him in the Red Army Park. There was a time when I jogged in this nearest park to 'Sad Sam' and I agreed to meet him. He is standing near our meeting place, a statue of some marshal or another. He greets me. He looks around, nervously: 'I know the truth about Wallenberg,' he says.

'Really' I say. 'You do?'

'Yes,' he says. 'And I've got proof.'

I am interested. As it happens I have felt for many years that the Wallenberg mystery was no such thing. Raoul Wallenberg was a Swedish diplomat who disappeared into Soviet custody during World War II, after arranging safe passage out of Nazi-occupied Budapest for thousands of Hungarian Jews. He was interrogated in the Lubyanka for thirty months and as a result, died there in July 1947 of a heart attack. It took a long time for the Russians to admit to another dreadful crime, but in the end they did, blaming it of course on Beria, Stalin and the rest.

The Soviet version never satisfied some people in the West, who had formed lobbies to harass the Kremlin on the issue and had a financial and other interest in keeping alive the 'mystery' of the Swede's death. From time to time, reports surfaced from people who claimed they had seen him in Soviet prisons and labour camps. It was absurd – nobody, but nobody, could spend thirty or more years in such places.

The man tells me how he worked for the Ministry of Internal Affairs, the Soviet police, and looked after lunatic asylums. In one of them he met a man who spoke Swedish, who, according to his records, was aged seventy, and said he was Raoul Wallenburg. 'It was him, and I have the proof,' he says. 'I have his records. Complete with his fingerprints. It is all there.'

'Let's have a look at them,' I say.

He looks shifty. 'Just now I don't have them with me. But we could meet again. Tomorrow?'

I don't like it, but I agree. I am recalling a case a few years earlier when an American journalist had met a Russian in the street who said he was a scientist. After talking to the man and accepting an envelope about Soviet research into parapsychology, the science of extra-sensory perception, the journalist was suddenly arrested by the KGB.

I decide to take a chance – could it just possibly be true that he has Wallenberg's records? Could I be wrong about Wallenberg having died when the Russians said he had, insisting that the stuff about Wallenberg having been seen here and there in Siberia in the 1960s and 1970s was rubbish?

Jogging in the park the next day, I see him under a tree. He is apparently carrying something wrapped in a copy of *Pravda*. I do not take it from him but we walk together without speaking to a bench that I select, so that I can have a good look around... see if any nasties are gathering.

Suddenly, he thrusts the package at me, stands up and walks quickly away without even saying *do svidania* – goodbye. I am holding the package and thinking I don't like this at all and I put it on the bench beside me. I am fairly confident that I can spot a professional stake-out – you look for unmarked cars with several men in them, those sitting in the back holding cameras, and for other young men meticulously dressed and with a disgustingly-clean appearance. But I am not being set up with the Wallenberg story the bait. And curiosity gets the better of me. I pick up the package and unfold *Pravda*.

That is all there is. There are no hospital records, no fingerprints, no message. Just bloody *Pravda*. And not even that day's copy. I assume my friends in the KGB have me on film...

Your real, actual dissidents were different. No cloak-and-dagger stuff for them. No guarded telephone calls or furtive encounters. They didn't give a tinker's cuss about the KGB, bugged telephones, and being followed. You met them in their flats or you didn't need to bother. You took what they gave you openly, and if you used it, that was nice. If you chucked away their petitions and appeals and statements and didn't use a word of the interviews they gave you, it didn't matter.

Many of them paid the penalty for this openness. ACC, the figures were revealed. Between 1966 and 1986, 2,468 people were convicted under the two main political articles in the Criminal Code covering anti-Soviet activities and agitation. Most of these people finished up in labour camps. Many more were messed about by the KGB at work and in their homes. But virtually all of them went on struggling for the cause of human rights in the USSR. Successfully, as it happened.

I can contribute a sentence or two to the first chapter in the history of open political dissent in post-Khrushchev, or for that matter in post-Stalin Russia, which may be said to have begun in October 1967. For some two years before, the ineluctable pattern of arrest-protest-arrest had emerged. One day, I had a call from a remarkable English woman, Ivy Low, the wife of Stalin's foreign minister and the greatest diplomat of the Soviet era, Maxim Litvinov. She had stayed on in Moscow after his death in 1951, living by her writing. (Once, after visiting her she telephoned to tell me that she had watched me driving away from her flat and saw men shadowing me from behind trees. They jumped into two cars and proceeded to follow me out of

190

the yard.) Now she said her grandson, Pavel Litvinov, wanted to talk to me.

We met in his flat and it quickly emerged he was determined to carry on the family's tradition of courage. A tall, rather Irish-looking young man with a warm smile and a direct manner, he wanted to make a statement about the trial of another young dissident, Vladimir Bukovsky, who had been sentenced to three years in a labour camp. Bukovsky was the first 'troublemaker' to cross my horizon when, in the early 1960s, he began his campaign against the abuse of legal and human rights. I wrote a small piece about him being arrested by the KGB and he went on to spend years in prisons, labour camps and mental hospitals, until coming to Britain in an unprecedented exchange for the imprisoned Chilean communist, Luis Corvalan.

Litvinov's statement upped the ante in the dissident stakes. It was typed and he signed it. Now he was distributing it to foreign newspapers, and to Soviet ones, although he knew they would not publish any of it. I was the first Western journalist to have it.

'Are you sure you know what you are doing?' I said to him. 'I can take this statement and knock out a story for my paper. It will be used, I assure you. But you are sticking your neck out here a long way. From now on you will be clearly identified as a trouble-maker, and doubly so because of your family name. The KGB are not going to like this. You are changing the way the game is played and they will look upon it as a brazen provocation. So why don't I just write about a protest by some dissidents over the trial, and leave your name out of it?'

'No,' he said. 'I have thought about it a lot. This is my statement. I want my name on it. I will take the consequences.'

This story had labour-camp written all over it. In fact, the KGB let a few months pass before it dealt with Pavel Litvinov, apart from telling him not to be foolish and expressing the hope he would see the error of his ways. Which, ironically perhaps, was exactly what I was saying, only from a another standpoint. Instead, he took part in a small demonstration on Red Square against the invasion of Czechoslovakia. For that he got exiled to a squalid, distant and bitterly-cold Siberian village. When he returned to Moscow a few years later, he continued his human-rights campaigning and had several run-ins with the secret police.

191

Finally, while on his way to the traditional human rights vigil in Pushkin Square, the KGB detained him and made him an offer it was difficult for him to refuse. To go West into oblivion or be slowly destroyed in the USSR. He choose freedom and the dissident movement in Russia lost him for good. Except – ACC – he returned to his homeland to live and work...

But the most impressive of all the dissidents I knew during that extraordinary decade was Andrei Amalrik, a frail near-sighted young-looking intellectual, who was totally opposed to the Soviet system, another who proved his integrity by spending years in prison, labour camps and internal exile.

He was a different – very much his own man, shunning public demonstrations of opposition and rarely signing collective protests. It took me some time to appreciate his special courage. At first I thought he was a little mad, and there were persistent rumours that he was working for the KGB as a provocateur. Of course, he did no such thing. But he was strongly critical of many Western journalists working in Moscow because – and he was right – we had no guts. Some of us eschewed dissidence and dissidents because we didn't want any trouble with the authorities and the KGB. Better not get mixed up with that lot if you wanted to lead a reasonably quiet life and bank your salary in Switzerland. A colleague took a much more lofty view of why he gave dissidents a wide berth – he decided that the West had an exaggerated view of their importance within the Soviet system and it was wrong to concentrate on their plight at the expense of other aspects of Soviet life, for example rewriting *Pravda* to make it more readable. I discussed it with him and he chided me: 'Your trouble, John Miller, is that you are anti-Soviet.' Oh dear!

Amalrik, and his lovely artist wife Gusel, lived in a large communal flat off the Arbat, now a pedestrian walk-way and souvenir mecca for tourists, but in those days – a busy street. True, many millions of new units of housing were built after Stalin's death, but probably a quarter of the population was living in communal flats right up to recent times, and millions still are, even as Russia goes capitalist. This meant that as many as twenty people were living on a floor of a building, with each family having a single room for sleeping, working and eating and

192

everyone sharing the single kitchen, albeit with perhaps two or three stoves, a toilet and the one bathroom.

A woman I knew once told me a story about how she had lived all her life – she was forty-three – in the same communal flat in Moscow. Her husband was a professor and an expert in the field of venereal diseases. One day he was asked to treat a senior Moscow Communist Party official, who had a particularly severe dose of the clap. During one of his visits, the professor complained bitterly about his living conditions. 'Oh,' said the official, 'that's not a problem. I know you will not want to charge me for my treatment, and you'll keep your trap shut, too, so I will see you are all right. Leave it with me.'

Within weeks, the woman and her husband moved out of their dreary, smelly and overcrowded home into a new and well-situated flat. 'Yes,' she said, 'I know that we had become as corrupt as these bastards who control our lives, but I don't care. I lived all my life in that communal flat. Arguing over the electricity bill, listening to the snores of drunken sons-of-bitches down the corridor, and the fights between husbands and wives. Have you had to share a toilet with several families for more than forty years? To queue almost every day of your life for a crap or for a bath or to use a gas stove? I had had enough. I would have given that official my body to get out of the place – but I am sure that, with what he has got wrong with him, he will behave himself for some time to come.'

Amalrik's was a typical communal flat. There was a dingy, dimly lit entrance hall. A long corridor led past a steamy kitchen smelling of cabbage, and a bathroom with laundry hung up to dry. Packing cases and suitcases were piled outside doors of different kinds and colours. At the end of the corridor was the Amalrik flat: just the one room dominated by a grand piano – which neither Andrei or Gusel could play. There were many books, a grandfather clock and a few plants. And everywhere, paintings – on the walls and propped up against the furniture. Half-seriously, Amalrik told me he sometimes blocked up the doors with the paintings so as to make it harder for the KGB to listen with their directional microphones. There was a small bed, but no dining table – there was no room for it.

During the trial of Aleksander Ginzburg and others on charges of anti-Soviet activity, the Western press was excluded, but Andrei and members of the family were allowed into the court. The evidence would be memorized and Andrei would telephone either myself, or Bob Evans, and invite us to come round to his flat and hear it from him.

We would drive to the Arbat, park at the end of his road and walk to the flat. It worked well for a week, but the KGB had clearly been thinking about the leak and where it was coming from.

One afternoon, we parked the car and as we got out we were greeted by a tall, young, blond-haired man who worked in the Press Department of the Soviet Foreign Ministry, Alexander Gresko.

'Hello,' says he in a friendly way. 'Fancy bumping into you two in the Arbat.'

'Fancy,' we say, 'and what a coincidence that you should be here, too?'

'Yes, isn't it?' he says, 'I would have thought you were too busy to get out and about in Moscow on such an afternoon. There must be some interesting stories to do.'

'There are, Mr Gresko,' we say, 'there always are in the USSR.'

'Yes, I know,' he says and the smile is still on his lips. 'But because I like you two gentlemen, and I know you are serious journalists, I would like to offer you some advice.'

'And what is that, Mr Gresko?' we ask.

He looks up and down the road, and bends forward so that passers-by cannot hear. 'My advice to you,' he says in his very good English, 'is to find less interesting, less exciting, less... dangerous... stories.'

Bob and I look innocent. I ask: 'Have you come from work specially to proffer this advice to British journalists you just happen to meet in the middle of the Arbat?'

He waves in the air the string bag he is carrying and which contains a bottle of milk. 'Oh no,' he says, 'I have just popped out to do some shopping.' And off he went.

As I said to Bob Evans at the time, it was nice of Alexander Alekseevich to warn us, but we didn't take much notice of it; nothing happened to us or to Amalrik just then, although Ginzburg got eight years in a labour camp and three in internal exile. A few months later,

I bumped into Gresko and he told me he was taking a job as the Public Relations Officer for the Ministry of Internal Affairs, effectively the ordinary Police.

For all I know, he may have landed such a job, which would have been unique. However, his name cropped up in 1971 when he was among 105 soviet agents expelled from Britain at a blow. Among his activities was trying to bribe science writers to give him secret, technical-information. But perhaps looking after the media was really his forte, because at one point in his career he was the 'spokesman' for the sensational Soviet gymnast, Olga Korbut, thereby ensuring she said all the right Soviet things. And when the Soviet Union hosted the 1980 Olympic Games there was Alexander Alekseevitch secretary-general of the preparatory committee. BCC, it was very hard to keep a good KGB man down.

They harassed Amalrik, but didn't arrest him until two books he had written appeared in the West, one of them being: *Will the Soviet Union Survive Until 1984?* In this, he predicted a devastating war between the Soviet Union and China. He got that wrong. But what he nearly got right, if a little prematurely, was when he said that there would be a withdrawal of Soviet troops from Europe because of this Sino-Soviet hostility, which would effectively destroy the Soviet bloc and lead to the break-up of the Soviet system and empire. He saw that coming a lot earlier than most of us.

They didn't like his '*1984*' and he got three years for writing it, which, just two days before his release, they changed to five because, they said, they had found other charges. They then said it would be a good thing for him to leave the country, otherwise he would be eternally harassed. He went, only to die within five years in a car crash in Spain.

The long arm of the KGB? A car crash engineered by specialists? I think not. By all accounts it was a rotten piece of driving. But I could be wrong...

17 - Moscow Nights, and Days

At first, Moscow struck me as a graceless, ugly city, the metropolis of the common man, part factory-hooter, part clarion-call. By no means was it a dream, but neither was it a nightmare. It had more the quality of a hangover, and I had experienced a few of those living and working in Russia's most typical, commanding city.

Some of the sights of Moscow stopped me in my tracks: war-wounded beggars without legs propelling themselves along street gutters – in summertime on little wooden trollies, in the winter on tiny sleds; snow-covered Red Square at night; overflowing spitoons lining the streets; two drunken cripples setting about each other with their crutches; corpses of two old ladies, faces like grey stubs of burnt-out candles, encouched in flowers in coffins in a church; kittens and puppies at the pet market, suddenly produced from the secret warmth of overcoat pockets and offered for sale with tattered, forged pedigrees; Red Army soldiers with rifles and fixed bayonets guarding Moscow bridges; a gigantic Russian epic at the Bolshoi with knights, serfs, horses – yes, real horses, a frenzy of bronze helmets and chainmail, banners, flames, flashing beacons and a huge open-throated chorus; the metro, a proletarian Disneyland, with vast stations of marble, mosaics and chandeliers; queues at ice-cream kiosks in weather minus twenty-five degrees Celsius; Moscow at dawn from the Lenin Hills, as the first rays of the sun strike the golden domes of the Kremlin…

Some of those things will never been seen again or experienced – for example, the amputees were rounded up in the late 1960s and dumped in cities in Central Asia, out of the sight of foreign visitors. The Plan did not call for the production of artificial limbs. Over the years, Moscow became less of a mystery to me, less suffocating, less fearful. The sense of alienation, as though you belonged to some unrelated visiting species, never totally went away, but it significantly diminished.

For Moscow was home. It was where we hung our hats. We began to appreciate its fusty, musty dated flavour. We became as used to the gothic bombast of Stalin's seven skyscrapers as we did to the Khrushchev boxes, row after row after row of stark, low, utilitarian blocks, like great shuttered batteries on some nightmarish chicken farm, punctuated every now and again with a wide window of a neighbourhood food shop, which always had empty shelves.

And the people of Moscow – Muscovites hardly fits the bill as two million out-of-towners pour into the city every day with string bags to buy anything that's going, and gawp – came less and less to seem to be unattractive, mindless puppets. Because I soon grasped just how much Moscow was the capital of an empire extending far to the east. Hence the Uzbeks, the Mongols, the Azeris, the Georgians, with their slant-eyes and high-cheeks, lighter shades of brown, and strange hairy men wearing Astrakhan hats and clutching knobbly sticks. They had to be as individualistic as most of us, and if I got to know them they were often much more fun.

Living in 'Sad Sam' had a great deal to do with my thinking about Moscow and the Russians although, paradoxically, only a few Russians worked there. None lived in this somewhat down-at-heel block of flats on Sadovo Samotechnaya, a section of the city's ring road, because it was a foreigners' ghetto, a building set aside for journalists, diplomats, businessmen and the like.

It wasn't our fault that we lived neither wholly within Soviet society nor completely outside it. We were put there by officials who wanted us isolated, nervous about our contaminating effect. They were also anxious to impress us that conditions in 'Sad Sam' were much better than those experienced by most Soviet citizens.

This beige, nine-storey block was put up by German prisoners after the Second World War, and it showed. It was a solid, stolid Teutonic building – unlike other blocks built for foreigners in the sixties, which prompted the gibe that one may have seen slums before, but never slums being *built* – and the flats were comfortable and warm with high ceilings and big windows. I lived in half a dozen different flats in 'Sad Sam' and had I bought them, I would now be a wealthy man. Many of them became offices for major Western news organizations with roomsful of computers, word processors, televisions and teleprinters before, inevitably, real Russians were living there. A kitchen in which I had breakfast for many years and from which I watched traffic trail as if for ever up and down the ring road is now a reception area for Reuter's business clients.

198

'Sad Sam' had a grotty yard and it sometimes looked like a building site after a downpour; but our children loved it. So did the Russian workers who were responsible for the plumbing, the heating, ensuring the rickety lifts were running and generally keeping the block tidy. They did small jobs for you – a drunken Russian electrician, at the top of a ladder fixing the lights, was like a scene from an early Hollywood comedy. Payment was only in whisky, vodka or brandy and the workers disappeared to the cellar for the rest of the day.

There was a time when 'Sad Sam' was the greatest concentration of gossip, rumour, intrigue and infidelity behind the Iron Curtain. Some of the best stories of the Brezhnev era were thought up over a bowl of borsch and had become hard news by the time the brandy was served. There was no lasting bad feeling if you screwed one of your colleagues by turning a rumour into a good story. And the wives of the indefatigable, endlessly toiling Reuters correspondents, always seemed to be having it off with laid-back young men from Agence France-Presse.

Some great party-givers lived in the 'Sad Sam' honeycomb which had a swinging, all-night summer soirée in the yard with British Airways flying in the bangers, and eggs and bacon being served at dawn. Russian kids would sit on the wall surrounding the yard looking down in disbelief at the behaviour of these strange, tipsy foreigners dancing to a jazz band. Now and again, they begged for chewing-gum – which was precisely what I did as a boy when spotting an American soldier during World War II.

The Kremlin could have declared war on the West and not a journalist or diplomat of worth in the city would have known or cared because they would have all been at 'Sad Sam' enjoying themselves.

A lot of drinking was done to fight off attacks of the so-called 'Moscow Blues' when you woke up in the morning feeling that you couldn't face reading another page of *Pravda* or a TASS item, or make another totally fruitless telephone call to an official. The Blues could strike quite suddenly and at any time – a new correspondent for the *Daily Express* arrived from London on a plane and succumbed that very night at a reception in his honour. He was shipped back home the next day.

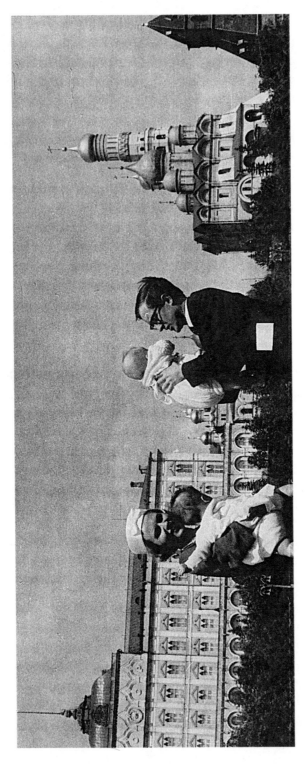

13. The Miller twins were christened in the British Embassy and had their first view of the Kremlin.

14. The Miller's first child, Dodik, went to the nearby school No. 186. He is third from right in the front row.

15. Tim Miller ice-fishing at Zavidovo, near Moscow.
The Russian fisherman has used a huge hand drill to force the
hole in the iced Shosha River.

16. The three Miller children, Dodik, Jane and Timothy, in the front row are at the big New Year party for children in the Kremlin.

I was attacked but once and took to my bed like Oblomov, the main character of Ivan Goncharov's novel of that name, overwhelmed by apathy and inertia. Oblomov has become a symbol of the agreeable laziness which is held to be a typically Russian characteristic, but the 'Moscow Blues' couldn't last long if you worked for a Fleet Street newspaper. The *Telegraph* was told I had flu, and after two days of refusing to get out of bed, I was back at work.

Other things conspired to cause Moscow Blues and one of them was being monitored, real or imaginary, by the KGB. A couple I knew saw their psychiatrist before coming to Moscow and the wife raised the problem of being overheard making love. The psychiatrist said: 'All I can suggest is that you do it a little less nosily.'

The presence of policemen – known as *milimen* – on guard, working rotating shifts, twenty-four hours a day at the one entrance to the courtyard did not help. They were there ostensibly to protect us and our property from unwarranted intrusions. But from their cramped sentry box they monitored our movements and screened casual contacts with Russians.

If you wanted a Russian to come to your flat, you had to meet him out on the street and escort him past the *miliman* who would usually let him pass, but not without giving him a hard stare and reporting the visit to the KGB on the telephone.

Milimen loved to talk with you and I enjoyed chatting to them. I suspect we embodied the forbidden and forbidding world outside and seemed fascinating. The only time they came into the building was to use the lavatory in the office of the Russian 'Kommendant', who dealt with our requests and our complaints. But once there was a burglary and the *miliman* left his box and came the flat to investigate the crime and prepare a report for his bosses, the KGB, who needed to know about these sort of incidents.

The thief appeared to have been another foreigner and had stooped to a bit of minor vandalism by scrawling a message in chalk on the outside door. The *miliman* insisted on knowing what it said and asked the wife of a British correspondent to write down exactly what was on the door in his report book.

At first she demurred, but he insisted. So she did what she was told and wrote: 'FUCK OFF, YOU BASTARDS'. It must have generated some amusement when it was translated into Russian at the KGB headquarters.

But we lived safe and sheltered existences in 'Sad Sam' – a Russian knew that stealing from a comrade was one thing, stealing from a foreigner was something else. He would get a longer sentence for a crime against a foreigner, for, apparently, bringing shame on the Soviet Union's image, whatever that meant.

I walked a lot in Moscow and was never mugged or robbed or threatened. A favourite stroll was out through the tunnel, past the *miliman* and into Yermolova Street, named after a tragic actress famous for her Ophelia and Lady Macbeth. If you turned right you were on the broad, ten-lane ring-road with its ceaseless roar of heavy traffic, a kind of urban M 25. Far into the night, the ring road was busy, used by the Soviet Air Force to move top-secret aircraft just off the assembly line. At three in the morning, police cars raced up and down with loud hailers telling drivers to pull into the side of the road. There was the growl of heavy vehicles, then flashing lights as lorries came into view, on each of their trailers a jet-fighter covered in tarpaulin. NATO military attachés living in 'Sad Sam' would be at their windows calculating, guessing which fighters they were seeing trundling past. But was this a touch of the Potemkin Village coming to 'Sad Sam'? Were these two or three Floggers/Fulcrums/Foxhounds or Flankers being trailed round and round the Ring Road to inflate the West's estimates of Soviet military air force production?

If you turned left and walked away from the hurly-burly of the ring-road there were small squares and gardens, quiet backwaters where *babushkas* in headscarves and aprons sat gabbing in the sun and kept an eye on their grandchildren playing in sand-pits. Here and there were crooked, slatternly houses with carved shutters and friezes, what were once elegant mansions. I watched them emptied – the occupants moved to blocks being thrown up miles from the centre of the city – slowly becoming more and more dilapidated, as roofs collapsed and walls bulged and cracked.

There was no money to repair these buildings of character, if not of comfort, and their end was symbolic perhaps of the decay and collapse of the Soviet system.

Taxi-drivers knew the area as the foreigners' ghetto; but it was better known to young Russians because Vladimir Vysotsky had lived in a block of flats on Yemolova. Vystosky was a jaunty film star, actor and balladier in the Bob Dylan tradition, who became a cult figure. He became the voice of the post-war generation with songs ridiculing the cruelties and banalities of the system. He died of drink at the age of forty-two during the Moscow Olympic Games, and they still flock to his grave or leave flowers on the door-step of his home.

There was no plaque on the wall for Vysotsky, but further up the road and round the corner, there was one for Krupskaya, Lenin's wife. She had lived in a single-storey building which had fallen on bad times, like so many others, with peeling walls on which kids were writing rude words and getting away with it because Communism was on its way out. Next door was a factory making clothes which had its own small 'palace of culture' where political lectures were given and films shown. I was astonished one day to see that a film starring Norman Wisdom, the funny man, was being shown. Called *The Round Peg*, it was how Norman, an army private, made his own officers and the Nazis look ridiculous during World War II. The cinema was packed and the Russians screamed with laughter throughout much of the film – which, of course, couldn't have been made in the Soviet Union: Red Army officers were not figures of fun and there was nothing funny about the German army and its behaviour.

My walk took me past a bakery where I learned from the *babuskhas* how to select the freshest black bread – by squeezing it with a metal spatula provided by the shop. For political, i.e. ideological reasons, there had to be cheap bread for the workers and the state heavily subsidized prices. Despite huge harvests, precious hard currency was spent on importing grain so bread was ridiculously cheap. A price increase in the 1980s was the first for fifty years. In the end, the government acknowledged that bread was so cheap that boys were using loaves as footballs and peasants were feeding their pigs with it.

Behind the bread shop and a scruffy milk-factory was the area's *detskii sad* – a small, two-storey kindergarten which the toddlers attended. Here they enjoyed friendly, if enforced, conformism. The teachers tried to persuade my son to stop writing left-handed so that he could write the same as every Soviet child, but desisted when we discussed it with them. Essentially, my children had the same political indoctrination as little Russians, learning songs and poems about Lenin and the *rodina* or 'motherland', which were invariably recited for visitors, and reading books with yucky and arguable phrases, such as, 'The first country of socialism in the world became the first country of children's happiness in the world'.

Long-gone were the days when small children were told to emulate a horrid little creep and national hero by name Pavlik Morozov, a twelve-year-old Young Pioneer who shopped his own father for hoarding grain from the police. But the 'socialist family' principle extolling the supremacy of the collective over the individual was put into practice whenever and wherever possible. And Lenin was presented to my children as the most perfect human being who ever lived – he never forgot to clean his teeth at night – and was the best friend of children everywhere.

From the start, I made it clear to my children that Lenin was not 'Grandpa' or 'Uncle Lenin', and although they have waved red flags, collected red stars and all sorts of Lenin badges, uttered the occasional paean to the Revolution and the Motherland and may have done a Morozov and denounced me to the *detskii sad's* KGB representative as a British spy, the kindergarten propaganda had no lasting effect on them.

I doubt if Lenin and his cause is buried somewhere in their subconscious. Come to that, given the sudden and total collapse of Communism, all that indoctrination doesn't appear to have done much for countless millions of Soviet children, either. ACC, they have found no trouble at all adapting to the new world of McDonalds, Reeboks, chewing-gum, commercials and rubbishy American films. Those badges of Lenin as a cherubic child might be worth a bob or two one day.

You passed the *detski sad* on your walk to the central market, the biggest in Moscow, a place of plenty in a land of chronic shortages. State shops may have been empty, but the market's long concrete counters displayed every conceivable fruit and vegetable in the summer.

Russian collective farmers brought their carrots, cabbage, beetroot and other vegetables to Moscow by train or lorry. Aircraft brought the melons, cherries, walnuts, apples, as well as the roses, tulips and carnations grown by Georgians and Azerbaijanis. I often visited this market just to look, and one day I saw brussel-sprouts on a stalk being sold for next to nothing. I bought all the stalks the weather-beaten old collective farm woman was selling, proudly carried off all I could, and said I would return for the rest.

Seven times I was stopped by women all asking the same question. 'What's that vegetable, young man?'

'*Bruselskaya kapusta* (literally, 'brussel cabbage'),' I told them. – 'So what are you going to do with it?'

'Eat it, of course.'

By now they had twigged I was a foreigner. They looked at me closely, studied my clothes. 'But in our country we feed *bruselskaya kapusta* to pigs,' they said.

'You shouldn't,' I advised, 'It is delicious. And this is how you cook it. Remove the little *kapustas* from the stalk. Put them in boiling water and boil for five to ten minutes. Don't overcook them. Remove, drain, add a knob of butter. Enjoy them with your Sunday roast…' And that was where I lost them.

Only I never saw brussel sprouts again in the Central Market, or elsewhere.

Not far from the market was a shop selling liquor whose opening hours depended on the prevailing wind – if there was an anti-alcohol campaign taking place it would be open for only a few hours of the day and instead of selling vodka or Armenian cognac offered customers beer or wine or a foul, probably lethal, fortified wine that Andrei Sakharov, the human rights campaigner, perceptively suspected was being deliberately foisted on Russians by the Government to keep them docile.

Queues formed long before the shop opened – usually at eleven in the morning and commonly known as the 'hour of the wolf'. This phrase was related to the façade of the Puppet Theatre on the Ring Road which provided a mechanical display of puppets on the hour. And at 11 am precisely, a grey fierce-looking wolf appeared. By that time, and if vodka was to be sold, dozens of poorly-dressed, haggard-looking men stood in line. These queues were desperate and so unruly that police had to maintain order, stopping customers pushing in or fighting. There were always women in the queue, suffering insults and

17.   Miller coming home from the nearby Central Market with a
bag of potatoes.

humiliation – all they wanted was a bottle of champagne or wine to celebrate a birthday or a wedding.

The men, some of them office workers, were desperate for a pint of hard stuff – and just before the collapse of Communism that was exactly what they were allowed, vodka was rationed and expensive. There is an old 'three on a bottle' tradition – one man stood around holding up two or three fingers signifying he was prepared to share a half or a third of the bottle. The foil top was ripped off and the vodka drunk there and then, sometimes with a small piece of black bread or a slice of cucumber.

The stumbling drunks that were a common sight outside this liquor shop did not drink wine, that was for cissies. As it happened, the capital's biggest wine-bottling plant was only a block away. Having passed it on one of my walks, I popped into the yard from time to time to see what was going on. The wine was brought hundreds of miles from Georgia to Moscow, slushing around in the sort of tanks petrol was carried in, and poured into huge filthy vats. Rats scurried about in the bottling plant, totally ignored by the people working there.

I swear that on more than one occasion I heard the sort of plopping noises you might get from rats falling into vats; from that day to this, I have never drunk Georgian wine bottled in Moscow.

From 'Sad Sam' you could walk to the Bolshoi and in twenty minutes be in another world. In the sixties, the Bolshoi Ballet still enjoyed the world-wide excellence it had established in the mid-nineteenth century. But in the seventies its glory began to fade. A magnificent company, one of the most important jewels in the Soviet cultural crown, it suffered – like the Soviet Union – from stagnation and stifling conservatism.

Yet, going to the ballet at the Bolshoi Theatre was one of the great experiences of living in Moscow. It was ludicrously cheap – and still is – although once it was realized that there was hard currency to be made from selling tickets to foreigners, the experience became increasingly rare for ordinary Russians. They would stand outside the theatre before a performance shouting: 'Anyone got a spare ticket?'

ACC, touts took over. Now they queue at the box office buying as many tickets as they can get their hands on cheaply for roubles, then selling them on the pavement to tourists for dollars. The laws of supply and demand are at work in the new Russia.

There was a time when an evening at the Bolshoi was obligatory for visiting big-wigs. They took pot luck on what they saw and heard – the programme was out of their hands – but both the ballet and the opera companies were obsessed with the classics and indifferent to the experimental. On these occasions the theatre, which holds over 2,000 people, would be packed with KGB officials and their families, and others in the Communist Party and government bureaucracy. This was how the men in the Kremlin could be sure of an absolutely reliable audience. If they themselves went at all, they sat in the grand state box, looking bored and glazed-eyed.

On such evenings there was no guarantee of the Bolshoi putting on a full-blooded performance. Stars had danced the piece dozens of times before and couldn't be bothered to turn it on for secret policemen and party hacks. Maya Plisetskaya, an indomitable and exciting prima ballerina with a remarkable vocabulary of swear-words, said she hated performing for the party *svolochi* (*bastards*)and admitted she was sometimes physically sick before and after dancing. Plisetskaya lived in style and commanded respect and affection, but she regretted not having had the guts to defect along with so many other dancers. That would have been a story on a par with the defection of Rudolf Nureyev.

A Russian friend once asked me at the Bolshoi if I knew what a quartet was. 'A Soviet symphony orchestra returning home after playing concerts in the West,' was the right answer.

The Bolshoi is a magical place. A neo-classical building, inside all is red plush and gilt, intricate plasterwork and chandeliers. Tier after tier curve around the auditorium, and they have been filled to overflowing since the theatre was opened to the man-in-the-street in 1917. It is the lush melancholy of Tchaikovsky's music and the fairytale world of ballets like *Sleeping Beauty* and *Swan Lake* that grab Russian ballet fans, and the ornate productions that blend the grandeur of royalty's pageantry with make-believe and melodrama, that pack them in for the interminable operas.

Many foreign visitors however go the Bolshoi not because they like ballet, but because it is on the itinerary; it is like visiting the Kremlin or Lenin Hills. They can sit down, they do not have

211

to listen to Russian, and in the interval they can rub shoulders with real Russians in the buffet, have a glass of champagne and a caviar sandwich or stroll in a foyer thick with cigarette smoke.

I became a scourge of a certain kind of Western tourist – the man or woman who took their camera to the Bolshoi, thought he or she was still on Red Square, and decided that a photograph of a stage full of ballerinas whirling in endless pirouettes would be nice to show the folk back home. I came to dislike these people, who almost certainly knew nothing about ballet or opera, otherwise they would have known how to behave, and who flatly ignored notices in Russian, English and French asking patrons not to take photographs.

Once, at a gala performance to mark the anniversary of the Revolution, I went over the top in audacity and ruthlessness. *Sleeping Beauty* was the ballet and when the wicked fairy appeared a group of Belgium women near me began snapping away, flashlights popping, cameras clicking. I leaned over, waved a finger reprovingly and hissed: 'You cannot take photograph. No photographs. It is not allowed. No. *Nein. Non. Nelzia.*' It worked. They stopped.

The last act. The wonderful wedding ball. Schmaltzy music, pulling at the heartstrings. A young West German disgraced himself and went to work with his camera with such enthusiasm he was half out of his seat. Click, flash, whirl, click, flash, whirl.

It was too much. I got up from my seat in the aisle and went out into the foyer. I spotted a short, square, tough-looking woman, a Bolshoi usherette. I told her the problem. She understood straightaway that a dreadful crime was being committed in her theatre, and what had to be done. As the music swelled she stormed into the auditorium, and strode down the aisle. The enormous audience was gripping its seats or craning from the high, gilded balconies above the chandeliers. The orchestra was in a quivering fortissimo and with a flash of the hand the conductor wiped the sweat glistening on his bald head.

My Bolshoi friend said something to the young man and when he pretended not to understand, she reached across another terrified foreigner and jerked him from his seat. He was marched up the aisle and out into the street.

The curtain fell. Bunches of carnations wrapped in cellophane rained down from the gods. Shouts of 'Bravo' and the distinctive

Soviet rhythmic clapping went on and on. With a small bow I acknowledged the applause – I had had a cultural vandal thrown out of the Bolshoi Theatre. A rare, proud achievement.

18 - Houses of Ill-repute

There was only one joke about the Lubyanka: 'Why has this evil heart of the apparatus of terror the finest view in Moscow?' 'Because from its windows you can see straight to Siberia.'

Other jokes may have been made up by the countless tens of thousands of residents in the building over the years but neither they, nor those that managed to find anything funny or witty to say about the place, appear to have survived.

The Lubyanka long exerted a fascination for me, albeit a macabre one, because I do really believe that buildings may even have more interesting stories to tell than people. If I could think of nothing else to do in Moscow, I would take myself off to Dzerzhinsky Square and walk around the Lubyanka, working out how it could centre in a novel. It would be about a British spy, who became the first man in history to withstand a devilish interrogation at the hands of the KGB before breaking out. After all, George Blake climbed over the wall at Wormwood Scrubs and got clean away to safety if not comfort in Russia.

In his magnificent *Gulag Archipelago*, Solzhenitsyn writes about that very thing, escaping from the Lubyanka. He suggests it should not have been difficult. Through endless interrogations, a prisoner could get to know his way around the long corridors which were well signposted – it had to be because it was a ministry as well as a prison. So many people were coming and going in the Lubyanka that the guards could not know everyone by sight. As for a pass to get in and out, Solzhenitsyn says it would have been possible to have attacked your interrogator with, for example, the marble paperweight on his desk, donned his uniform, stolen his pass and you were on your way to freedom...

He didn't try it himself. Nor did any of the dozen or so Britons who spent time in the Lubyanka between 1918 – the first was diplomat, Robert Bruce Lockhart – and 1965, when the London lecturer, Gerald Brooke was briefly held there. Nor, as far as I know, did anybody else – Russians and citizens of a hundred countries who were taken for interrogation, and often death, to the headquarters of the secret police in all its various forms, from Cheka through the NKVD to the KGB.

So what was it about the Lubyanka that has fascinated me over the years? To begin with, of course, it was actually difficult to get into the building – I managed to do so on one occasion and that was when Communism was collapsing, it had become KGB offices, and nothing more, and I was there as a visitor, and asking the questions.

It always intrigued me that this notorious prison and interrogation centre shared a grand square with the country's great toy emporium, a dingy, cavernous place called 'Detskii mir', where parental indulgence had become a national cult. We, being British, were an exception, managing to lose our son Tim, aged two, in the place. Shopping there with the twins, Brenda temporarily mislaid him as she coped with the system – queuing to buy something, queuing at the cash desk to pay, queuing again to get the purchase. It was a nasty moment, but he had been taken to an office where he was bawling his head off, surrounded by a clutch of admiring, clucking women store-assistants.

In effect these two buildings were monuments to deeply-rooted instincts in Russian culture. Or, outward and visible symbols of the Russians' split personality, one segment grim, unbending and cruel, the other kind, possessed of a passionate love for children, for whom nothing is too good.

The Lubyanka has been described in hundreds of books. For decades, it was not a good idea to be seen taking a photograph of it – many a time someone has emerged from the solid phalanxes of citizenry trailing up and down surrounding streets to tell you to stop it, and even hand over the camera for the film to be removed. Certainly taking a picture of its main entrance – at the back of the building and without a name plate – was asking for trouble.

Once I decided to try and provoke the KGB and parked my car among the black Volga saloons in front of this entrance. I had a pretext – the wife of Gerald Brooke, who had been arrested by the KGB for bringing messages to Moscow for an *émigré* organization, was going to meet him in the Lubyanka. It is unlikely that the building had been door-stepped by a Western journalist before. Russians didn't even dare to tread the pavements around it, preferring to cross to the other side of the road than to walk in its shadow. No ice-cream or soft-drink seller set up a stall outside it. You certainly didn't knock on its door to ask directions, although I once heard a story about a man whose

18.   Moscow, August 1957. An ice-cream lady is doing good
       business. In those days traffic crossed Red Square.

drunken friends played a dirty trick on him during the Stalin era. He was telephoned by one of them and told to report to the building within an hour. He put down the phone, packed a small case, kissed his wife and children goodbye and took a taxi to Dzerzhinsky Square. He presented himself at the desk inside the Lubyanka entrance, but they wouldn't let him in – he wasn't listed for an interview. The more he insisted he had been summoned to the place, the more they told him to clear off and stop bothering them. Fearing it was a trap, and that if he walked out and went home they would come and get him later and give him a longer sentence, he shouted at them to arrest him. The KGB duty officer only laughed, pointing out it was April 1, and that he was victim of a Fools' Day prank.

Hanging around the entrance was not without interest. A van drew up and the driver and his mate opened the back and went back and forth to the building carrying armsful of cans of film. Shots of foreigners caught red-handed with their trousers down? Recordings of bugged telephones?

A lorry arrived at the huge black gates further along the pavement. The driver hooted once and the gates slowly opened, giving me the chance to catch a glimpse inside the Lubyanka before they closed again. All I saw, of course, were some buildings; not a soul was in sight.

Predictably, they didn't like someone hanging around outside the headquarters of what was then, probably the world's most effective counter-intelligence organization – not that MI5 would be overjoyed if you carried on the same way outside any of their many offices in London. Out came a grim-looking, plainclothes secret policeman.

'All right,' he said, 'you can clear off.'

'Just a minute, Comrade Colonel,' I said, flattering him by giving him a rank much higher than he could possibly have had. 'I am a British journalist and I am covering a story.' I flashed my *udostovorenie*, the little blue cardboard correspondents card with its photograph.

That had him. He stared at it intensely, clearly trying to memorize my name, then handed it back. 'Anyway, you can't stand on the pavement outsided this entrance, or this building come to that.'

'I'm not in anybody's way. I am not interfering with pedestrians. Or vehicles. I am not holding a demonstration. I am not passing out leaflets. I am minding my own business,' I said.

'Nobody stands around outside this building,' he said. 'It is impossible. It is not allowed. In the old days...' his voice trailed off.

'Can I come inside and wait then?'

He laughed out loud. 'Oh, do what you like,' he said and disappeared. Mrs Brooke turned up and we talked, but much more interesting was that I learned you can make a Soviet secret policeman laugh if you try hard enough.

Across the road from the Lubyanka was one of the best-stocked food stores in the entire Soviet Union – you couldn't have your brightest and best going hungry; even before the Cheka, Lenin's political police, took over the area it was the site of a huge open-air market. There was a fountain in the middle of the square, but they knocked that down in 1958 to put up a bronze statue of Felix Dzerzhinsky, the sadistic, fanatical Pole, who modelled the Cheka on the Committee of Public Safety in the French Revolution and showed what punitive terror was all about. That statue came crashing to the ground after the abortive August *coup* of 1991, prompting Mikhail Gorbachev, foolishly, to whinge about hooliganism and cultural vandalism. What he would have said if the Lubyanka had been sacked by the mob that night as it deserved to be and as happened to secret-police headquarters across Eastern Europe, I have no idea. It did not, apparently, occur to him that a statue to a man like 'Iron Felix' should not have been raised in the first place.

Why the Cheka took over the Lubyanka area in 1918 is not recorded, but one reason was probably that it was a few minutes from the Kremlin. There were also some convenient office blocks and the Bolsheviks were confiscating private property. One lovely building seized was owned by Count Fedor Rostopchin, Moscow governor at the time of Napoleon's invasion and held responsible for the city burning, although it was a major factor in the French emperor's withdrawal and disastrous retreat.

The Cheka gobbled up the offices of several big insurance companies, including Lloyds, and added new blocks, and there is something ironic about the fact that state insurance can be abbreviated in Russian to *Gostrakh*, which can just as easily mean 'state terror.'

For years the Lubyanka was a double-purpose building housing the KGB and its predecessors, and many of the high-ceiling rooms of the Rossiya Insurance Company were little changed until recently. But after Stalin's death, No 2, Dzerzhinsky Square, was never the same. The spy arm was moved to a nondescript building on the main ring-road around Moscow, and Lefortovo prison became the detention and interrogation centre for dissidents. When a restaurant named Lefortovo opened near the prison and advertized its grills, I saw the funny side and thought it called for a visit. It turned out to be tucked away next door to the entrance of the Moscow military barracks. I had to share a table with two majors who stopped talking to each other when they realized I wasn't Russian. The food was execrable.

The KGB also began building a massive new complex across the road and even nearer to Detskii mir. Rounding Dzerzhinsky Square one day, I asked a taxi driver what was going on there. 'That was for the fathers,' he said pointing to the Lubyanka. Nodding in the direction of the new building, he added: 'And that is for the sons.'

Not for long. Because – ACC – the KGB's days were numbered. And this was why I got inside the Lubyanka – and into its extraordinary museum, a pantheon for KGB chiefs, and the agency's native and foreign spies – for a talk on my terms. It was just in time – a week before the *coup*.

I presented myself at a door at the front of the building, rang a bell and was taken in a lift by two young uniformed security guards to meet the head of the KGB Centre for Public Relations. Sweetness, light and coffee had replaced the scowls, *nyets*, and Mickey Fins. Crystal chandeliers in the cosy café had replaced the interrogator's lamp and cells.

That day, a truly terrible statistic emerged which, if nothing else, underlined how well secret police records were kept over the years. The Lubyanka had in its files the names of 4,256,781, men and women who had been 'groundlessly' repressed, i.e. killed, by the Soviet government since the 1917 revolution. Two million were killed in one year at the height of the Great Terror, say 1937 and 1938, which is an awful lot of killing, and of whom 23,000 were from the NKVD itself, the men who had been doing the terrorizing and carrying out the executions. The revolution devouring its own...

But I failed to get the information I really wanted from my visit to the Lubyanka.

'I suppose you wouldn't like to make my file available,' I asked Colonel Oleg Tsarev.

Ask a silly question and you get another silly one. 'What file would this be?' he countered.

'My file. About me. All my real or imaginary crimes. Black-market operations, leg-over situations, traffic violations, visits to dissidents. I'm sure you have something on me about my years of anti-Soviet activity. Something about my crafty spying. You've got to have a file on me. Given the years I have been coming to your country it is inconceivable that you haven't. Say you have, please say you have.'

I was desperate. Surely they must have cared about me enough over thirty or more years to have started a file? Even a small one would be better than nothing. All right, so I wanted to feel important; but the KGB must have appreciated that I was a considerable Cold War warrior who spent his working life trying to bring down the system.

He distilled a few words of seductive wisdom: 'I don't know if you've got a file. And I couldn't get it for you even if there is one. But think about it for a moment. Just supposing we did give it to you. There might be something in it that you might not like. Something you would rather not like revealed. Something to break up your marriage, your friendships. Some little item, perhaps, of double-dealing and betrayal that might ruin your life.'

And that was where we left it.

But he knew of my interest in the past and in that building, and from the room he pointed out of the window and across a yard to a five-storey building with rows of small barred windows.

'That was the cell block,' he said. I shivered a little. 'Are you sure you know what you are talking about?' I asked. 'Because all the best authorities on the Lubyanka that I have read, all refer to the cells being in the basement. And that was where the executions were carried out.'

'It's a myth,' he said. 'There were always only thirty-six cells. And they were above ground.'

But later that day he confirmed that the killings were carried out in the cellar, done by stealth with a single fatal shot, delivered without warning by the NKVD executioner walking behind the prisoner down a corridor until they entered a room. Bang. Revolutionary justice, endlessly repeated, and at a time when Stalin said: 'Now we live better. Now we live more happily.'

But if Moscow has any haunted houses, two are top of the list. The first is the Tunisian Embassy, a squat inconspicuous dwelling set behind a high wooden fence, bordered on two sides by a bit of garden, and situated just off the broad Sadovo-Kudrinskaya. For Beria lived there and any place connected with him must be permeated by evil spirits.

Beria, Stalin's last secret-police chief, was an interesting man, and an odd bird. Like Stalin, he was a Georgian but did not greatly resemble his fellow countrymen who tend to be dark, noisy and aggressively masculine. He looked like a clerk, and his glasses gave him a pedantic, bland look. There is no doubt he was a womanizer – his bodyguards scoured Moscow to find him suitable girls – and women feared to walk anywhere near his house in case they were grabbed and served up to him. He was for ever afraid he would get a dose of clap, but in the end he succumbed to a bullet in the back of the head in the Lubyanka – his headquarters – on a Christmas Eve. Beria had considered his police to be his private domain, superior to both Communist Party and government, and this had produced an intolerable situation. After Stalin's death, Communism had to be made safe for the leading Communists, so Beria was doomed.

Stories are legion about Beria's nasty ways, but a legendary Soviet soccer player, Nikolai Starotsin, once told me how he spent twelve years in the GULAG after clashing on and off the field with the man. Starotsin played against Beria, a 'stocky, somewhat crude right-half' in the 1920s in Tbilisi, the Georgian capital, running rings round him. Some fifteen years later Beria, now the NKVD chief, reminded him of it, but to laughter from his bodyguards added: 'Well, Comrade Starotsin, you won't be able to get past me now.'

Starotsin went on to captain the Spartak side which eclipsed Moscow Dynamo, the Secret Police club of which Beria was chairman, during the 1930s. And after Spartak beat Tbilisi in the 1938 Cup

Final, watched by Beria who showed his annoyance at the result, Starotsin was doomed. He was arrested with his three brothers, all of whom were footballers, and sentenced to ten years in a Siberian labour camp for heading a gang of 'terrorist-footballers plotting to kill party and government leaders'.

Soviet football fascinated me for several years, probably because the first Russian I ever saw – and with great difficulty – was a goalkeeper. He was Alexei 'Tiger' Komich who kept goal for Moscow Dynamo, when the side visited Britain in 1945. I saw the game against Arsenal - who had in the team my hero Stanley Matthews, the Wizard of Dribble - in the fog at White Hart Lane with Komich with his unique acrobatic style a few yards in front of me. In those days there were often fogs over London called 'pea-soupers' and this was a classic. Visibility was down to about twelve yards and you only saw any of the game when it came very near. Moscow Dynamo won 4-3 but the team had played twelve men for twenty minutes and the Russian referee was the thirteenth, or so they said.

I never managed to get an invite to a Tunisian National Day reception, but from time to time a few gates were crashed and I got inside Beria's house. I compounded my villainy by asking my Tunisian hosts if the place could just possibly be haunted – it was widely known there had been suicides and several accidents in the house. Indeed it was, they told me cheerfully. At night the house was full of groans, unexplained footsteps, the slamming and banging of doors. Meanwhile unusual lights hovered over the building and black cats congregated in the yard. They confirmed everything I had been saying for years about the house that Lavrenti Beria lived in.

The other fearful, if not haunted, place in Moscow is its most famous block of flats, 2, ulitsa Serafimovicha, sitting like a bloated-bullfrog on the south bank of the Moscow river, diagonally across from the Kremlin. Once it was called the House of Soviets. Then the House of Government. Now it is known on as the House on the Embankment. And it is unlike any house in Soviet history. To begin with, it was the first Soviet high-rise and built on poisoned land – a site used mainly for executions. And it contains more than just some of the best flats and the best views in the capital of Russia – it also houses descendants of the founding comrades, and the ghosts of its pernicious demons.

In this unique building lived the highest-ranking Bolsheviks and their top aides, and everything they desired was within reach – cafeterias, a post office, a bank, polyclinic, cleaners, a theatre, a store, hairdresser, and even an indoor tennis-court.

During Stalin's years 'Entrance No. 12' became one of the most terrifying places in history. Almost his entire Politburo had their spacious five-room apartments there, living a life of luxury and privilege – although modest as compared with the champagne-and-caviar days of the Brezhnev era. But as the purges got underway, the House became paralysed by fear. The NKVD moved in. Dozens of government, Party and military aides were arrested – usually at three in the morning – and disappeared. Their families were moved out – sometimes to the GULAG – and other families moved in. Not for long. The pattern repeated itself. More arrests, more newcomers, more arrests, more newcomers...

When I first arrived in Moscow, the House sat like a concrete sphinx, effectively closed to the outside world as the survivors of the Stalin years kept their mouths shut, keeping the building's secrets to themselves. Once or twice, I nosed around the building looking for wicked old Lazar Kaganovitch – I was told he sometimes played chess in the yard and I had an urge to ask him if he really had signed the lists of railway workers drawn up by the NKVD for execution.

And then one day, I managed to get inside the building. Not only that, I sat in one of those flats built for the top Soviet people, and talked with Stalin's grandson, appropriately enough called Joseph, and about his mother, Svetlana Alliluyeva.

I wince when I think about Svetlana, the tormented, highly emotional, headstrong, prickly daughter of one of the most powerful and murderous tyrants in history. Because she could have been the Great Scoop of my life, instead of being the Scoop that nearly was.

Victor Louis tipped me off that she had gone to India with the ashes of her fourth husband, Indian Communist, Raja Brajesh Singh. He told me that the the decision to let her out of the country had been taken by Alexei Kosygin, the then prime minister whose own wife was dying of cancer and who felt responsible for her happiness.

After much discussion and argument in the Politburo, he persuaded them that she should be allowed to go to India. Victor also said that the KGB were becoming nervous about her – she had a visa for two weeks but now, three months later, she was letting it be known she was in no hurry to return to Mother Russia and would only do so in her own time. What a story – Stalin's daughter was in the West and apparently enjoying it!

'But,' Victor said, 'Don't write it just now, I beg you. There will be a time, but don't do it now. Promise?' And I promised.

It would have been a sensational story in the paper, and with enormous repercussions. Hacks would have descended upon Lucknow from all over the world to interview the girl nurtured in the womb of the Kremlin where her father plotted his political slaughtering. And it occurred to me in a blinding flash, that it would have been enough to warrant the KGB 'heavies' from the Soviet Embassy in India acting decisively to 'protect' her, an important Soviet citizen, from harassment. They would have had her on the first plane to Moscow.

I didn't write it. I should have done. Four days later, while I was agonizing, she walked into the United States Embassy in Delhi and defected. And indeed it was a sensational story. And to this day, I do not know what game Victor was playing – on the one hand leaking an important Kremlin secret and making me promise not to publish it, until he gave the signal. Perhaps he didn't expect, or want, me to keep my word...

So Svetlana defected. The Kremlin princess had rejected the Soviet system and chosen freedom in the West – for seventeen years, until she changed her mind and went home. The propaganda blow of her defection was, for the Kremlin, seismic. But it was more than a propaganda *coup* for the West: it was a symbolic event in the moral imagination of millions of people. And it was very embarrassing for Kosygin, who felt he had been let down by an ungrateful woman that he had been nice to and helped, and there is some evidence that it did him considerable political harm.

I knew she had lived in the House and found the flat simply by asking the *dvorniks* (caretakers), where the Indian gentleman had lived. They all knew who I was talking about, although they could not have known that Svetlana had become the most famous defector in history.

Joseph, her nineteen-year-old son living in her flat, was stunned by it all; only a few minutes earlier he had heard the news on *Voice of America*. I was the first Western correspondent to call on him and he was trembling. But when he spoke it was much more in sorrow than in anger. He was sure she would be returning to Moscow, he loved his mother and he knew she loved him. Later, when other Western correspondents – and the KGB – got to him, his tone changed. His mother was a wicked and confused woman and he rejected her. She clearly did not care for her children and only thought of herself. She had no right to desert her Motherland where she had every comfort, happiness, and so on.

After her brief visit to the Soviet Union she took on the name of Lana Peters, lived in a London hostel ran by a charity before returning, now in her eighties, to the United States. She was a brave, impulsive, deeply unhappy and, above all, impossible woman.

But then her father was a latter-day Ivan the Terrible, who left a bloody trail of broken bodies and hearts, as he dragged his massive, sad country along. When she went back to Russia with her daughter after eighteen years living in the United States and East Anglia, she was tracked down by a poker-playing friend of mine, an American correspondent, Stuart Loory. He told me about the exchange.

As she walked along a street with her KGB minder he asked her: 'Miss Alliluyeva, can you tell me, please, why you have returned to the USSR? The world would really like to know.'

'It is none of the world's bloody fucking business! Piss off!' she said.

Which showed she was a lady not without spirit.

19 - The Gruesome Twosome

A word about Vladimir Ilyich Lenin. Ever since the collapse of Communism, the greatest thinker of the Twentieth Century, 'Uncle' to millions of good little Soviet children, the leader whose effigies were for so long a compulsory feature of every Soviet city, town, farm, railway station, cultural club and military base and lots, lots more, has had a terrible time of it. And there is absolutely no possibility he will make a comeback.

Lenin's fall from grace, and from his pedestals across Eastern Europe, showed the way the winds of change were blowing. Poles, Czechs, Hungarians, East Germans and others enjoyed trampling on the symbols of Communist rule that had been imposed for four decades. Countless bronze, concrete and plastic statues were taken away, broken up and dumped. Hundreds of thousands of 'Big Brother' pictures of him were removed from government buildings, offices, factories and workshops of the former Soviet satellite countries. Many millions of small, shining, ball-shaped heads painted silver and gold, once articles of worship, were thrown out.

Lenin was then massively purged in most of the former Soviet Republics. Having been daubed with paint or disfigured so badly that he was unrecognizable, his statues were pulled down, while street signs carrying his name were painted over or replaced. And now in the new Russia, too, Lenin is fast fading from consciousness.

That Lenin is finished is shown not only by the fact that his head has come off banknotes or that his name has disappeared from squares, avenues and entire cities – remember Leningrad? – but also by what has happened to the most bizarre and ghoulish tourist attraction in the world.

For the Mausoleum, the chunk of dark, red granite on Red Square, no longer draws the crowds as it did during the years of Communist authority. Having for so long contradicted not only the Soviet Union's avowed atheism, but also the wise old Russian proverb that you can't die twice, and you can't escape one death, Lenin in his sepulchre is doomed.

He shouldn't have been there at all, of course. His wife, Nadezhda Krupskaya, was horrified at Stalin's insistence that the body of the founder of the Soviet state was going to be on view for ever in a specially built mausoleum. 'Don't make an icon out of Ilyich' she begged. 'Do not raise monuments to him or palaces to his name.' She pointed out that he had wanted to be buried near his mother in St Petersburg's Volkovo cemetery, and where a splendid family plot awaits him. Stalin, however, made it clear nobody was to take any notice of Lenin's wife. He had decided that Lenin belonged to the working class, who revered him, and so he had to be given a kind of immortality.

There were other reasons. Russian history is full of imposters – think of the false Dmitris – and the comrades wanted to be in a position any time to demonstrate that Lenin was really dead. Or that in the new religion that was then taking off, Lenin was a demi-god and it was only fitting he should be visible to all, as were Christian saints in early days.

It also underpinned the propaganda slogans 'Lenin lived, Lenin lives, Lenin will always live,' and the equally yucky 'Lenin is more alive than the living.'

Thus, preserving him dramatized the claim that his teachings remained to guide the Soviet state he founded – an attempt to deny his death. I also suspect that, although Stalin probably never considered the idea that one day he might die, he decided that if he did, there would be room for him in the Mausoleum's funeral hall, too.

Lenin's remains only just made it to the original wooden mausoleum. They had a bit of luck, since he died during an abnormally cold winter and he could be kept in natural deep-freeze conditions, while two scientists got cracking on embalming him before the spring thaw. They worked round the clock to get it right, including experiments on other bodies. For the next seven decades they had a huge team of pathologists, biochemists, cell researchers and anatomists making a living from preserving the dead, preventing Lenin's – and briefly Stalin's – body from decomposing.

They didn't do too badly. 'How do they keep that guy looking so fresh?' Danny Kaye, an American film-star/comedian, asked me as we were leaving the Mausoleum. (When he left Moscow after a visit, he offered to telephone anybody in London and pass on a message. 'Yes, please, Danny,' I said, 'speak to my mum in Enfield and tell her her son

19. Miller claims he viewed Lenin and Stalin together in the
Mausoleum on Red Square about half-a-dozen times, often
with visiting British politicians.
He dubbed them the 'Grusome Twosome.'

is having a lovely time.' True to his word when he got to London he telephoned my mother and said he was Danny Kaye. 'And I'm Queen Victoria,' she said.)

I confessed I didn't know the mixture for keeping Lenin looking in rude health, which, incidentally, was hailed as a great feat of Soviet science. Indeed, like so much else, the formula was a secret. All that was known was that a chemical solution filled the cells, displacing both water and bacteria, and thus hindering the decomposition of body tissue. Lenin has a check-up twice a week, dust lightly-brushed from his waxy skin, here and there a dab or two of the secret tincture, and throughout, the temperature kept at a constant 15° C and unchanging humidity.

Every few years the Mausoleum would be closed for a major overhaul of the world's most visible corpse. Yet it always baffled ordinary Russians; they could not believe that there was a way of preserving Lenin indefinitely when Soviet science was unable to find a way of keeping milk fresh overnight.

There must be a statistic of how many people are calculated to have taken a peek at Lenin – for that is all you get – since 1924, but I don't happen to have it; an average of 15,000 a day has been mentioned. But, of course, he has not been open to viewing every day, and during World War II, when the German army was beating on the gates of Moscow, they evacuated him to the Urals in the back of an army lorry. However, my pocket calculator suggests that some 200 million could have made the pilgrimage to see the Communist juju.

It figures. Whenever I saw him before the collapse, perhaps half-a-dozen times – including twice when he shared the Mausoleum with Stalin, whose pock-marked, spotty and discoloured face presented his embalmers with a formidable task that they had to get right, or else – it meant a long and punishing morning.

It was during the World Youth Festival that I first joined the queue, like every good, fully paid-up card-carrying comrade in Alexander Gardens, the narrow park along the Kremlin's north wall. There followed several hours of shuffling along before getting within spitting distance of Red Square and the holy of the holies. In those days, this was an extraordinary queue. The longest in all Russia, and not until McDonald's opened and Lenin was on the way down did the situation change. And there were many security checks along the way. Sour-faced Kremlin guards frisked everyone in the queue, and were enraged if they came across a camera. More than that, they didn't like buttons to be undone or pullovers to be carried or hands to be in pockets. Nor was there smoking on Red Square.

Just before the clock in the Redeemer's Tower, the Soviet Union's Big Ben, struck the hour, the queue would be stopped. From the Kremlin marched three young sentries of its spick-and-span brigade to relieve those guarding the Mausoleum – a slightly sinister piece of theatre in itself.

Like clockwork soldiers these KGB élite troops advanced on Sentry Post No. 1 in a slow, measured goosestep, absolutely controlled, right arms swinging across the chest to the bayonet-fixed Kalashnikovs, looking straight ahead. I was once told that after two years in the job they were finished, hairline cracks developed in their kneecaps! Much more likely now is that they will be retired along with other such ostentatious trappings of Communism.

At the bronze doors of the tomb, you again came under intense scrutiny, were told to take your hat off, and silenced with a glare. Huge wreaths flanked the entrance and gave off familiar funereal odours and suddenly the Red Square heat was replaced by Stygian cool and you shuffled in semi-darkness down a few steps leading into the granite tomb. It never turned me on; more like entering the foyer of an underground cinema than a sanctuary for saints. On that first visit Stalin was there, having died three years earlier, to the relief of millions who had never managed to get as much as a glimpse of him. Now they could, close up and for free.

Right, then right again, and suddenly you saw the grisly bedfellows, lying in glass sarcophaguses so finely-polished that the glass was all but invisible. Glowing with an eerie incandescence, the features of these makers of twentieth-century history stood out with sharp clarity. You were only a few feet from them. It was hard to think of Lenin working away in the British Museum, popping out of his lodgings to buy a loaf of bread, and of Stalin bouncing his daughter on his knee, giving her a cuddle and a kiss.

Lenin lay on the catafalque with his arms outstretched. His right fist was clenched, a nice touch. He was wearing a black jacket, white shirt and a dark tie patterned somewhat surprisingly with polka-dots. He seemed incredibly short, but then half his body was covered with thick shrouds from the waist downwards, with lengths of black crepe cast at his feet. Lenin's familiar stubby beard was tinged with red, but the rest of his face and his hands had the vague luminescence of moist chalk. He had the hint of a smile playing about his lips – sardonic enjoyment over all the fuss he had caused? But he looked ill and deranged in the long-suppressed photographs his sister took of him after he suffered the stroke which was to kill him at fifty-three, prompting Winston Churchill's brilliantly-perceptive quote that the worst thing that happened to Russia was Lenin's birth and the next worse, his death.

Stalin looked more austere in his military tunic and he had an impressive show of medal ribbons. His grey hair was brushed back, and there was that familiar grey moustache drooping below the prominent nose. A wonderful example of Russian irony was that Stalin sent the doctor who embalmed Lenin to a Labour camp. He was returned to Moscow to work on the old tyrant's corpse, tempted, no doubt, to do unspeakable things to it.

The air in the tomb was sinister with idolatry, but I only thought to myself that first time about how much of a bastard Stalin had been. I paused in mid-shuffle to study him a little more, but it was impossible to stop even for a mid-second, before there was a peremptory whisper from a KGB officer: 'Keep moving. Walk quickly on.' They wouldn't have known what 'please' and 'thank you' meant.

I clocked myself in and out of the tomb that first time and it scarcely changed over the years – two minutes and forty-seven seconds.

For some, in the days before Stalin was officially condemned as one of the great monsters of our time, and Lenin's statues came a-tumbling down, it was a deeply emotional experience. I've heard sobs coming from grown-ups who should have known better. Once a woman fainted. On another occasion, leaving the Mausoleum, there was a woman behaving hysterically.

Not any longer. Fans of Stalin crawled into their holes light years ago, and those of Lenin are a dying breed. Even the Lenin statue factory, which turned out the stylized Lenin either striding or in a 'hailing a taxi' pose, went out of business, a victim of the ideological recession. The one big order it never landed, incidentally, was when a 900-foot high statue of the great man was turned down by the Ministry of Culture because someone observed that in low cloud you might only be able to see the great Lenin from his flies downwards – and that was undignified.

The last time I popped in on Lenin in the Mausoleum I was embarrassed for him. So few people – mostly foreigners – wanted to see the Greatest Revolutionary of Our Time that there was no queue at all. There were as many policemen standing around as marshals, as there were customers. Once relieved of your camera you proceeded up the hill by the Historical Museum, and across Red Square at what can only be described as a fast clip. You could do Lenin in under fifteen minutes.

The few children dragged along for the occasion were not in the slightest bit awestruck as they popped their bubble gum. They won't be going again, that's for sure, to see a boring, and very dead, old fart.

Moreover the sense of dignity has gone – despite a notice to the contrary you can even light up on Red Square now and drop your fag-end on the ground right outside the Mausoleum. You can shout insults, make rude gestures, carry placards. (Elderly Communists even up to this day carry placards saying 'Long Live Stalin!')

Some say the writing was on the Kremlin Wall when Stalin was unceremoniously lifted off his own personal catafalaque, dumped into a coffin, taken outside and dropped into a nearby grave, and at the dead of night too, so as not to cause any fuss. I was there when it happened and it was all because a dotty little old lady rose to her feet at the 1961 Communist Party Congress and told delegates: 'Yesterday I asked Ilyich for guidance and it was as if he stood before me, alive, and said to me: "I don't like being next to that man, Stalin."' They had Stalin out of the Mausoleum that very night. Lenin was alone again.

It wrote *finis* to the old joke about the two peasants emerging from the Mausoleum, one saying to the other: 'Just like us – dead but not yet buried'.

It quickly transpired, of course, that Comrade Squeaky Clean had one or two little skeletons in the cupboard, or rather, locked away in the archives and well out of sight of those making a good living out of bringing to light his every utterance and act. Moscow's Lenin

Museum, the white-marbled Communist shrine at the bottom of Red Square, with some 7,000 hailing the man and his Revolution, showed the way with an exhibit of a letter in which he urged the hanging of Russian Orthodox priests. Also revealed was his telegram to local Bolsheviks in the Penza region on how to deal with some revolting peasants – 'hang at least a hundred so that people will see, and find a hard man to get on with it.'

This well-educated intellectual also wrote about his political enemies as 'prostitutes, bastards, dirty scum, blockheads and Russian idiots'. And it is now clear to Russians that his family, the Ulyanovs, were well off. He only worked as a lawyer for two years of his life, handled five cases and lost them all, and never earned any money. He didn't need to: his mother was sending him money regularly until the day she died, and he was over forty.

They kept his letters to Inessa Armand out of sight, too, because being deified he wasn't supposed to have got up to hanky-panky with a lady not his wife. One of his little notes to her, I suggest, gives the game away. It reads: 'Dear Inessa, will you let me know the size of your galoshes. I am hoping to get a pair of them for you. Please write.' Why was the leader of the world's first workers and peasants state, so concerning himself about a young lady's feet if there wasn't something going on between them, we may well ask.

After visiting Vladimir Ilyich you couldn't go straight home and get on with living. You came out at the back of Mausoleum into the blessed daylight, and they had arranged it so you had to take in the Soviet Union's most exclusive graveyard, the one at the Kremlin Wall, a monument to more than seventy years of Soviet history, to the epoch of totalitarianism.

One after another the graves mark the road Soviet society travelled, the road of faded hopes and ideals. But none of the Soviet Nobel Prize winners are here, nor some of the country's great figures of the twentieth century, such as Eisenstein or Prokofiev or Bulgakov or Stanislavsky. This graveyard is founded on different values. It is a pantheon of Communist heroes, nearly 150 of them.

Here are many of the top villains. This is truly a roll-call of disgrace. Read the gravestones and you are reading the names of mass-murderers, psychopaths, degenerates and sick people, without exception members of the Soviet Communist Party between about 1920 and the coming of Mikhail Gorbachev.

There are twelve disciples of Lenin in a row behind the Mausoleum, all with a bust so you can recognize them, and for years they would all have a bunch of flowers on their graves, if only sometimes of plastic. There is Klim Voroshilov, Civil War hero, close-buddy and drinking companion of Stalin until the end when Stalin decided he was a British spy. This has to be another example of Stalin's paranoia – after all would MI6 have seriously employed an alcoholic Communist marshal? Come to think of it, Philby did make General, albeit in the KGB.

There is Yury Zhdanov, whose name, like that of Voroshilov, has also disappeared from the map of Russia. Another one of Stalin's henchmen – the ideological elements of Stalinism were largely his creation – he unleashed a crackdown on the Soviet artistic world with such considerable ferocity it drove some to suicide and others to labour camps. He was said to have been murdered in 1948 by nine Kremlin, and Jewish, doctors at the behest – you will not be surprised – of British and American intelligence services.

There is a whole bunch of unpleasant Communist politicians of our time, Brezhnev, Andropov, Chernenko, Suslov, and others like them, who ruined Russia and held on to power as long as they could. When they all died one after the other in the 1980s, the frequent state funerals and the mode of transport used for their last journey to Red Square became known as the 'gun-carriage race.'

There are two outstanding nasties, Dzerzhinsky, who founded the first secret police and cranked up the Red Terror after the Revolution, and his successor Menzhinsky. The other five of the first seven chiefs of the secret police were executed and dumped in a pit full of quicklime, so they didn't qualify.

Some of the other psychopaths didn't manage to rate their own grave and a bust, but at least they got a niche in the Kremlin Wall itself. Such as Andrei Vyshinsky. Now there's a name to recall – the man who conducted the show trials of the 1930s with such frightening rancour and vindictiveness, and showed the same venom at the United Nations in his attacks on the West. Dreadful man. Did anybody shed a tear when he died? Remember him fondly, or even at all?

There's some communist small fry too. Such as People's Commissar, Vadim Podbelsky, who cut his foot during a day of 'voluntary' labour and died of blood poisoning in 1920, and a Dora Vorovskaya, who died from a nervous breakdown after her *apparatchik* husband was assassinated. The couple's urns are side by side, the only family burial in the graveyard for Very Top Red People. And what about one Arthur McManus, chairman of the British Communist Party, who got his 1927 deathbed wish granted – to be buried in the capital of the workers paradise. I bet he regrets it now. But at least he was buried with a bit of dignity. Another British comrade, William Marshal Wheeldon, went off to Russia in the 1930s and worked as an interpreter for Comintern, the Communist International, which preached world revolution. Unfortunately he got in with a bad lot – Stalin's Old Bolshevik enemies – and when the OGPU sadists rounded them up for trial they included Mr Wheeldon on their list. He was charged with counter-espionage and carrying out subversive activities for a foreign power, and sentenced to death. They deliberately set out to spoil his Christmas; he was shot in the back of the head in a corridor in the Lubyanka on December 25, 1937. Mark you, the Soviet government did the decent thing and he was postumuously rehabilitated in 1957.

The clamour for shutting down this graveyard began on the day Communism collapsed in Russia. But there are some practical problems with setting history straight. Such as who wants the remains of Joseph, Felix, Leonid and the rest, not forgetting Albert's ashes?

Once, China's Communist leaders may have been interested in taking Stalin off Moscow's hands, but then only to spite the 'revisionist Russians' because the historical fact is that Stalin behaved arrogantly and rudely towards Mao Tse Tung and the Chinese revolution. Now off-loading Stalin on the Chinese, or anywhere else, is a non-starter.

History's remorseless dustpan and brush has already dealt with a formidable list of transient Soviet top people. Khrushchev showed what could be done more than thirty years ago when the inhabitants of Stalingrad, the courageous World War II city, woke up to discover they were living in Volgograd. This rewriting of the script, however, has become something of a national joke. Lugansk, in the Ukraine, was changed to Voroshilovgrad after the Marshal set the pace in

20.   John Miller broke the story for Reuters in 1961 of
Khrushchev's decision to change the name of Stalingrad to
Volgograd. He was at the opening of the 725-metre long dam
that crosses the Volga river the following year.

eulogizing Stalin. After he clashed with Khrushchev, it got its former name back. But in 1970, when he died, Brezhnev ordered it to revert to Voroshilovgrad. It is now Lugansk again.

And across the length and breadth of Russia the old names have come back at last. I was working in Moscow when Mokhovaya ulitsa (Moss Street) was merged with Okhotny ryad (Hunters' Row) to become Marx Prospect, and Menage Square became the Square of the fiftieth Anniversay of the October Revolution. Now I can write the song that has been buzzing around in my head for years: 'Goodbye, Marx Prospect! Farewell, Square of the 50th Anniversasry of the October Revolution!' because these streets and several dozen others have reverted to their old names. More than that, I can again use the 1914 Baedeker's guide to Moscow.

Other names too have gone, or are unlikely ever to burden a generation again. It is hard to imagine a Russia without Ivans or Borises or Natashas or Svetlanas, but there was a time when children were given names like Traktor or Elektrifikatsia, Avangard and Utopia. Many such unfortunate names have faded along with ideals and few of today's Renats are aware that they are namesakes of Revolutsiya, Nauka, Trud (Revolution, Science, Labour) or Melors that they are linked with Marxs, Engels, Lenin, October Revolution.

Lenin must bear the responsibility for a whole catalogue of dreadful callings including Vladlen for Vladimir Lenin, Ninel for Lenin spelled backward, and Vilior, the acronym for Vladimir Ilyich Lenin, Initiator of the October Revolution.

And what to do with the Mausoleum with its two dozen rooms and halls when Lenin is given a decent burial at last in St Petersburg? Because, given that there is plenty of room in Volkovo Cemetery beside his mother, two sisters and brother-in-law, that is where he should finish up.

Why not turn it into a nightclub called the 'Gruesome Twosome'?

238

20 – Margaret and Harold and Denis and George

However disagreeable it may be to some people, it remains a fact that there was a period when the most popular woman in Russia was British. Certainly she was the best-known of all the British political or cultural figures who had dealings with the Soviet Union. There are no Lenin Prizes for guessing who I mean – the Russians call her Margarit Tatsher.

They took to her the day that a Soviet newspaper sneered at the '*Zhelyezhnaya Dama*,' the *Iron Lady*. Ostensibly, what upset the tightly controlled Soviet press was her saying that the Soviet Union with its policies and its arms build-up posed a threat to the West. This was not acceptable to the Kremlin, the self-styled bastion of peace, with its tens of thousands of peace-loving tanks, guns, rockets and aircraft.

It was more than that, of course. The attack on the Soviet leadership came from a woman – and the few women there were in Soviet politics were not supposed to have opinions and were supposed to keep their mouths shut. They may have held a few figurehead positions, but the reality was that Soviet men ran the country.

In six decades of Soviet power there was one exception, and I met her two or three times. Yekaterina Furtseva was the first, and only, woman to make it to the Politburo, and it had a lot to do with her relationship with Khrushchev; for which she had a vulgar nickname – 'Nikita's Gate'. Though stout, she was attractive with rich, yellow blonde hair done in a big, twisted bun, apple cheeks and candid blue eyes.

When she was Minister of Culture she gave a small press conference and after I introduced myself she patted a chair next to hers and said ever so sweetly: 'Ah, *Gospodin* Miller, why don't you come and sit next to me?' There was a faint smell of vodka about her, but it could have been a popular perfume of the time known as 'Svetlana's Breath'.

Furtseva came across as a passionately dedicated Communist, and some of her pronouncements were paralysingly dull. Not even Mrs Thatcher at her most wearisome could have delivered anything such as: 'The reactionary forces of the capitalist world fear peaceful competition and international cooperation like the plague, because they do not believe they can win in such a competition. By following the policy of militarism in war, the arms race and preparations for military adventures – which fabulously enrich the capitalist monopolists, while bringing the people privation and poverty – they hope to check the processes of historical development.' And this stuff from a woman burning and blindingly intellectual.

Furtseva hung onto her job for ten years after Khrushchev was shafted, but when I heard rumours she was involved in a scandal over paying cut-rate prices for building materials for a dacha, I knew she was on her way out. As the gossip spread, she coughed up the full amount, but the scandal was too much for her and she committed suicide by slashing her wrists. Not a word of Furtseva's problems ever appeared in Soviet newspapers. But the Kremlin told editors to snipe at Mrs Thatcher, and the 'Iron Lady' tag began to crop up more and more frequently.

It did Mrs T. a power of good in Britain. She was perceived as a woman who was not going to be pushed around by Moscow or cowed by Soviet rocket-rattling, an image which Labour politicians never managed to cultivate.

Some, being soft on Communism, never tried. And the leadership preferred to blame the United States for most, if not all, the dangerous developments that occurred during the Cold War – whereas Moscow was generally given the benefit of the doubt.

In the Soviet Union, the denigration of Mrs Thatcher cut no ice at all. The Russians took their newspapers with a load of Siberian salt and became excessively cynical in the Brezhnev years. The more the lady was attacked, the more they felt she couldn't be all that bad and perhaps was right after all. Attacks on her in *Pravda* and other propaganda organs were simply counterproductive.

I was in Moscow when she became prime minister and I was tipped off that Soviet editors had been told to drop the Iron Lady bit. The fear was that she might make an official visit to the USSR and it was felt in the Kremlin corridors of power that there was no point in adding to her image as a tough, no-nonsense British leader.

Being a Thatcher fan at the time and having picked up and flogged the Iron Lady theme for all it was worth – such as votes – I thought that was a pity. But I kept my eyes open and, sure enough, the

Soviet Communist Party's Agitation and Propaganda Department had somehow failed to get the message. Suddenly, its presses rolled off tens of thousands of copies of a new crude poster of the Wicked Witch of the Cold War, none other than our Margaret.

I saw the nine feet by four feet poster in the window of a children's library in central Moscow. It was the work of Boris Yefimov, the country's best-known, i.e. nastiest, political cartoonist, who arguably did his finest work during the Stalin years. Charitably, I wrote at the time that Mrs Thatcher would have had trouble recognizing herself as she rode a broomstick over the Houses of Parliament, wearing stringy yellow-hair and with a ghostly face, twisted in hatred. Appropriately, she wore a black witch's hat and a black cloak and was being cheered on by NATO top brass. In big letters the caption read: 'Mrs Thatcher, trouble hatcher. Tory leader, Cold War pleader'.

There was some more drivel which needed the fine hand of Bob Evans, the Reuters Bureau chief – his Russian embraced its heartbeat – and we caught the Soviet spirit of the time with:

'They say that having blabbed her fill
And poured out slander to fit the bill
This Mrs Witch flew to the skies
Hoping for a heavenly prize
That Mr God would help restore
Tension in Europe for evermore'.

The poster was withdrawn within days of the appearance of my story that the anti-Thatcher campaign had not died out, which, if nothing else, showed that the Soviet diplomats in London read newspapers as well as spied.

Yefimov must have been on to a good thing, because the following year he produced another huge drawing of the prime minister, this time for the cartoon section of an exhibition to mark the sixtieth anniversary of the Soviet Union.

Huge crowds were presented with Mrs Thatcher as an enraged lion with bloodstained paws. Wearing a black dress and high-heel shoes, she was walking the waves towards an island with 'Falklands' written on it. On her head was a policeman's helmet, and she was wearing a holster with a pistol in it, around her neck, a dollar medallion. Her lion's tale was twisted in the shape of a pound sign.

BCC, the Russians were not used to seeing cartoons about their own leaders, and they loved it. They were also impressed by the way Britain went to war to get back the Falklands, and with the British leader's firmness and vigorous style. For a long time their leaders had come across as boring, ill and even senile.

So, it was not really surprising she was mobbed by large crowds when finally she paid her first official visit to Moscow. Her host was Mikhail Gorbachev, 'the man with whom' – in her memorable phrase – 'she could do business'. There were a lot of Russians who would have been quite happy to swap Mikhail for Margaret.

Nobody ever mobbed Harold Wilson, or George Brown, or Michael Foot, or Denis Healey, or, come to that, even Sir Alec Douglas-Home, when they pitched up in Moscow to discuss Anglo-Soviet relations, to strut the world stage, to get away from domestic political problems, and hopefully to win votes.

Wilson was something of a regular visitor to Moscow for four decades, first as a civil servant during World War II; as a businessman when he was arrested for taking a photograph of a woman carying a child's tricyle; as Opposition leader and finally, as a Prime Minister. His last visit came shortly after Edward Heath had kicked out 105 Soviet spies and he was anxious to kiss and make up with the Kremlin. Leonid Brezhnev hadn't been seen around Moscow for nearly two months and it was said he was very ill, but he turned out for Harold and James Callaghan, the Foreign Secretary, and they said he was lively and mentally-sharp.

I rarely believed information of this kind. Foreign visitors to Moscow were grateful for, and overawed by, their reception in the Kremlin by one of the most powerful men in the world, so they habitually put discretion before unpleasant truths. The scene can be summed up with a Russian saying – that the cuckoo is flattering the rooster because the rooster is flattering the cuckoo. They made use of a nasty regime without worrying about giving it what it craved for – respect.

But what do the statesmen of the age talk about as they preen themselves and pose for the media at the ice-breaking sessions, before getting down to discussion and negotiation about our futures? The answer? Trivia, as the Wilson-Brezhnev meeting brought home. As one of the two pool journalists allowed into the Catherine Hall in the Grand Kremlin Palace, I listened and took a note of who said what, how, and to whom.

Wilson: 'How are you Mr Brezhnev? Are you well?'

Brezhnev: 'I'll tell you later… you are looking younger than when I last saw you.'

Wilson: 'It's the beer I drink.'

Brezhnev: 'We drink mostly vodka in this country.'

Callaghan, pointing at Prime minister Alexei Kosygin: 'He looks the fittest of all of us.'

Brezhnev: 'Yes, he's been on holiday. But he has now used it all up for this year.'

Callaghan: 'Foreign Ministers like Mr Gromyko and myself never have any time for holidays.'

Later Wilson praises Soviet mineral water. Brezhnev pushes over a bottle to him and said: 'We will sell you some at a specially-reduced price. To you, fifty kopeks.'

Kosygin: 'That would ruin us. No, we want seventy kopeks a bottle. We have got to make some money out of you. After all, you are rich capitalists.'

Wilson: 'You are the ones who are acting like capitalists. Can't you get the price down?'

Brezhnev, nudging Kosygin: 'There you are. We make them a good offer and they start trying to bargain with us.'

There was a lot more of this, but the conversation, which has always stuck in my mind, was the one I had with Harold Wilson in a men's toilet in the park at Petrodvorets, the former imperial palace, outside what was then Leningrad. This was a simple wooden and corrugated-iron construction, with a rudimentary metal-channel for urinating in. Like most public toilets in the USSR it smelled abominably.

As we stood there, Harold Wilson turned to me and said: 'There's a lot of writing on the wall. I didn't know they did that sort of thing in the Soviet Union.'

'They do it all the time,' I said. 'Usually it is in the form of slogans striving for peace, working harder, and how the Party and the people are one.'

He laughed. 'Yes,' he said. 'But I bet that's not what some of those words are saying.'

'No, it's not.'

'All right,' he said and pointed at the wall in front of him. 'What's that word?'

I had to lean sideways to see that that some dirty minded devil had written the word *pizda*. I said: 'Well... er... Mr Wilson... it er... it is an exceptionally rude word for a part of the female anatomy.' I couldn't resist it, and added: 'It is also used sometimes to describe a politician.'

He thought that funny. 'Well, I've known the Russians for years,' he said, 'and I've always said they were human beings, just like us. And that proves it.' He pointed to another word. 'What's that one say?'

It was *yebat*. The Russians have a rich, swearing vocabulary but for lavatory walls they keep to basics and this four-letter word was certainly that.

'Fuck,' I said, determined to treat a serious question from a leading British politician in a serious manner. 'As in 'fuck you', 'fuck off', and 'gofuckyourself'.'

'Hmmm,' he said, 'That's a useful Russian word to know. How's it pronounced?'

I coached him as he buttoned his flies and we strolled out into the sun. He got me to repeat the word several times, much to the amusement of his Russian guide, the KGB minders and the rest of the party, but he never managed to get it quite right.

⁂

The visit to Moscow by a Labour party delegation headed by Michael Foot, and including Denis Healey, was also entertaining if you had a front row seat. But their performance was not very creditable. They didn't actually suck up to the Russians – perhaps more like cosy up to them – spending hours talking to dreary dead-beats in the Communist Party's Central Committee. They were apparently impressed by Brezhnev's thoughts on disarmament, and sympathised with the Kremlin's concern about the Reagan administration.

Foot's and Healey's audience in the Kremlin with Brezhnev summed it up. This was a traditional set-piece ceremony in Brezhnev's office and as they awaited the arrival of the two men, I heard the Soviet leader ask his aide, a horrid old *apparatchik* Boris Ponomaryev, who he was meeting. Ponomarev told him it was a British Socialist Party delegation headed by *Gospodins* Foot and Healey. 'Never heard of them,' said Brezhnev, then aged seventy-six, and he scowled.

In came Messrs Foot and Healey. They strode across the room and Healey reached the Soviet leader first with inches to spare. He seized Brezhnev's hand and bowed so low I thought for a moment he was about to kiss it. It was a remarkable moment, and somewhere on film. I knew the Kremlin photographer and asked him for the picture, but he was frightened to sell it to me.

I noted the small-talk as hands were pumped – it included 'Very happy to see you', 'marvellous to be here' and 'good of you to see us'. Finally, Brezhnev had had enough of all the glad-handing and said: 'Let us get down to work, Gentlemen. We must not waste time.' He showed them to their places at a long, wooden table covered in green baize for one of those useless 'top-level discussions', after all, the Labour Party then had no clout at all, and its opinions on disarmament were of no consequence. More photographs were taken and it was on this occasion that I became a non-person.

The art of eavesdropping on the conversation in the Soviet leader's office was to position oneself as near to Brezhnev as possible. So I stood with his aides behind him and heard exchanges about vodka – a sensitive issue with Labour leaders ever since Hugh Gaitskell drank nineteen tumblers of the stuff during a similar visit to Moscow in 1959. Perhaps I shouldn't have been there, because the next day *Pravda* duly published the picture and I had disappeared, been eliminated, obliterated. I was in good company, however. The same thing had happened to Foot's press spokesman, Sir Tom McCaffrey, who was actually sitting at the table right next to his leader, and had helped himself to a fistful of Kremlin pencils.

The urge to mess about with a photograph and effectively distort the truth was nothing new, of course.

And it has happened to people a lot more important than Tom McCaffrey and me. When Stalin took over after Lenin's death, Trotsky was quickly painted out of every photograph and picture of the Revolution he had been in. If Stalin was in a photograph with Lenin, he was cleverly moved up a few places to be at the leader's right hand. And as the purges got underway, the Old Bolsheviks being shot to death in the Lubyanka were at the same time obliterated from all official photographs.

✻❧✻

George Brown was different. Unlike Foot, who told Brezhnev that many Soviet proposals on disarmament echoed those of the Labour Party, and Healey, whose anti-Americanism led him in Moscow to publicly embrace Soviet propaganda stratagems, George Brown didn't stand for any nonsense from the Russians.

When Khrushchev visited Britain, the Labour party gave him a dinner in the Commons. It was a famous occasion marked by a bitter clash between Brown and the Soviet leader, after Khrushchev had tried to defend and justify Stalin's pact with Hitler. 'May God forgive you,' said George, who may or may not have had drunk too much. Later, when a Labour Party delegation called on Khrushchev to smooth over the row, he asked: 'Who is this George Brown? I never knew such people existed. We haven't seen them in Russia for thirty years.' (They were all shot, of course.)

Khrushchev was four years out of office when Brown, now Foreign Secretary, flew to Moscow for talks with his counterpart Andrei Gromyko. He was still a cheeky chappie, calling Gromyko by his first name, although the protocol-bound Soviet Foreign Minister always addressed him as *Gospodin* Brown.

Brown endeared himself to the British Embassy staff by bringing in ten kegs of beer at the special request of the MI6 station chief, Tony Motion, who said it would be good for the Embassy's morale. Ronnie Payne, a colleague from the *Daily Telegraph,* asked me what I wanted brought from London.

'Kippers,' I told him.

Not a pair, but a box of kippers was flown in on the Foreign Secretary's plane. For us, this was a special treat, but Brenda gave a kipper-party at 'Sad Sam' for any of the journalist pack who cared

246

to come. For me, it proved to be an embarrassing occasion for as the kippers were about to be served up to my guests – effectively my competitors – I had a telephone call from London. Because George Brown was in Moscow the Foreign Office had asked the BBC World Service to withdraw a programme in its Russian service about Alexander Solzhenitsyn's *Cancer Ward*.

Would I go and see him and ask him if he approved of this example of censorship? Having asked Brenda to save me a kipper or two, I drove to the Embassy. George was still dining with Gromyko when I got there but eventually he came through the heavy wooden door, staggering and supported by his wife. He had had several hours of talks with Gromyko and a dinner, and clearly, he had had a long, hard day.

But I had to ask him about the programme, and introduced myself. 'Foreign Secretary,' I said, 'Do you know the BBC Russian service has dropped a programme at the request of the FO because you are in Moscow?'

The Foreign Secretary swayed. 'What are you on about? What Russian Service?' he asked, and his speech was slurred.

I repeated it again. I don't think he got my question even then, and he swayed even more dangerously. Mrs Brown now took over the interview.

She made it clear: 'The Foreign Secretary is not going to answer any more questions. He has a press spokesman who is paid to do that. Mr Brown has finished work today and is going to bed. Goodnight.'

That was that. She helped the Foreign Secretary up the elaborately carved, grand staircase. The incident had been witnessed by the guard who sat at the reception desk in the hall. He was chortling. I asked him what was funny, and he told me. When he came on duty that evening he had been bollocked by George Brown for wearing a pullover with deers' heads on the front – the Foreign Secretary said he wasn't properly dressed.

He had seen George Brown staggering up the stairs after a skinful and he was a happy man. As I was when I got back home and found a pair of kippers waiting for me.

When Sir Alec Douglas-Home came to Moscow for talks with Gromyko he couldn't wait to conclude them and get off to Leningrad to visit the Hermitage. Discussing the international situation with the Soviet Foreign Secretary was boring – Gromyko played the same old record time after time. There was nothing new to say to each other. But there was always something interesting to see in the Hermitage, which, after all, is one of the world's finest art museums.

In those days, the quick way into and around Soviet art gallerys and other institutions was to hitch yourself to an official delegation. The word *delegatsia* had a magic of its own. It meant you didn't have to join an enormous queue to get into the building, and then another one to deposit your coat. You turned up at the Hermitage with the delegation and you were in and viewing within minutes. The big draw back was that it was obligatory for a delegation to have a guide, and most guides were conscientious loyal and ideologically sound servants of the state.

A wily bird was Sir Alex, and a gentleman too. So he listened politely to the stuff about the storming of the Winter Palace and how Kerensky's cabinet was arrested in the White Dining Room, and he showed interest in the Palaeolitic and Mesolithic artefacts, among them tools and primitive figures, and in the several rooms devoted to classical antiquities. Then he made his move and asked to see the Joshua Reynolds and the Gainsborough before moving on to the Picassos and the Matisses, which was why we were there.

And it was at that point I was picked up, literally, by the KGB. It was not a nice experience. Standing by a statue of Jupiter and listening to my Foreign Secretary showing off his knowledge of the contents on the Hermitage, I was confronted by two men.

'*Dokumenty*. Show us your documents,' one of them said in the manner of a secret policeman, and he clearly thought I was Russian.

'Show me yours first,' said I, and they didn't like that at all. These were Sir Alec's KGB minders, and I should have uttered the magic password *delegatsia* – but I didn't. They were professionals and they had no intention of discussing the matter further. Quietly but firmly they moved each side of me and picked me up off the ground by my arms. As we proceeded away from the scene I protested in Russian and English – but not too loudly so as to make a scene, because that wasn't how gentlemen behaved in a place like the Hermitage.

To my relief, we passed a diplomat from the Embassy whom I knew. 'Ted,' I implored, 'tell these two goons to put me down. Tell them I'm with you.' Ted Orchard, who spoke the best Russian in the Embassy, heard me. And turned away – later he said he hadn't recognized me.

A few yards further on they put me down and took me to a small room near the entrance. 'All right, Comrade,' one of them said. 'We don't like what you were doing. Why were you hanging around the delegation from England? Making a nuisance of yourself... sucking up to foreigners?'

Before I could answer, the other man added: 'To change money? Buy some dirty jeans? Hand over anti-Soviet slander?'

'This is ridiculous. I'm not Russian,' I said. 'I'm British. A journalist.' Now I showed them my Foreign Ministry pass, then my British passport. Shock and dismay. They were crestfallen, unhappy, even embarrassed.

'*Gospodin* Miller, this has been a terrible mistake on our part,' one of them said, and he meant it. 'We are extremely sorry for any trouble we have caused you. We thought you were a Soviet citizen who was going to make a nuisance of himself. As you know, our duty is to protect your Foreign Minister. These days one cannot be too careful, can one? Even in your country there must be a lot of funny people about, people who have bad intentions.'

I forgave them, but I didn't know whether to laugh or cry about being mistaken by the KGB as terrorist stalking Sir Alec Douglas-Home in the Hermitage. By that time he had done the collection of French Art of the nineteenth and twentieth centuries and gone off to ride in the driver's cabin of an underground train. For some time I stood on my own looking at the Child Harlequin in White with Blue Buttons. It was badly lit, but it was wonderful.

While Sir Alec dined that evening with the Mayor of Leningrad, they made it up to me. I was drinking in the bar of the Astoria Hotel – the hotel near St Issac's Cathedral, and where Hitler had planned to hold a victory dinner when the German army seized Leningrad – when Viktor Sukhodrev came over.

Viktor was the most brilliant of all Russian-English interpreters, having been brought up in England during World War II when his father was a diplomat at the Soviet Embassy. He was so good that he could speak several dialects. To escape the London Blitz, he was evacuated to a school in the north of England where he learned to speak English with a Yorkshire accent. But he spent time in London, so he could slip into cockney, when necessary.

He became famous as Khrushchev's interpreter. We shouted questions at him – 'Viktor, Viktor, ask Khrushchev if he is going to go to war over Berlin?' or 'What does he think about Macmillan, Viktor?' Or 'Viktor, ask him if he is serious about arms agreements with the West?'

Viktor always came up with an answer of some sort, and on several occasions he cleaned up Khrushchev's salty rhetoric. He was an intelligent and friendly man, and with his black wavy hair and good looks, he could have gone far in business in the West. As it was, he was stuck for years as being his master's voice, the No 1 Soviet interpreter and was privy to so many secrets that it held up his progress in the Soviet Foreign Ministry. Later, however, he found a niche in the United Nations Secretariat. And before he retired to his dacha near Moscow, he was given a really daft title – Envoy Extraordinary and Minister Plenipotentiary First Class in the Soviet Foreign Ministry.

'You don't want to sit here drinking with your mates,' he said. 'Come and sink a few with some real comrades.' And he took me into a kitchen behind the bar where several men were sitting and drinking at a large table. Viktor and the boys were having a party. This was the Soviet support unit for Sir Alec's visit. Two men – but not the goons I met in the Hermitage – were clearly KGB and they flashed silver teeth at me in greeting. One person I knew – Sasha Gerasimov, the diplomatic correspondent of the Soviet News Agency, TASS. Gerasimov had a truly rotten job. He spent his working life taking statements drafted by the Soviet Foreign Ministry and telephoning them to TASS.

His story on Sir Alec Douglas-Home's visit to Moscow read 'Today, Soviet Foreign Ministery A.A. Gromyko had a talk with British Foreign Minister, Sir Alec Douglas-Home. The talks took place in a good atmosphere.' Which didn't give him much scope for good writing or diplomatic reporting. Gerasimov smoked incessantly and died three years later from throat cancer.

There were two friends of Viktor who said they were from the protocol department of the Foreign Ministry and they might easily have been, because they greeted me pleasantly. This band of comrades were there in order to drink. There was some food – a few bits of cheese, some ham, bread and butter – but more attention was paid to the many bottles of Armenian and Georgian brandy, vodka and red wine.

Some of the bottles were already opened, and empty. I thought to myself that I needed to be careful in case I woke up the next morning naked, in bed with a beautiful blonde with gorgeous cornflower-blue eyes and flaxen hair, and with the photographs developed and printed. But I sat down. A glass of vodka was slammed into my hand like a rifle butt.

'*Pod stolom*,' said Viktor.

'Under the table'. Oh dear, it was going to be one of those evenings. I did what I was told, then put the upturned glass on my head. Not a drop came out. I had shown my credentials as a man who really did drink to the bottom of the glass.

It was a good start, I thought, but TASS was staring at me, and suddenly he said: 'You, John Miller, you are a British spy. You shouldn't be drinking with us. You are a spy. You hate us. You want to destroy us. It is very unpleasant to sit here drinking with someone like you.'

Not a word about peace and friendship. And I knew why he was behaving as he did. The previous year he had visited London with Gromyko and when I met him at the Foreign Office, he had taken me aside. 'John, I want to ask a favour of you,' he had whispered. 'This is my first time in Britain, and I would like to visit a whore-house.'

'I don't think there are such things in London these days, Sasha,' I said, innocently. 'They are illegal. I certainly don't know of one.'

'All right,' he said, 'I would like to see some pornographic films. They are not shown in our cinemas in the Soviet Union.'

'That's very honest of you to tell me that, Sasha,' I said, 'but I can't help you there, either. I don't watch porn movies myself.' I suggested he spent his time visiting the National Theatre, the Tate Gallery, Hyde Park Corner, etc. He had not forgotten…

Now one of the KGB men with a face like a football backed him up. 'It is well known,' he said, 'that John Miller has a file that thick' and he held his hands about a foot apart.

'Nice of you to say so,' I said. 'But have you seen it? And where's it kept?'

Sasha Gerasimov looked triumphant. 'You see,' he said, 'he is asking questions. He wants to know where our archives are. Get rid of him.'

Viktor, who had been sitting there glowering, suddenly erupted. He called Gerasimov *vyyebannoye barakhlo,* which can be translated as a 'fucked-out load of old rubbish'. There were other colourful expressions including one about a syphilitic toad climbing up a sticky prick. Viktor said he had known me for fourteen years. I was a guest. Russians were known for their hospitality. If I went, so did he.

The table fell silent. Football-face was the first to speak. OK, I can stay, he said, but I was still a spy. And one of the men from the Foreign Ministry protocol department said that I must first pass a test. So we played an old Russian drinking game, and I thought of Tolstoi's *War and Peace* and the drinking party when Pierre takes part in a madcap game with a wine bottle on the window sill.

Protocol showed me what had to be done. He poured brandy into a glass nearly to the top. He placed it on the back of his hand and he raised it to his lips. He drank the brandy, threw the glass into the air, and caught it. Bravo, we shouted and clapped.

Now it was my turn. I suspected that they all wanted me to fail, if only to underline that only the Russians knew how to drink. I disappointed them. I have small hands, but the glass was as firm and as steady as rock on the back of my right hand as I leaned forward and began to drink from it.

I downed the brandy, tossed the empty glass into the air, grabbed at it… and missed. The glass crashed to the floor and splintered into pieces. There was a brief silence, then they laughed uproariously. I could stay – 1 had passed the test as I had finished the brandy without spilling a drop.

So the game went on. Every now and again an old woman would slip into the room with a Russian brush broom and a pan and clear broken glass off the tables or sweep it up around our feet without saying a word. No notice was taken of her at all: she might not have been there.

It was gone midnight and I stood up with difficulty. Viktor was very drunk, came over to me and took me into the corner of the room. 'Look, John,' he said, and he put his hands on my shoulders, to support himself. 'Look ole mate, I've got something to tell you. It comes out of the talks in Moscow between Sir Alec and you know whom. My boss. You're a journalist and you've got to hear it. It's for you to use as you like.'

He closed his eyes and put a finger to his lips and then to mine. He looked around to see that the others were not listening to our conversation.

'I hear you, Viktor,' I said. 'Speak, man. You can trust me to be discreet.'

He leaned very close. 'Listen carefully,' he said. 'It's a state secret. But I'm going to give it to you because I like you. We're mates. But don't tell anybody who you got it from otherwise... ' He held an imaginary pistol to the side of his head and pulled the trigger.

'That's right, Viktor,' I said. 'Good mates. So... what's the story?'

He pulled himself up. 'John, John,' he said. 'What we've been telling Sir Alec is this... The Soviet Union... the Soviet Union is for peace... The Soviet Union wants to be friends... peace and friendship... peaceful coexistence... *détente*... no war...'

It was as though conveying the Soviet Union's worst-kept secret to me had lifted a burden from his shoulders. He sighed and suddenly collapsed into a chair and closed his eyes.

'Thanks, Viktor,' I said. 'Thanks very much. That's nice to know. That's important. Leave it to me. I know how to handle it. I'll write it.'

⁂

Later Viktor made up for all that Sovietspeak tosh by giving me a good story. He showed me a piece of wood and lowering his voice he said: 'Have a look at this.' It was about a foot long, some six inches

253

across and three or four inches thick and it was once painted white. 'So what', I said.

'That piece of wood,' he said almost triumphantly, 'was part of the door the last Tsar and his family passed as they were taken into the cellar in Ipatiev House in Yekaterinburg in 1918. And we all know what happened next. They were all shot dead by the execution squad.'

'How did you come by this?' I asked him.

'Well,' he said. 'Quite simply the Ipatiev House is no more. It has been pulled down, levelled. It was a sort of historical-Revolutionary museum but people were treating it as a kind of memorial to the Tsar and his family. So it had to go – and I managed to get my hands on a bit of it as a souvenir.'

Much later, ACC, it became a major place of pilgrimage when the impressive Church on the Blood was built on the site and dedicated to the Romanov family.

✺🙂✺

I saw President Charles de Gaulle in action in Moscow, the only time I have been in awe and overwhelmed by the personality of a visiting VIP. He sent the comrades reeling and they may even have regretted inviting him. Their idea was to woo France into greater independence from the Western Alliance and they laid on very special treatment for him – he became the first non-Russian to be taken to Baikonur to see a Soviet space satellite blasted into orbit.

The most extraordinary event in his visit, however, was when, after talks with Brezhnev, he was taken on a tour of the Moscow City Hall. But when he got there, he said he wanted to address the people from a balcony. By now, some 6,000 Russians had gathered, and not all them were rent-a-crowd either, bringing Gorky Street to a stop.

'Mon Général' appeared on the same balcony where Lenin had harangued the masses during the Revolution and where a microphone had magically been installed. The moment he started to speak in French, there was a terrifying flash of lightning, a tremendous clap of thunder and the heavens opened. As the Russians say, it rained like water from a pail. It was the worst rainstorm to hit the city for years.

You could see the wet clothes clinging to the bodies of the crowd, and de Gaulle, who was seventy-five, was also exposed to

254

the downpour. Rain dripped off his *képi* and ran down his face. He ignored it and continued to speak concluding, mischievously: 'Long live Russia. Long live friendship between the peoples of France and Russia.'

Nobody apparently had told him he was visiting the Union of Soviet Socialist Republics. But I wondered: was the old boy being his usual provocative self? Or did he have an insight into the collapse of Communism and the end of the USSR?.

Something, perhaps, to do with *Après moi, le déluge?*

21 – Sex and the Married KCMG

The British Embassy in Moscow is a grand and elegant yellow and white mansion, built for a wealthy sugar baron some one hundred years ago. Lovingly restored and looked after by a succession of British ambassadors, it has one of the finest ballrooms in the capital, white and gold like a set from *War and Peace*, surely the greatest and longest film ever made. Romantic tales are linked to this room, such as the time when a British parliamentary delegation was dining there one evening and a Russian naval officer, acting as an aide, was called to the telephone. It was from his mistress in St Petersburg telling him their affair was over. Without replacing the receiver the officer drew his pistol and shot himself in the head.

For years the Embassy was an irritant to the Soviet government. From some points on his Kremlin estate, Stalin could see the Embassy with a large Union flag fluttering above it, and one of the final acts of his rule on Christmas Eve in 1952, was to order Britain to find another residence. He died. So we stayed put, refusing newer, larger and better sites offered.

It has a most splendid view of the city. Across the river is the high bank of the Kremlin with its red-brick battlements, and you can count the thirty gold cupolas of the cathedrals and churches, marvel at the soaring pinnacle of the Ivan Veliky Bell Tower, admire the façade of the great Kremlin Palace. I've spent a good many man-hours in the Embassy, attempting to wrest secrets from Her Majesty's servants, enjoying their hospitality, and all the time enjoying this matchless view.

News gathering in Moscow was never easy in those days, especially when it involved your own side. After all, the Cold War raged for much of the time. Our beleaguered men in Moscow were continually on guard against being penetrated by the KGB, and their caution was extended to include relations with British journalists. Some ambassadors were of the old school who believed that never, under any circumstances, should a journalist be trusted, and certainly he should never be told anything of any importance. For why? For because he might put what you told him in the newspaper, God forbid!, upsetting delicate, desperately important negotiations, and causing the Foreign Office in London to come down on the Embassy like a ton of bricks. Be damned to the great British public's right to know! Others didn't like us for our personal habits – we drank too much, mixed with Russians too freely, scrounged and didn't treat diplomats with the respect they deserved. Which was all true.

An ambassador I never liked was Sir Geoffrey Harrison. One of his first acts when he took over the embassy was to close the doors of the embassy shop to the small British press *corps*; I told him that this was unfriendly. Admittedly, it was a privilege, albeit a small one, but in those years the shop that the embassy ran in its basement was a life-saver to many of us, especially those with children. The Soviet Union was a land of shortages of almost everything and diplomats and their wives imported virtually everything they ate or used – from cornflakes to toilet paper. This saved them having to shop and rub shoulders with the natives, but in any case there was nothing to buy.

We did the best we could from the local market and Brenda made splendid stews. Another dish she perfected was fried crab balls, but it was not easy finding tins of the wonderful, meaty Kamchatka crab. There was bread, including the superb black variety, in those Khrushchev years, but there were also bread queues. If anybody told us they were visiting Moscow and asked us what we would like, we would urge them to smuggle in a pound or two of sausages, or tomatoes, or a pair of kippers, or a jar of coffee, or some bacon, or a pork pie. If they dared, because indeed it was a criminal offence to bring meat products, vegetables or plants into the USSR, along with guns, roubles and drugs. Customs officers at Moscow airport must have seized and consumed as many English bangers as they did dirty films and books.

Meanwhile, the basement of the embassy was an Aladdin's cave. A shop, known as the Commissariat, opened to sell food to the staff and once a week to the tiny British community. Here was nearly everything, from fresh meat and milk to tinned or packaged food, or toiletries. And not forgetting duty-free Scotch at 5 shillings a bottle, and Soviet vodka for half a crown, so cheap in fact, that if you were short of anti-freeze you would pour a couple of bottles in the car's radiator.

Sir Geoffrey threw us out. Goods sold there, said he, were intended for the use of diplomats and, anyway, the Russians threatened

21. The old British Embassy directly across from the Kremlin and the former mansion of a merchant Pavel Kharitonov. Despite being inefficient and outdated, it was the cosy home of MI6 in the Cold War struggle against the KGB. The new embassy opened in 2000 is on Smolenskaya Embankment.

to close the shop down entirely – by being awkward over deliveries from Britain – if the handful of British journalists were not barred. I never accepted this and told him so. The reason was that Harrison didn't like us. And he didn't like us coming and going in the Embassy because, as he often reminded his staff, we were 'security risks'.

We protested about the ban as being unfriendly to the British community which, in those days, was really no more than us. So they did us a favour. As we were still the Queen's subjects, a special concession was made. Once a year at Christmas, we could order a turkey. More than that, with some trimmings, i.e. a pound of sausages or Brussels sprouts or a jar of cranberry sauce (but not all three). And we were warned – don't, whatever you do, tell anybody else, like the Russians, and certainly don't share any of the turkey with them. Otherwise the privilege might be withdrawn... old boy.

Needless to say, the United States Embassy was not going to be dictated to by the Soviet Foreign Ministry and the KGB as to who could, or could not, use their shop. American correspondents were always made welcome, even when the hard-currency shops began opening in Moscow in the 1980s, selling food, unobtainable elsewhere and affecting the way foreigners lived and worked in the capital.

So Sir Geoffrey very much got off on the wrong foot as far as we were concerned. Tall, suave and chinless, he made it pretty clear that we were a nuisance. Much, much later, it emerged how much of a nuisance we might have been. Because Sir Geoffrey had been naughty and, had we got wind of his behaviour, he might have been embarrassed, if not publicly disgraced, at the very end of his career.

Not for the first time, and decidedly not for the last, sex reared its head with a man in a position to have known better. In this case, sex with a Russian lady. More than that, sex with a Russian lady who did his washing, ironed his shirts and made his bed. And who also had to report on his extra-marital activity to our old friends in the KGB.

Galya was (perhaps still is) a terrific-looking woman and in a very Russian way, which can be summed up – she was blonde and buxom. When George Brown, Foreign Secretary in the 1960s, and a renowned slap-and-tickle man, stayed at the Embassy he was captivated by the lady. After a hard day's negotiating and several G & Ts he was incorrigible.

260

Soviet foreign policy was being discussed when Galya entered the Blue Room with coffee and brandy, wearing a tight little black dress and white apron. Leaping to his feet, George gave Galya a big hug, and then a kiss, saying. 'That's a lot better. I've always wanted to do that to a Russian lass.' I thought at the time that the ambassador was giving his Foreign Secretary a funny look.

I somehow doubt if the Foreign Office file on Sir Geoffrey will be made public. But this was a classic honey trap set by the KGB. There were even photographs of Sir Geoffrey and Galya when they took that romantic, overnight express train to Leningrad for a cultural weekend.

When the crisis over Czechoslovakia blew up, the KGB began making Sir Geoffrey aware that they knew his maid was performing extra services at the Embassy when it closed for the day. They had photographs of the couple making love in the residence's laundry which, if nothing else, showed just how good the KGB was at its job. It was the time of the Prague Spring and the Kremlin was becoming concerned, about to make up its mind what to do about it. So the KGB went to work, suggesting that Britain's ambassador in the Soviet Union should be much more sympathetic to Soviet aims in Czechoslovakia, i.e. maintaining Warsaw Pact unity and Soviet hegemony in Eastern Europe. And he should tell the Foreign Office as much.

Realizing the game was up and he had been stupid, Sir Geoffrey confessed all to a gob-smacked Foreign Office and returned to London. At the time it was thought he had been withdrawn as a sign of Britain's disapproval of the Soviet invasion. That wasn't the case. And what went unnoticed was that he did not pay the traditional call on the Queen before going into retirement.

I was told about Sir Geoffrey's affair shortly after his distinguished diplomatic career came to end. But he kept his secret from the media for thirteen years. Then he complained he had been stabbed in the back – quite deliberately. Not by me – the source was Harold Wilson's circle.

Galya was fired by the new British ambassador. Later, a Russian told me that she had not only been working for the KGB, but she had been the sister of an infamous intelligence officer, Lt. Commander Eugene Ivanov, who had been involved in the so-called Profumo affair in London a few years earlier. And that she had given birth to twin boys who resembled their father...

❧❧❧

I suffered the ultimate disgrace of a British journalist in Moscow – being banned from the embassy, told never to darken its doors as long as the ambassador was Sir Terence Garvey. It was a pity, because Sir Terence was an able and experienced diplomat – an obituary described him as an inspired draughtsman of crisp and timely despatches and telegrams – and a nice man.

A couple of paragraphs in the Peterborough column of the *Daily Telegraph* would have had me on the rack if the embassy had had one. It was winter. Harold Wilson was poised to visit Moscow to smooth out the ripples caused by the expulsion of the 105 Soviet spies. He flew to Moscow with a large pack of hacks and stayed at the British Embassy.

The wife of one of Sir Terence's diplomats told me of Lady Garvey's determination to brighten up the Embassy during those gloomy winter days with masses of flowers. Which was not an easy thing to do in the 1970s. Harsh weather bought chaos to the Soviet flower supply and if the growers could not get their supplies to Moscow, prices went through the roof. This happened that year. Roses and carnations were costing more than a £1 a stalk and even then, they were hard to find. So, according to my informant, Lady Garvey had shopped around. When she discovered one of the Russian staff at the Embassy grew flowers in a greenhouse, her problem was solved. I thought it was worth a mention – it would do no harm telling Britons that their Embassy in Moscow was not going to waste its money on buying expensive flowers for its prime minister to sniff if he noticed them at all.

The item read: 'Mr Wilson's return-lunch to the Russians on the eve of his departure from Moscow next Monday is causing some problems for Lady Garvey... She has personally searched the Moscow markets in the last few days for flowers at a reasonable price. Appalled to find that carnations cost the equivalent of £1 each – a sum she considers too high for the Foreign Office purse – she has managed to find a Russian working for the Embassy who has promised to provide roses at twenty-five pence a stem.'

Pretty innocuous I would have thought. Certainly I had no wish to upset the ambassador and the embassy – don't spit in the well, as the Russians say, you might want to drink from the water. But that night at a party given for the visiting journalists by the British Embassy's press secretary, Nigel Broomfield, I learned that the item had not gone down well with the Garveys. Ironically, the journalists had not wanted to attend the party: they had only a couple of nights in Moscow and were planning to go on the razzle rather than be entertained by a Foreign Office mandarin. I pleaded with them to have drinks and a meal with Nigel Broomfield and got them to his home.

Nigel took me aside. He was white-faced and clearly disturbed. 'The ambassador has seen the piece in the *Telegraph*. He knows you did it. He is furious.'

'Come off it, Nigel,' I said, 'You can't mean it. What's his gripe?'

'It is insulting both to him and Lady Garvey. It suggests they were too mean to buy flowers at the market price. But that is no longer important,' he said, and added portentously, 'more than that, he has told me to tell you that you are banned from the Embassy. If you do show your face anywhere near it, you will be ejected.'

'Thank you,' I said. 'You have just given me another item for the Peterborough column.'

'Maybe,' he said,' but that is the last time you get anything from me. In fact, if I had known about the piece before I issued invitations, you would have been off the list, anyway.' Finally, he added: 'I never wanted to be a press attaché. I don't like the press. I never have. I never will.'

Of course it was soon forgotten. Many times since then I have visited the Embassy and been wined and dined there by the ambassador. Nigel Broomfield survived the incident too, got his KCMG, and became an Ambassador to Bonn.

※❦※

Most British ambassadors to Moscow I have known have been likeable, unpompous, shrewd observers of the Soviet scene. Also, unlike American ambassadors, they spoke passable and often very good Russian. One American ambassador had considerable trouble walking into his own Embassy. When Soviet police stopped him, he insisted on saying: '*Ya amerikanski potom*'. The more he repeated it, the more they resisted. He should have said '*posol*' the Russian word for ambassador, and not '*potom*' which means '*then*.'

Our men in Moscow, who knew how to deal with the Russians, included Frank Roberts, nicknamed the 'Clockwork Mouse' on account of his diminutive stature and inexhaustible energy. At a Kremlin reception I saw Khrushchev go up to him, apologize for a speech he had just made – about Britain being a mangy lion who had lost his teeth and tail – and pick him off the ground in a bearhug. Another was Howard Smith, who did something unique when he told the Kremlin he was leaving his Moscow post having been appointed head of MI5 – a fact withheld from the British public and press. A third was Sir Curtis Keeble, who once told me he was sorry, but he wasn't a ball of fire and couldn't therefore promise to provide exciting news stories.

It had to be tongue-in-cheek because he was a fund of good stories about his spell in Russia during the boring Brezhnev years. One, was the day he left the Rolls-Royce at the embassy and drove to Suzdal, a tourist town 120 miles outside of Moscow, in his Range Rover.

As he was locking the vehicle in what seemed to be a car park, an old man with a severe limp hopped towards him. He didn't say a word – just beckoned with his index finger for the Ambassador to follow him. They went to a small tumbledown hut where the man ordered the ambassador to sit down in an old and greasy chair.

Sir Curtis declined. 'You do what you are told,' said the old man. 'Don't argue. We are going to sort you out, if takes all day.' The parking attendant opened a cupboard and got out an exercise book and a book of receipts.

'Name?'

'Keeble.' The old man slowly wrote the name down.

'Nationality?'

'*Anglichanin.*'

'Passport.'

'Not got it with me,' said Sir Curtis who couldn't see why his diplomatic passport had anything to do with parking. The old man was not happy with this, so Sir Curtis produced the vehicle's technical passport. Very slowly the old man read it until he was satisfied. He then asked: 'Make of vehicle?'

'Range Rover.'

The old man had not heard of the name before. 'No such vehicle,' he said.

At this point another man entered the hut and he was drunk. He joined in the conversation. 'That's right,' he said. 'There is no such thing as a...' He couldn't pronounce it either.

They showed off their knowledge of foreign cars. They were not – they wanted him to know – Russian village idiots. They rattled off the cars they had seen and ticketed... 'Fords, Volkswagens, Mercedes, Volgas, Zhugalis...'

Suddenly the drunk, who has been trying to read the technical passport, shouted triumphantly: 'The make of the car is here. It's a Gerbert, of course, we've had them before in Suzdal.'

The drunk had seen the ambassador's first Christian name on the technical passport. It was Herbert the 'H' in the Russian language is replaced by a 'G'. The two Russians were delighted at cracking the problem. There was no diplomatic incident and Russian honour was satisfied. The ambassador got a ticket to park. Suzdal, a treasury of architectural monuments of the thirteenth to seventeenth centuries, had seen its first Gerbert.

✵⟊⟊⟊✵

British military attachés would travel a lot in the Soviet Union too, and many of them liked some fun. If they could, they caught trains to outlandish places and spent the trip looking out of the window in the hope of catching a glimpse of a Foxhound or a Galosh or a Gazelle or perhaps a Pill Box radar, anything faintly military that would justify getting out of Moscow. They were often in danger – the KGB didn't think twice about roughing them up if they got too nosey, and they were sometimes expelled, usually as a *quid pro quo* for us tossing out a Soviet military intelligence officer for being too brazen in Portsmouth or elsewhere.

I never spied with Air Commodore Ted Williams, senior military attaché at the British Embassy, and he never shared his top secrets with me. But we once met in a bar in Pushkin Street down the road from the Bolshoi Theatre, and that was a pretty nasty experience. Called the Yama, or the *Pit*, it literally was that; but I had seen the queue from the road and thought this was a slice of Soviet life worth looking at.

Ted was a snappy dresser and distinguished looking, and he stood out as we joined the queue to feed a twenty-kopek piece into the automatic gate. The price of admission included a sausage, or a plate of shrimps and a slice of bread. A pint of beer was twenty kopeks and it was served from an *automat* into a glass, which you had to find and clean yourself. The trick, we learned, was to use empty milk cartons.

We got our beer and joined the workers at small chest-high tables. The tables and the floor were covered with crumbs, shrimp-heads, bits of sausage and spilt beer. The company was exclusively male, and there was a strong smell of sweat, cigarette smoke and urine. BCC, this was Moscow's most popular bar, and it was grim.

We had scarcely begun to drink when two uniformed policemen entered the bar, checking passes and driving licences of the drivers. But not ours. We were ignored; we may not have been there. There was a fair bit of grumbling from some of the drinkers and there were many references to mothers. What was it all about? A crackdown on drinking and driving? A hunt for villains? Or was it related to the presence of a Western military attaché? Was he meeting Russians in a bar, chatting with them in the hope of gleaning state secrets? Or was the KGB concerned about our safety – catching a dreadful disease from the dirty glasses?

We stumbled up the steps and out into the daylight, declaring the place lived up to its name and really was the *pits*, swearing never to return. Never were the warm vodka and the cold, tired chips of the National Hotel restaurant more welcome.

22 – Saying No with Bare Hands

It was a shock to the system to hear it said about me, and to my face. 'You are behaving worse... much worse... than the KGB,' shouted my hero, Alexander Solzhenitsyn. He was looking straight at me and he was a very angry Nobel Prize winner, an enraged writer of titantic achievements.

He hadn't finished. 'Look at you. It's disgraceful. It's a scandal. You are walking all over somebody's garden. You are crushing down plants, destroying shrubs. You are killing living things. Clear off, all of you.'

True I was standing on some plants in a Swiss gentleman's front garden, but it was an accident. I had been pushed willy-nilly onto a flower bed by other hacks. We had surged forward across a front lawn when Solzhenitsyn emerged from the house in Zurich where he was staying after being expelled from the Soviet Union. Being well to the front, so as not to miss anything the Great Oracle said, I inadvertently stamped on some plants and shrubs.

It was unfair of Solzhenitsyn to equate our behaviour with that of the KGB. But it was understandable. Solzhenitsyn had a thing about the KGB. After all, he had spent eight years in the GULAG and the KGB had done its best to crush him. Only a few days before he had been arrested, stripped, interrogated, held incommunicado, accused of treason, threatened with execution and forcibly thrown out of the country – a fate he once described as spiritual castration – like a character in one of his books. The KGB was responsible for all of this.

Later, during those mad days when we chased him all over Switzerland, he referred several times to his old tormentors, comparing them almost favourably with French *paparazzi*, refusing to leave him in peace. At least I was only going about my lawful occupation of getting as close to the man as I reasonably could.

Solzhenitsyn's meeting with the Western media must have been bewildering and downright terrifying. One moment he was sitting in a quiet cell in Lefortovo, the KGB interrogation centre, the next he was the centre of a media circus, hounded by a crowd of baying journalists, persistent photographers and determined cameramen. He wasn't used to it. From time to time the Soviet press had slandered and abused him, but it was under total control. And, more or less, in Moscow he had got away with using Western journalists as tools he could turn to in an emergency, but otherwise ignored.

When he was stripped of his citizenship, exiled and put on a plane for West Germany, there was a general election campaign in full swing in Britain and I was seconded to the paper's news desk, sent to cover a press conference given by the Scottish Nationalists. Within minutes of the Solzhenitsyn story breaking on the wires, Ricky Marsh, the Foreign Editor, phoned the news editor.

'Solzhenitsyn's been exiled. I'm sending John Miller to West Germany. Tell him to come and get some money fastest,' he said.

News Desk looked up the list of engagements. 'He's not around,' he was told. 'He's covering the Scottish Nationalist Party.'

Mild-mannered Marsh exploded: 'You stupid buggers! You've sent him to Scotland? Well for Christ's sake get him back. I want him in Germany now... today.'

When they checked around they found the press conference was at Euston Station, London. Another reporter was dispatched to replace me while I went off to find Solzhenitsyn, Russia's most famous living novelist.

That night I got to Langenbroich, a hamlet in the Eifel hills, west of Bonn, where Solzhenitsyn was staying with Heinrich Böll, the West German writer, but so had hordes of journalists and cameramen from all over the world. We staked out the farmhouse, which was bathed in the bright light of arc-lamps, prowled around the house, peered into the back windows, dozed in our cars or looked for a bar.

There wasn't one.

Solzhenitsyn had made a short statement before I arrived and concluded by asking the press to go away and leave him alone. Shrimps might whistle, as the Russians say. The next day he moved on to Zurich with the world's press in hot pursuit. He insisted on going by train, so several hundred journalists joined him. I flew to Zurich and then took a train to one of the stations on his route. It worked, and I boarded the express from Cologne and worked through it to find where there was a crush of hacks.

There was no chance that anyone would be able to sit with him in his compartment and talk about those terrifying experiences in Moscow, when he was arrested after taking his son for a walk and dragged off to Lefortovo. But I did exchange a few – and for me – memorable words with him when the train arrived in Zurich to scenes of pandemonium that not even another historically well-known arrival, that of Lenin's at the Finland Station to get the Revolution rolling, could equal. When the train stopped, I was wedged up against the lavatory in the corridor and right near the door from which he had to leave. Down on the platform, hundreds of Swiss commuters and journalists pushed and fought to catch a glimpse of the author – now front-page news round the world, except, of course, in the USSR – or simply to get to safety.

Incredulous, Solzhenitsyn watched the scene unfolding. Then he turned and fixed me with his eyes – they were stunning, a very brilliant, intense blue, the like of which I have never seen before or since. These were eyes that could do the talking for him, but he said in his pure and genuine Russian: 'Terrible. This is terrible. I never expected anything like this. Can't something be done about it? It is not safe for some of those people on the platform.'

I pointed to the train door on the other side. 'That is the only other way of leaving the train, and you cannot go that way. People out there want to see you. They respect you. They welcome you to Switzerland. They applaud you.'

'That's right,' he said.

We opened the train door with difficulty and he stepped down on the platform. Cursing in several languages, television cameramen fought the police. Women screamed as they were pushed aside and trampled on. Solzhenitsyn was swept along the platform to his car and after he had got into it with difficulty, we chased him for two miles through Zurich to a block of flats in the suburbs.

It was rush hour and we created chaos, refusing to stop at red lights, snarling up traffic for miles around, travelling at outrageous speeds and performing all sorts of dangerous manoeuvres, so as to keep Solzhenitsyn in our sights.

Solzhenitsyn's mistake was not to hold a press conference, which would almost certainly have satisfied most of the pack and got rid of some of them. But he didn't, so we staked out the flat where he was staying, ensuring that the silly game of cat-and-mouse continued.

Door-stopping Solzhenitsyn in Switzerland was a full-time job. You had to lay siege to his flat for most of the daylight hours – you couldn't turn up and find he had gone off God knows where. So I followed him when he went shopping, as he walked in the street, when he took a tram ride and when he went to the cinema. Not surprisingly, he became more and more angry.

Once he lost his temper and shook a suitcase at me and a bunch of photographers, shouting: 'You have pursued me all the way from West Germany and I cannot stand any more of it. Leave me alone. I am a human being and what you are doing is an affront.' I agreed with him

Later, I went back to Zurich when he was reunited with his wife and family. At the airport I asked him; 'Can we say it is all's well that ends well?' – a phrase which trips easily off the tongue in Russian. And he replied: 'Yes, you can say that. You can see we are all together again.'

I never had the interview I had always wanted with Solzhenitsyn, for all sorts of reasons, one being that in Moscow you were carefully checked out by his friends before you met him and I had been a friend of Victor Louis, whom he detested.

So I still haven't had that chance to decide whether he was the giant figure on the stage of Russia's tragedy or a reactionary crank; the voice of Russia's conscience or the spokesman of Russian nationalism; unquestionably the greatest living Russian writer or an unparalleled producer of historical sermons. (ACC, and after twenty years in exile, he went back to Mother Russia.) After all, as the Russians say, to be a guest is fine, but home is best. He died there in 2008, aged eighty-nine.

The other super dissident was Andrei Sakharov, and he was an extraordinary, as well as a lovely, man. Unlike Solzhenitsyn, a commanding personality, Sakharov was shy, unpretentious, homely. A gentle old cat springs to mind when I try and recall the times I saw Sakharov in his flat on the Garden Ring. He would sit perfectly still for minutes on end, head rolled thoughtfully to one side as he studied a newcomer, legs crossed and with his hands crossed and resting just above his knees.

He was a gentle, kind and reflective man, modest in gesture, dress and surroundings, who invented his country's hydrogen bomb in a programme ordered by Stalin and controlled by Beria. 'Father of the Soviet H-Bomb' was the label we fixed to him and, typically, he always denied it.

'I was just one of several scientists working on the project,' he would say admonishingly. But whatever he did or didn't do for the Soviet nuclear arsenal, he became a VIP. Never permitted personal fame, he received the Stalin and Lenin Prizes and was thrice named a Hero of Socialist Labour (even Brezhnev only gave himself two such awards), and there were all the other perks of the *nomenklatura*, the twenty million or so top people that ran the Soviet Union, such as the chauffeur-driven car, the dacha and a big salary. When he was thirty-two he became the youngest member of the prestigious Academy of Sciences.

At about the time I began working in Moscow, and when he had access to the pinnacle of the Soviet system, he personally took on Nikita Khrushchev over the decision to carry out an atmospheric test on an extremely powerful one-hundred-megaton hydrogen bomb. Khrushchev told him to stick to research and not meddle in policy matters – it was necessary to match the imperialists, bomb for bomb, and protect the Motherland.

Next, Sakharov 'came out' as a dissident by writing a letter of protest to Brezhnev – not that he would have received it – over the KGB's arrest of four young people for so-called anti-Soviet activity. Came an essay establishing his liberal humanistic credentials: mankind can be assured of a safe future only if Communism and capitalism converge, and there was an end to the arms race. Having amassed a huge fortune, some 150,000 roubles, he donated it to the Red Cross for cancer research – it was blood money. Later, he regretted what he had done – the money could have been used much better by helping dissidents who had lost their jobs or their flats.

Sakharov was taken off secret work – you can't really blame them – and he became more and more involved in the dissident cause. When I and other Western journalists were beating a path to his flat, he was effectively the head of the activist dissident community. Periodically, he issued statements about cases of human rights violations or instances where political dissidents were locked up in psychiatric hospitals.

Going to see Andrei Sakharov was a remarkable occasion. You were being received in a Russian home – and that was rare! – and much more than that, you were sitting having tea with one of the great humanists of our time. It was a two-roomed flat he lived in with Yelena Bonner, his second wife, and typically, it was unpretentious. One room was dominated by a large double-bed. During the day the bedclothes were removed and this room became the living room, where he would welcome visitors. There was a glass-fronted bookcase, a typewriter, an old-fashioned gramophone. Once, I used the Sakharov lavatory and you could scarcely get in the door for stacked suitcases, two pairs of cross-country skis and ice-skates hanging on a hook in the wall.

It was always tea time at the Sakharovs, and usually taken sitting at an enamel-topped table in the small and cluttered kitchen, remarkable for the number of fallen wall-tiles that had been unsuccessfully stuck in place with scotch-tape. I never cared for Sakharov's tea. It was served Russian-style, plain or with redcurrant jam. Sakharov also offered you a rather nasty tea with chunks of hard green apple, which I feared would upset the stomach. He poured his hot tea into a saucer – like my granddad did – and blew gently on it before sipping it. Most Russians drink tea accompanied by loud noises, as though it was soup. Sakharov had one idiosyncrasy – he liked everything warmed up, including herring and Russian-salad.

It was a very Russian ceremony. You were welcomed, made to feel at home, part of the family. There was no bullshit, no propaganda, no whingeing and no humbug. And the Sakharovs were not afraid.

What came across when meeting Sakharov was his utter integrity, his generosity of spirit, his absolute independence of mind and his simple kindness for the victims of the Soviet system.

In the living-room, he would hold the press conferences that so annoyed the KGB and the Soviet Foreign Ministry. Invariably he had on a tattered sweater – he may not have had a suit until much later, when he became an MP – over a cowboy shirt and faded blue-jeans. He either padded around the flat in stockinged feet or badly

272

worn leather bedroom slippers. His domed, bald head and cracked spectacles gave him the appearance of a slightly dotty professor.

But when he told you in his flat, quiet voice with its slight lisp about some injustice or called-for reforms or argued for *détente* or greater freedom, and looked at you with his sad compassionate eyes, you knew you were in the presence of a man of remarkable inner strength. A man who could never be stifled.

They tried to, though; my God, they did! When he won the Nobel Peace Prize, the Soviet press predictably whipped itself into a frenzy of mendacity and slander. He was referred to as a 'laboratory rat', although of course Soviet readers were not told what sort of laboratory he had worked in. Another newspaper of the officially-atheist state managed to introduce the Bible into an article comparing the Nobel Gold Medal and the £60,000 awarded to Sakharov with Judas and the thirty pieces of silver.

Sakharov heard the attacks on him while sunning on a beach in Sochi, listening as he was discussed and denounced as a traitor by those nearby. He asked some of them what this Sakharov had actually done; but they either didn't know or were uninterested. His wife hustled him away before he said any more.

Sakharov was a very serious man but not without humour and once he told me a joke at his own expense. Two Soviet scientists were discussing him. One said to the other that he couldn't agree with what Sakharov said about the Soviet Union's rotten medical care and educational system.

'Why not?' the other scientist asks. 'Do you think our medical service is all right?'

'Certainly not.'

'Well, do you think our education is any good either?'

'No, I don't,' says the first scientist. 'If anything, Sakharov could have spoken out even more strongly about how bad it is.'

'So what's the problem?'

'I'm afraid,' the first scientist says, 'that I cannot go along with a man who insists on throwing himself in front of a steamroller.'

Which is what he did and why they treated him so shamefully, and for so long. He took a lot of punishment, including having a

KGB sponsored visit from two Arabs; they were members of the Black September terrorist group and suggested he stopped saying anything nice about Israel or else they would kill him.

Finally, they sentenced him to a lifetime in exile in Gorky, the armaments city closed to foreigners. It was a wicked act and typical of the time, but they got away with it, up to a point. Even there, they made life hard for him, stealing his personal papers and documents, drugging him on one occasion, seizing and opening his mail, depriving him of a telephone. Visitors would have to show their papers to a policeman on guard round-the-clock at his door. The idea was to shut him up and they more or less succeeded.

He went on a hunger strike – not for himself, but in the hope of forcing the Kremlin to allow his wife to go abroad for medical treatment. They could not let him to die in Gorky, so they brutally force-fed him, and stories began circulating that he was seriously unwell. It was this development which tripped up Victor Louis, who foolishly became involved in selling to the West a KGB film of Sakharov in internal exile. It may well have been that he had little option.

It could be argued that Western television companies should not have spent tens of thousands of dollars buying KGB material of this kind. But, of course, they were quite prepared to do the KGB's work and contribute to its coffers if there was a scoop in the offing.

Walking in the woods near his dacha, I taxed Victor about the footage of Sakharov in Gorky, and told him that it was a nasty and disgraceful operation. He wouldn't admit it was a KGB film and I never expected him to. Nor would he agree that Sakharov was a great man and the treatment meted out to him by the Soviet state was abhorrent.

But Victor did let something slip that day – that there were people at the top who were against the exiling of Sakharov and that one day he would be released. He spoilt what he was telling me by portraying Sakharov's wife as a wicked woman who manipulated Sakharov and led him astray, suggesting that the dissident leader could be freed quicker if only she curbed her anti-Sovietism.

That she was never going to do. She went on encouraging him to speak out whenever he could against injustice, as she did herself. But what Victor forecast came to pass when Mikhail Gorbachev made the remarkable gesture of personally telephoning Sakharov to summon him back to the world, after some seven years away. At that point I knew that Gorbachev himself shared some of Sakharov's qualities of courage, integrity and generosity; that he really was prepared to tackle the question of human rights and create a 'law-based society'. More than that, much more than that, Gorbachev's telephone call signified that the Soviet Union was never going to be the same again.

Sakharov returned as the conscience of the nation and his voice was impossible to stifle. They hadn't managed to break him with exile and harassment, though this and his protest hunger strikes and the subsequent forced-feeding undoubtedly shortened his life.

Captured on television for me and a hundred million viewers was that wonderful moment and extraordinary confrontation between Sakharov, the Russian Holy Man, and Gorbachev, the politician. At the end of an unprecedented debate in the Soviet parliament, Sakharov suddenly made his way uninvited to the rostrum. He had been given a bad time by many of the deputies who knew their time was up – they hated him for his utter refusal to tell lies in a country where despite glasnost, the truth was still obscured by the ghosts of millions of corpses and the need to talk in circumlocutions. Already he had incensed them by accusing Soviet helicopter-crews in Afghanistan of killing their comrades to prevent them being captured. But he didn't have very much serious evidence to back it up. Sakharov's mistake, as a politician, was a terrible error of judgement: Russians are nothing if not intensely patriotic, and here was someone insisting that our boys, *nashi rebiyata*, had murdered each other.

Looking quite impervious to his surroundings, as though he didn't hear the abuse hurled at him, he tried to speak above the hubbub – mostly on the theme of Gorbachev's failings and the Government's mistakes – and although he exceeded his allotted time, he refused to stop talking.

This was Gorbachev's show, however. As chairman he was charged with wrapping up the proceedings and sending everybody home satisfied. You could see him getting more and more fed up with this behaviour and he didn't like being ignored, either. Finally he snapped. 'Andrei Dmitrievich. *Vsyo! Vsyo!* (That's it! That's all!) Please respect the Congress...'

And Sakharov replied: 'Yes, I do. But I respect the people and those who listen to me more, and I respect mankind. I have a mandate that goes beyond this Congress.'

Of course, it was a stand-off between two great men. They respected each other. Russia needed them both. Six months later, after spending an evening with guests in the same modest flat that had served for so long as the centre for the fight for freedom and democracy in the Soviet Union, he said: 'I'm going to turn in now. Tomorrow is going to be a tough day. There is going to be a real fight in the Congress.' And those were his last words – he died in his sleep.

The next day, Gorbachev spoke movingly to the Parliament about Sakharov and said his memory would be cherished for ever in Russia's history. Gorbachev tasted power for another two years.

23 - Me and U-2

'A Lockheed U-2 spy plane,' it read, 'was presented by the US Air Force to the Imperial War Museum at Duxford, near Cambridge, yesterday.' A paragraph of just twenty-two words in a newspaper at the bottom of the page, but it was enough to send me scampering down memory lane.

Given that Duxford is in Cambridgeshire, and not in neighbouring Suffolk, it cannot be said accurately that the U-2 had come home after a lifetime of service in the frontline of the Cold War. Because it never flew from Duxford, a World War II base for American Thunderbolts, Mustangs and where the 'Old Groaner', Bing Crosby, was known from time to time to croon to assembled airmen.

But many years ago, as a cub reporter on a local newspaper, I had heard about one flying from an airfield in Suffolk. And for some time after that the huge dark wings of the U-2 cast a shadow over my life, as it did over the lives of many other people during the height of the confrontation between Communism and the West that marked the fifties and sixties.

For the U-2 was an extraordinary, perhaps even wonderful, aircraft. At the time, it was capable of aerodynamics no glider or jet had ever accomplished before. In the business it was known as the Black Lady, and it bore no markings. It had a wingspan of eighty feet, a speed of 500 miles an hour, a range of 2,600 miles and a ceiling of 70,000 feet. And it was equipped with high resolution cameras that could distinguish two men standing ten feet apart on the ground. The first aircraft was in service in 1956, just as I started work on a newspaper in a small Suffolk town.

It was the straight wide wings – to facilitate gliding flight and thereby preserve fuel – more than the sinister, black look of the aircraft which first caught the attention of the local people who worked at the US Air Force base at Lakenheath in the fearful fifties. There was the secrecy, too. Other aircraft, such as the early jet bomber, the B-47, were seen and heard, and raised little interest when they took off to fly along the rim of the Iron Curtain, showing the flag and intimidating the comrades, before screaming home for supper, thumping down on the runway, mission accomplished.

From the start the U-2 was different. They parked it in a hanger out of sight of the road. They guarded it twenty-four hours a day. When it flew, it took off and landed at night. And those in positions of authority brushed aside questions about the plane with a 'none-of-your-business' response. Or so I was told in the pub where I drank to pass away the time, put myself about, pick up the gossip, and write stories for the newspaper.

'It's like one of those German Horsa gliders used during the War,' said an informant, a man who had dropped over Arnhem, and never talked about it. 'It's weird. It makes a strange noise and its wheels fall away when it takes off. And it's secret. Top secret. Try asking them about it up at the base. Mark my words, they won't tell you anything.'

But he was wrong about that: the Americans at the base were polite and helpful and, for all they knew, I could have been a Soviet spy. After all, in those days there were a lot of English people speaking the language perfectly, and with much better accents than mine, who were working for the Kremlin.

More than that, they were prepared to give me some news when I told them I was a reporter for the *Thetford and Watton Times*, a weekly newspaper of some authority in those parts. They did need to refer my question to the base commander, but this was purely routine, of course, and they would call me back with something that would be publishable.

They did too. And it was. The U-2 was neither top secret nor merely hush-hush. It was only a new high altitude weather research aircraft and it was being tested under an openly announced programme.

But what about all that security... the special treatment... only flying at night... and so on? Well, Mr Miller, that is because the base tries to maintain one hundred per cent security all the time, and the aircraft works better at night. No, they couldn't invite me up to the base to have a look at it. Sorry, Mr Miller, but it had just flown away, wouldn't be back for sometime. Pakistan or some other faraway place was not mentioned.

That was fine. So read all about it: 'PLANE RUMOUR IS DEBUNKED: Nothing hush hush – a research machine' the *Thetford and Watton Times* told that little bit of the world centred on the Brecklands. Life went on. The high altitude weather research plane

Chinese Nationalist pilots had done when their aircraft 'flamed out' over China. Powers parachuted to earth where he was grabbed by some collective farm labourers and turned over to the military. As it later transpired, the CIA were not pleased that he had decided not to use the suicide pin, charged with shellfish toxin and hidden in a silver dollar, and had allowed himself to be captured.

Powers did not carry out orders – who would in such circumstances? – giving Khrushchev a wonderful opportunity to milk the flight for propaganda purposes. For crafty Khrushchev had not revealed that Powers was alive and well, being interrogated and singing like the proverbial canary.

So the CIA and the White House were wrong-footed and short of a creditable cover story. They got into a terrible mess, denying the U-2 was a spy plane, suggesting that a plane may have strayed off course and coming out with other daft statements, which were soon exposed as lies when Khrushchev stood up at another session of the Supreme Soviet a day or two later to tell the rest of the story.

Such as the fact that Powers had been caught red-handed. In the wreckage of the U-2, they had found a map with his flight plan and had developed the incriminating pictures he had taken from the air. They knew the plane's point of origin, its route, its destination and its mission. They were fed up with these overflights – as the old Russian proverb says, no matter how many times you fetch water from the well in the same pitcher, sooner or later the day will come when the pitcher breaks.

Khrushchev was funny with it, though. Ridiculing Powers's emergency equipment, he said the French gold francs were 'nicely wrapped in cellophane in the American style', there were the two gold watches and seven gold rings – 'perhaps the pilot should have flown higher, to Mars, where he was no doubt preparing to seduce Martian women?' And of the 7,500 roubles – 'had the pilot come to the Soviet Union to convert old roubles into new?'

There was much rough invective against America, too, and Khrushchev gave us several opportunities to hear him vent his anger. The wreckage of the U-2 was brought to Moscow and displayed in Gorky Park. This was the first and last time I got near to the U-2, and it was not a pretty sight, being in several parts and badly damaged,

281

having fallen from a great height. It was nothing at all like I had envisaged it when it was flying out of Lakenheath. In an official Soviet photo, I am seen looking closely at the tangled heap of metal that was once the fuselage.

More interesting was to observe Khrushchev in action, when he suddenly appeared in the park's chess pavilion where the wreckage was laid out. Holding an impromptu press conference, he leaped onto a whicker chair with such force that he could have gone through it. Then we heard him sound off about the CIA and the US military establishment, expecting the chair to collapse at any minute.

Khrushchev had tried hard to let Eisenhower off the hook by not blaming him personally for the flight. But, Ike let him down, and made him look a fool by breaking all the rules of diplomatic protocol and assuming personal responsibility. Yet he could be forgiven, after all, George Washington, the cherry tree, and telling a lie is a famous American story.

So the summit was doomed to failure. Khrushchev went to Paris, where he rampaged about France, ranting about the wickedness of the Americans. He had no intention of going through with the summit unless Eisenhower apologized. But the demands of American and Soviet dignity had become so great that Eisenhower simply could not do this. He did, however, announce that further U-2 flights had been cancelled.

This wasn't enough to satisfy Khrushchev. He commented: 'That's a lackey's way. When a gentleman slaps a lackey's face and then gives him a sixpence, the lackey at once says, "Thank you... But we know who we are and whom we represent".'

In Paris, Khrushchev appeared like many a Soviet Samson, intent on pulling the temple down around him, and the failure of the summit seemed to herald terrifying events to come. As it happened, his temper and the U-2 incident were not allowed to deflect the direction of Soviet policy towards a better accommodation with the West.

But Khrushchev always insisted that his political downfall dated from the shooting down. After that, he said, he never regained full control over the government, he had to pay more attention to what the Politburo and the military were saying. He had to share power with

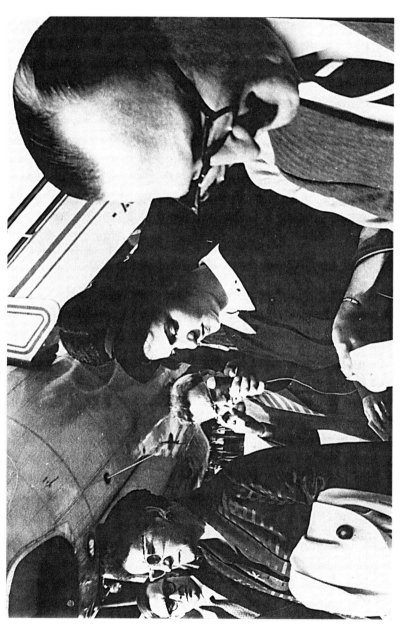

22. Mrs Barbara Powers arriving in Moscow for the trial of her husband, Francis Gary Powers, the U-2 pilot, in August 1960. Miller was there.

those who believed that only military clout would enable Moscow to deal with the West and, particularly, the United States.

One or two other people were hurt. Powers got a ten-year sentence for spying after a spectacular show trial in Moscow's House of Trade Unions, site of the purge trials of the 1930s. But within two years he was exchanged for the Soviet masterspy, Rudolf Abel, in one of the most dramatic East-West spy swaps ever made. In the end, Powers was never charged with failing to have committed suicide and was awarded the Intelligence Star, the CIA's highest award. There were medals too for several Soviet rocketeers and for a couple of air force officers who were never heard of then or later and may easily have been shot down by their own side while tailing the U-2 at a lower altitude. Fate caught up with Powers seventeen years later, when he was killed while piloting a helicopter for a Los Angeles television station.

Disgraced, my U-2 was more or less put out to grass.

Certainly it didn't dare make another overflight of the USSR, although one of the aircraft was used during the Cuban Missile Crisis the following year, and was shot down, killing the pilot.

By then a new generation of spies-in-the-skies was coming along. It was not only a question of other aircraft doing the job better and faster, but also the use of unmanned satellites hovering between 80 and 200 miles over the scene, surveying photographically even small objects and electronically recording sounds and impulses down to telephone-call level. Crammed with new marvels, they had names like Big Bird and Keyhole, and for years they have criss-crossed the skies, detecting nuclear-test explosions, rocket-launchings and troop movements.

Finally, with the end of the Cold War, the Americans and the Russians got together and began signing one disarmament treaty after another. Now American army intelligence officers turned inspectors can sit at the gates of factories that the U-2 flew over and had targeted, watching lorries leaving, and they have the right to examine any created object over a certain length, the length of a missile. As it happens, these factories now make washing machines and prams and vacuum cleaners – or that is what they should be doing.

And the U-2, the aircraft I never saw in the air and yet will never forget, had become a museum piece.

※꽃꽃꽃※

Not so. That was what I thought. But I was wrong. A week or two after writing the U-2 chapter, I was playing golf on Southwold Common with my friend Mac, who as a golfer is one of the finest cartoonists in Britain. I had rifled my drive down the second fairway and was poised to hit my second shot, so as to leave it lying up short of the bunkers in front of the hole. I pulled out my trusty Sundridge Technik 3-Wood and wound myself up.

At the top of the back-swing I heard a noise. An unusual droning noise. Not the sort of noise that the Tornadoes and the F-16s made, as they hurtled at a 1,000 feet across the golf course, scaring the dogs and the little old ladies and drowning out warning shouts of 'Fore' and Mac's inexhaustible supply of rude jokes. I looked up into the vast blue Suffolk sky – and there it was, flying rather slowly at a height of some 10,000 feet, with its long wings and its engines each side of the body. The hairs on the back of neck didn't act like they did that day in the Supreme Soviet, but I felt distinctly funny. There was no doubt in my mind what I was seeing. It was a U-2 up there.

'Mac,' I said. 'Mac, do you know anything about the U-2.'

'It's an Irish rock group,' he said. 'Very popular. Make a lot of money. Last big hit was Achtung Baby. And rather a bigger hit than anything you can manage with a golf club.'

'No, Mac, no!' I said excitedly. 'The U-2 is a beautiful and famous aeroplane. And there it is.' I pointed it out to him as it disappeared over the neighbouring village of Reydon. 'That's it! That's the real thing! The U-2. The world's most historic spy plane.'

But what was it doing flying over Southwold? The Cold War was over, so there were no Soviet nuclear submarines lying off the Suffolk coast. There were no military sites in the area. Was it interested in the nuclear power station at Sizewell? Curious about the new free-range pig farms opening up in the area? Puzzled about the ancient cannon sited on Southwold's sea shore and ready to tackle any foreign foe? Preoccupied over whether I had really seen a U-2, I promptly lost the game and handed over the £1 we played for, plus fifty pence for him being nearest to the hole on the ninth, and twenty pence for his birdie. Then I went to work.

At that time, the U.S. airforce base at Bentwaters was still functioning, although with the end of the Cold War the jet fighters based there had gone. I telephoned the base, told them I had seen an aircraft flying over Southwold golf course and asked: 'Could it have been a U-2.' Not flying from there, I was told. But it could have come from Alconbury in Oxfordshire. They gave me the number.

And the clock was turned back. I had a re-run of the conversation of thirty-six years earlier. Yes sir, they did have a U-2. No sir, they couldn't tell me what it did. But the Cold War is over, I told the young man. The U-2 was, is and will be, a spy plane. So it had to be spying on somebody or something.

He said he would call me back. And he did. My U-2 was on a training mission in accordance with NATO operational duties. There were several of them stationed at Alconbury and they had been there for a few years.

'The Base Commander,' he added ever so politely, 'has asked me personally to assure you, Sir, that if you did see a U-2 and we are not saying that you did or you did not, it would not have been... er... fulfilling intelligence tasks over Southwold. Have a good day!'

24 - A Very Russian Coup

Some things about the Soviet Union I got wrong. Mostly they were minor errors. I killed off the world's most skeletal-looking politician, Arvid Pelshe, a Latvian stooge, who became a member of the Politburo and head of one of the world's most boring committees – the Party State Control Commission. He was aged eighty-four and definitely unwell when I wrote his obituary. In fact, he didn't croak until nine months later. As the oldest member of the Politburo – he had known Lenin personally – he had a Red Square funeral which proved that someone loved him and may have kept him alive as long as possible.

Killing off prominent Soviet politicians for the sake it is not to be recommended, but in this case it was the result of being given a bum steer. Reuters, to its great embarrassment, mistakenly reported Nikita Khrushchev's death, sourcing it to a West German news agency citing a Soviet one. That caused ructions, the story briefly affected stock markets around the world. In the case of Pelshe, I was deliberately misled, but there was no question of anyone trying make to a quick buck. Kremlinologically speaking, a lobby wanted Pelshe declared dead – their man was ready for his job – and it was felt that my organ would serve the purpose nicely. Alternatively Pelshe's 'death' was meant as a reminder to all and sundry of the mortality of the gerontocracy running the country, and that the generation of the Revolution and World War II was on its way out. As it happened, no one appeared to take notice of the report greatly exaggerating Pelshe's death.

I was wrong, too, about the Soviet invasion of Czechoslovakia in 1968. It is easy, in retrospect, to see how. I was as naive, optimistic, and trusting, even with regard to the masters of the Soviet empire, as were the Czechoslovak Communist reformers. Like Andrei Sakharov and many others in the Soviet Union, I thought that the ghost of Stalin was unlikely to triumph once again and even that one of his heirs would resume the work that Khrushchev had started, developing a Soviet version of 'Socialism with a human face'. Which is precisely what happened some seventeen or so years later, when Mikhail Gorbachev came along.

For five months crises ebbed and flowed. Alexander Dubček – whom I tracked down many years later, when he was in internal exile, only to be warned off interviewing him by the Czech security police – basked in the moral splendour of the Prague Spring. This was a precocious attempt at perestroika and glasnost. Dubček really thought his country's renaissance was also doing a favour for the entire Communist Bloc, and that included the Soviet Union.

I summed up the situation in an leader-page article, doubting that a Soviet invasion was on the cards because life had moved on since the crushing of Hungarian resistance twelve years earlier. Then I turned out the light, closed the door of the office in 'Sad Sam' and took myself off to South Africa and a change of scenery.

Three days out from England and somewhere off the coast of West Africa, one August morning, the Windsor Castle's newspaper was pushed under the door of our cabin. The steward was about to bring morning tea, a read in bed was in order.

One glance at the headline *Russian Tanks Crush Prague Spring* and I didn't feel so good; and it wasn't due to sea-sickness either. A Warsaw Pact army of some 250,000 had gone in to put the uppity Czechoslovaks in their place. It was like firing a cannon at sparrows, as the Russians say. The Red Army met only with passive resistance. There was not much the Czechs could do about it. Come to that, nor could I, from somewhere in the Atlantic Ocean – a think-piece, datelined the Windsor Castle, about the use of Soviet power and attempts to reform Communism wasn't on.

I learned a lesson. Never to be bamboozled again by stuff and nonsense about Soviet Communism progressing irreversibly towards rationality, restraint and traditional norms in foreign policy, as well as towards a more human and responsive government of its own subjects. Never to lose sight of the fact that the Soviet state was a multi-national empire, in which harsh centralism was the simplest response to Nationalism stirring on the rim. Never to forget that the then ruling generation of Soviet politicians were a bunch of mediocrities who favoured repression, not reform. And in line with my theory that history turns on little events, I should not have ignored the sensational defeat of the all-powerful Soviet ice-hockey squad, largely formed from the Red Army team, by the Czechs in the Winter Olympics, a few months before the invasion. It prompted an explosion of joy in

Czechoslovakia, but enraged Brezhnev, a keen ice-hockey fan. And Russians were bad losers.

But the *coup* of August 1991, the three days that shook the world and which undid the October Revolution, I did get right. I saw it coming and said so in the *Herald*, the authoritative Scottish newspaper, exactly a week before it happened. And when it did, I knew it would fail.

I was in Moscow sniffing the air at my own expense a fortnight before the *coup*. And having breakfast one morning on the twelfth floor of a flat overlooking Komsomolskaya Square where three of the city's most important railway stations disgorge more than half-a-million people a day, I watched a military helicopter wapa-wapa-wapa its way over the roofs of central Moscow. It was a rare sight: I decided there and then that a *coup* was in the offing. Hunch, it may have been, but it was not difficult to back it up. There were rumours and warnings of a revolt against Gorbachev all over town. And he had taken himself off to the sun-drenched Crimea for his first holiday of a punishing year.

More than forty-five years ago, at the height of the Cold War, Nikita Khrushchev left Moscow for a holiday in his dacha by the sea. It was the biggest mistake of his life. His comrades in Moscow, disturbed by his tinkering with the old Stalinist system, patched up differences and decided to remove him. Khrushchev heard rumours of the intrigue and summoned the odious Semichastny, the KGB boss, to his holiday dacha. 'You're just a piece of shit!' Khrushchev shouted by way of greeting him. 'Don't forget it! I made you. I gave you the job. So what's going on in Moscow?' Semichastny swore everything was quiet in the Kremlin, but it wasn't.

Gorbachev's first error was to forget his Marx (or his Engels?) – that history repeats itself, first as tragedy, then as farce. But this was the most widely advertized *coup* in history. The very volume and intensity of the grumbling coming from his comrades – which I was picking up with my simple political antennae – should have told the Soviet president something was up.

He didn't listen when they said he had let the economy fall apart; ignored Boris Yeltsin's moves to destroy the Communist Party; left the glorious Red Army in the lurch; led the people into poverty; and,

289

last but not least, was shutting his mates out of the decision-making. They were right on every count.

While I was in Moscow that August, Gorbachev unveiled an ambitious programme designed to demilitarize the huge military-industrial complex, by beating its swords into colour television sets, tape recorders and refrigerators.

The top brass in the military didn't like it, and were saying so. For me that clinched it.

Perhaps the cry of wolf sounded old and tired to Gorbachev. Off he went on holiday with Raisa and the kids, while his comrades got together and planned a *coup*. And from the very beginning it was a typically Russian *coup* – bungled through bad organization, ignorance and misguided logic. The *vosmyorka*, the conservative, grisly Gang of Eight, were prime specimens of Soviet political Neanderthal – for years, I have had to deal with these people and their chief characteristic was their oafish brainlessness and second-rateness that characterized Soviet Power. And predictably, who was the leading light? Your friendly neighbourhood KGB chief, Vladimir Kryuchkov, of course. A workaholic, addicted to conspiracy theories, secret policeman for more than thirty years and with a private card index of 300,000 – would that I could see my name on it. There was Prime Minister Valentin Pavlov, nicknamed 'Porky the Hedgehog' who cried sick when faced with tough decisions. There was the figurehead, Gennady Yanayev, Gorbachev's vice-president and the quintessentially malleable *apparatchik*, shown on television looking hungover, hands trembling uncontrollably. And there was the stony-faced Defence Minister, Dmitri Yazov, who fought in the Second World War, a soldier of old-thinking and old-habits.

Of the other members of a dispirited, embittered élite, who backed the *coup*, I had met but one, Marshal Sergei Akhromeyev, who had been chief of staff and Gorbachev's adviser on military matters. I asked him a question at a press conference about Soviet casualties in Afghanistan and whether it was looked upon as an excellent training ground for the armed forces. The way he took the question suggested that if he had the power he would have had me running around his parade ground carrying a heavy-machine gun, or confined to barracks as the shit-house wallah for twenty years.

23. Miller questioning Marshal Sergei Akhromeyev about Soviet casualties in Afghanistan after the Soviet withdrawal in 1982. He refused to answer – to the applause of Soviet 'journalists'. After the abortive coup against Mikhail Gorbachev in 1991 the Marshal hung himself in his Kremlin office with a piece of curtain cord.

'I am not going to answer questions of that sort,' barked the marshal. 'Our casualties are none of your business and the rest of your question is outrageous.' The Soviet hacks duly applauded this answer and one of the resident British correspondents in Moscow, Martin Walker, turned to me and said: 'Any more questions like that and they won't let you in again.'

After the *coup* failed, Marshal Akhromeyev hung himself from the curtain rail in his office. His farewell note said he had backed the *coup* to protect the socialist achievements he had fought for all his life. He didn't spell out for us what he meant. And two other comrades, one of them top cop Boris Pugo, decided to escape the grasp of earthly justice and shot themselves. They shouldn't have bothered: they may have got away with it.

The three-day *coup* that shook the world was a bumbling misadventure launched by mediocre men. It was a tragic-comic operetta, embodying many of the contradictions that characterized a society that was changing so rapidly.

It was a military *coup*. But it lacked the support of the army. It was a *coup* launched in defence of the Communist Party apparatus that, in the end, declined to support its actions. It was a *coup* against Gorbachev and led by people he had chosen for office, his old friends, his neighbours, deadbeats and thugs. And how did the tank army get on – the one that for so long we have feared rolling across Europe at the start of World War III, brushing aside NATO's defences, and reaching the Channel ports in a day or so?

The tanks, successors of those that I took a close interest in some fifty years ago, should have acted brutally and quickly and with a massive show of strength. But instead of a coordinated manoeuvre bringing Moscow to submission, there was a shambles. Columns of tanks rumbled about ominously, but drivers did not know the route and asked pedestrians the way. Some tanks ended in ditches on the outskirts. Others stopped at red traffic-lights. The tanks proved no more effective than the Wizard of Oz.

The biggest mistake was not to kill Gorbachev and Boris Yeltsin. The plotters had the Leninist nostalgia, but lacked the Leninist temperament which can be best summed up as 'shoot the bastards'. At their ludicrous press conference on Day Two of the *coup*, they said nice things about poor Gorbachev, at the time isolated, bugged, locked up at his seaside dacha with his sick wife and reliant on foreign radio bulletins.

The plotters even talked about working with him again, when he was over his 'illness'. They failed to arrest any Gorbachev loyalists in the Kremlin. Nor did they get army units to invade the Russian Parliament building, seize Yeltsin and his supporters and end their resistance. And they should have shut down the country's television, telephones and other communications with the rest of the world.

Perhaps it was not a *coup* after all that undid the October Revolution. It was more like half a *coup*. But already, many are the myths. Did the people of Russia, for example, rise up on those August days to defend democracy and abolish serfdom in Soviet political life? Some did, but not many. On that Monday, few gathered at Yeltsin's White House. When, prompted perhaps by the Russian proverb 'when trouble comes also make use of it', he seized a moment of history and climbed impetuously onto a convenient tank – it reminded me of Henry V leaping onto a cart before Agincourt – to denounce the *coup*, watched by 200 citizens of a city of some ten million. Nevertheless, it was the first turning-point. For cameras and tape recorders were there. Pictures went round the world and words came back on the World Service of the BBC. But even that evening, when the first barricades went up outside the building, the turnout was not impressive. After all, it was a dirty night, cold and wet.

Yeltsin's supporters were still few in number, disorganized and some of them drunk. At that point, the 'Russian people' were neither united nor rushing to defend democracy. They were shrugging their shoulders – after all they had lived through the purges, a terrible war, and much more. They were sitting back, waiting for the outcome.

Only next morning did they show that at least they were were not afraid. A protest rally on Day Three marked the beginning of popular resistance. That night another myth emerged: how the Russian people rushed to the barricades to confront armoured vehicles and the guns, how three young people laid down their lives in the battle – the only ones – to defend the White House. It wasn't quite like that, either.

APCs had been sent to clear a barricade in an underpass which had blocked the Ring Road and caused traffic jams, infuriating

Moscow drivers. The crowd mistakenly thought it was a prelude to an attack on Yeltsin's White House, and formed a human chain. The lead APC would not, or more likely, could not, stop. Two young men failed to get out of the way in time. A third was killed by a bullet fired by a frightened crew, whose vehicle was alight.

It matters not whether their sacrifice was needless. Blood was spilt and democratic Russia had its first martyrs. And these deaths enraged the crowd and persuaded army commanders that any show of strength near the White House could lead to unacceptable bloodshed.

In my piece in the *Herald*, which appeared exactly a week before the *coup*, I concluded: 'Any attempt by the army to get rid of Gorbachev or Yeltsin could touch off a civil war and it would be unlikely to solve the underlying problems. They – Communist hardliners, army and KGB – are not going to ring the Kremlin with tanks because they do not know what to do on the second day.'

I got that right, too.

The swift, bloodless collapse of the August *coup* speeded-up the very process the plotters hoped to block or reverse. They themselves administered the *coup de grâce* to seven decades of Bolshevik rule. And it spelt the end of Gorbachev's political career. The events also shattered the nerves of his wife, the glamorous granny who seemed to have come from another planet, compared to the dumpy spouses of past Soviet dignitaries. Beleaguered in her dacha, Raisa was haunted by thoughts of the fate of the royal family shot to death in a cellar in Ekaterinberg, as well she might have been.

Distracted perhaps by Raisa's ill-health and shaken by his Crimean captivity, Gorbachev behaved like a Soviet Rip Van Winkle. He not only failed publicly to embrace Yeltsin as his saviour and a national hero, he had not realized that his policies were in ruins and the whole rotten structure had collapsed. Four months later, on the eve of Christmas, he left the world's political stage.

Gorbachev put himself out of a job. When he succeeded geriatric Konstantin Chernenko as Party boss, he knew his inheritance was rotten. The land was ravaged. The economy had broken down. The people were dispirited. The men in the Kremlin were hated. He wanted to destroy the old system. But he wanted to replace it with something so similar the people rebelled. We adored him in the West

– remember Gorbymania, the 'I love Gorby' badges and T-shirts, the Man of the Year awards and the Nobel Prize? – but at home he was deeply unpopular. And then there is a Russian proverb which neatly captured his problem – 'nobody groans at another man's toothache'.

I hold that things started to go wrong for Gorbachev the day he clamped down – for all the right reasons – on drinking. He decided that the demoralized and oppressed Russian people needed a little discipline. Young and energetic he may have been, but he was out of touch, unable to put himself in the shoes of the ordinary people, refusing to accept that drinking is a Russian way of life. So the vodka was poured drown the drain or not made, and the best vineyards in the country were destroyed. This led to Russians home-brewing on a massive scale. To do this sugar was needed in enormous quantities. The demand created an acute shortage, which in turn meant that across the USSR housewives were unable to make jam. Toothpaste disappeared or was sold only at a black market price – it was said that drinkers discovered it contained an ingredient which, when extracted, was guaranteed to give a kick. Eau-de-cologne became a favourite tipple. Contemptuously, they called the General Secretary the 'Mineral Water Secretary' and cursed him.

Gorbachev became a national joke. Such as, Gorbachev taking his grandson to the Kremlin for some of his colleagues to admire. Defence Minister Yazov says: 'The little lad is going to be a general. Look at the way he stamps his tootsies.' 'No, no,' says Prime Minister Pavlov,' he is going into business. See how he grabs things with his little fingers.' 'You're both wrong,' says Gorbachev. 'He's going to be a President, like me. You can tell by the way he soils his nappies and keeps on smiling.'

One of Gorbachev's nicknames was *'Comrade Boltun'* or 'Comrade Chatterbox', because as a typical Kremlin man he lectured and threatened constantly, but said nothing. There was a story how he and the Speaker, Anatoly Lukyanov – his best friend until the *coup*, when he joined the plotters – bought some rabbits in the country and Lukyanov took them to his dacha to raise. He calls Gorbachev a few days later and says the rabbits are starting to die.

Gorbachev tells him not to worry but to draw a square in white chalk on all the rabbit hutches. A few days pass but still the rabbits are dying. "Right,' Gorbachev says, 'draw a triangle in green on top of the square.' No luck. 'OK,' says Gorbachev, 'Put a circle in red around the design.' The deaths continue. 'Now I tell you what you've got to do,' says Gorbachev. 'Make a huge cross in blue through the whole design.'

'It's too late, Misha,' says Lukyanov. 'All the rabbits are dead.'

'That's a shame,' says Gorbachev. 'Because I've got a lot more ideas to try out.'

My law of politics says that once you become a national joke your authority is finished. Gorbachev may have looked to the West like the master of the Kremlin, but he was often merely the hapless steersman of the Soviet raft as it rushed out of control down the rapids. Right up to the day he left the stage he had occupied for almost seven years, he adhered to a fantasy that he could reform the unreformable.

To be fair to Gorbachev, he had a sense of humour. To this day he seizes any opportunity to tell his favourite joke about himself: 'There was this long queue for vodka when I launched my anti-alcohol campaign and some of those in it were turning nasty. One angry and thirsty comrade says to the man in front him 'Here, save my place for me. I'm going to the Kremlin to try and get hold of Gorbachev, and kill the fucker.' An hour later he comes back, looking really unhappy. 'Did you do it? Did you kill him?' asks the second man. 'Fuck it, no.' came the reply. 'The queue at the Kremlin to kill the bastard was even longer than this one.'

The most famous birthmark on earth, the man who ended the Cold War, the reason why millions of young people became interested in Russia, was stripped of his power and perks after the *coup* but had the sense to set up a think-tank-cum-fan-club, which has kept him going ever since. He has also tried his hand at light entertainment by appearing in a television advertizement for Pizza Hut.

It was sad, however, when he thought he still had more to offer Russia than merely playing the senior statesmen in retirement and stood in the presidential elections because it was crystal clear Russians had finished with him.

Gorbachev won only half a per cent of the vote.

25 – Sleeping in Brezhnev's Bed

'It doesn't matter how much you feed up the wolf, the elephant still has bigger balls' is an old Russian adage, and on every occasion I have been back to Russia since the collapse of Communism, there has been something to underline its truth and wisdom.

General and presidential elections returned me to the country that has been at the centre of my life not as a journalist, but as an observer. The job was to see that the Russians didn't cheat as they took their first steps along the road to democracy. Given that Russia is 118 times the size of Britain, it was not an easy task.

There was a time – and not so long ago really – when their elections were a farce. To martial music blaring from loudspeakers, tens of millions trooped to polling stations across the biggest country in the world for reasons which had little to do with real democracy.

The Kremlin bribed its long-suffering subjects with goodies. Every polling station had a buffet which sold, at heavily subsidized prices, such items as oranges, chickens, good sausage and even lavishly produced books. It was worth a short stroll to the nearest polling station to vote for the only candidate – a comrade – for the sausage alone, because there was none in the shops.

Not that it mattered if Ivan Ivanovitch Ivanov failed to vote, although voting was compulsory. Stalin was supposed to have said – no doubt in his soft voice – that it did not matter who voted. The only thing that mattered was who counted the votes. And so reliable comrades counted the votes and they always got the right result. Thus the turnout in Soviet elections was habitually ninety-nine per cent or thereabouts, and the Communist candidate was always elected.

This was a palpably absurd situation, a statistical impossibility, because more than one per cent of the population in any election was surely dead drunk, lost in the forest, departed this life since the last census, walking in the mountains or otherwise beyond the reach of the energetic, hectoring, squeaky-voiced Young Communist vote-collectors.

The first elections I was sent to monitor – ACC – took me to Saransk, some 250 miles east of Moscow, a dreary provincial city in an area once 'closed' because of its role in the military-industrial archipelago, and a labour camp complex which is still operating. Simply getting there was an experience because we flew with Aeroflot.

There is nothing romantic about flying in Russia. Aeroflot, once the world's biggest airline and one of the glues that stuck the USSR together, has been the subject of off-colour jokes – Aeroflop, Aeroslop – for as long as I can remember and many stories told about flying with it are true.

I have flown with Aeroflot with chickens, and once with a goat, and I do believe the story about a dog that lifted its leg on a passenger in mid-flight. A friend told me that he had flown in a plane with two escaped budgerigars flying around in the cabin. Another extraordinary feature was the amount and type of hand-luggage you were allowed. It was a common sight on flights to Moscow from the south to see boxes of tomatoes and cucumbers, sacks of apples and potatoes, and bags of flour being stowed in overhead lockers. In-flight entertainment like this made Aeroflot something special.

Aeroflot, with its fleet of 10,000 or more aircraft, has been another casualty of the collapse of Communism and it has been carved up between dozens of firms. Who flew me to Saransk I will never know, but the aircraft was a beaten-up, corroded carcass, which could have been a propellor-driven Antonov 24, more commonly used to fly platoons of Red Army soldiers to trouble spots.

Flying from Bykovo airport on the outskirts of Moscow sent my mind scurrying down memory lane because some thirty years earlier, when it was a military airfield, Nikita Khrushchev put on a stunning display there of the most advanced Soviet bombers and fighters – to the delight of Western air attachés, gob-smacked at their luck. Their reports home guaranteed sharply increased budgets for their own air force.

The end of the Cold War had shut down the air base. Its runways were pitted with craters and overrun with weeds. Its buildings looked like a collection of cattle sheds. There were no baggage carts – and only a fool would have checked in his baggage if he had wanted it to arrive with him – and no buses to take passengers to their aircraft. However hard you tried to keep your spirits up, the ground-staff, scruffy, rude, glum and unhelpful, tried to bring them down.

298

24. Miller is checking the amount of sausage in a local *gastronom*. It was customary to mark Soviet elections by local officials stocking polling stations and shops with foodstuffs.

The plane was no place for nervous types. Dark and gloomy, the cabin had broken seats and rotten carpets and only a handful of seat belts worked, and it exuded Aeroflot's special and unwholesome smell of sweat and urine. The stewardess weighed thirteen stones, or thereabouts, had a mouthful of gold teeth, sullenly counted the passengers and disappeared to spend the flight drinking vodka with two of the three crew, while the passengers had not so much as a glass of water. When I found her behind a tattered curtain and asked about a drink from the gallery, she said: '*Seychas*' which means 'now', but has come to mean 'when I get around to it, which might be never'.

The wolf and the elephant were alive and well and living in Saransk. The hotel was no ordinary hotel. Hard by the old Communist Party headquarters, it existed to accommodate top Party officials when they came down from Moscow on their inspection tours – and drinking binges.

Someone had decided that this was the only place suitable for a foreign gentleman. For almost without exception, ordinary Russian hotels are sad places, frequented by bedbugs, cockroaches, rats and whores. I once stayed in the Rossiya hotel near Red Square, which at that time claimed to be, with its 5,374 beds, the biggest hotel in Europe. Certainly it was big enough to loose oneself in the hundreds of yards of corridors and in the confusion of names for different areas. But at the same time, it was possibly the biggest whore-house in Europe, with fewer tourists occupying rooms than girls on the game, soliciting openly from their doorways. When it was shut down, however, it was because of the rats. (According to some estimates there are some eighteen million rats in Moscow for its nine million people). These had taken over some of the kitchens and could be seen by tourists as they ate in the huge restaurants. When the Rossiya's director was asked what the hotel's clientele thought of the closure, he laughed uproariously and said: 'They've not had time to think about it. They are all too busy chasing away the rats.'

The Party-Government hotel in Saransk was also caught in a Soviet time-warp, as far as its guests were concerned. Having been welcomed and shown to my room, I decided to take a bath after my journey from Moscow. The tiny bathroom, which contained a toilet, was badly in need of a lick of paint and the tiles were cracked and

300

stained, but this was Russia. I turned on the taps and I was not at all surprised when the bath water ran a brown rust colour. The bath slowly began to fill up. But the water remained cold. As the Russians say when confronted by an major and unexpected difficulty this was 'a spoonful of shit in a barrel of honey'.

I went downstairs to see the hotel's director. Her face lit up with pleasure when she saw me – the only guest in the hotel.

'Ah! *Gospodin*,' she says. 'Do you like your room.'

'I do,' I say, 'but there is a problem in the bathroom.'

'There are no cockroaches,' she says quickly. 'We have seen to that.'

'No,' says I, 'it's the bath water. It is cold. I have run it for a long time and but it is always cold.'

'That's right, *Gospodin*,' she agrees brightly. 'That's right. Alas, there is no hot water.'

I ask ever so politely, although I fear the worst: 'And when will there be hot water?'

She dodges the question. 'I have no hot water in my home,' she says. 'I have had no hot water for the past week. Nobody has. They are repairing the system. They always do it at this time of the year.'

'And when will there be hot water in the best and most important hotel in Saransk?' I ask.

She thinks about it. 'Well if today is the 15ᵗʰ, I think I can say... next week. You will still be here, yes?' I could have asked her why she didn't tell me about the situation when I checked in to the hotel. I could have asked her if water could be boiled for me in a kettle. I could have moved out to another hotel, which also would have had no hot water and would certainly have had animal life and whores. But this was Russia, so I went off to find the headquarters of the local Electoral Commission to see how they were getting on in the hot-waterless capital of the Mordovian Republic.

As it turned out, not very well, and they were not at all pleased to see a foreign observer. While so many remarkable things were happening in Moscow and St Petersburg during the Second Revolution, life in the provinces went on much as before, and an old-fashioned power struggle had been taking place in Saransk between reconstituted and hard-line Communists. It had not been resolved and suddenly a Westerner, and worse a Nosy-Parker turns up on their doorstep.

We all play our parts perfectly, just as in the good old days. After welcoming me to Saransk, they ask the damn-fool question as to whether I had visited the city before. 'Sadly no,' says I. And I diplomatically refrain from pointing out that Saransk has been 'closed' to foreigners, along with the whole of Mordovia, for many decades.

They offer every facility for my work: a car and driver, (to tell them everywhere I went), an interpreter, (to tell them everything I said) a fax machine, and a good telephone line to Moscow. I thank them profusely and ask to use the fax machine. Alas, they say, right now it isn't working. How about the telephone then? They sigh; it is very busy with calls to Moscow and the election headquarters. Perhaps later it might be free...

A large portrait of Lenin is hanging on the wall behind the head of the chairman, so I assume that Communists of some hue were going to win (they did.) A secretary sits in the corner of the room behind a table and there is a PC and two telephones on it. Several times the telephones ring, but not for long: with a bored expression, the secretary picks them up and drops them down on the cradle. This is a familiar Russian bureaucratic routine that I have seen countless times in offices during the Soviet era, and I permit myself a hollow laugh.

Polling Station No. 33 in a school classroom is so full of people that you gasp for air as you enter. There are Russians queuing with their passports to collect their ballot papers, and there are Russians queuing to enter the booths to cast their votes. But the area between is packed with some dozen elderly people, without exception festooned with medals and ribbons. They are Communists and proud of it. Actually they should not be there: campaigning is supposed to have ended the day before polling. But these are Russians who have been seriously left behind in the rush to a new society. They see me arrive and are stunned – after all, they have never met a foreigner before – and they move in and surround me. World Youth Festival, Moscow, 1956, comes to mind as they ask questions and open up about themselves.

These are veterans of the Great Patriotic War, the great touchstone that was the Soviet Communist Party's lingering reason for being. I have met men and women like these Russians before and I listen to them today, as I always did, even though I know that they portray their wartime victory as proof of Communism's strength – the system that saved the world. Of course, these people have a Stalinist view of history and nothing will change it. They carry portraits of Stalin across Red Square – when they are allowed – knowing, but wanting to forget, that Stalin repressed their fathers or their grandfathers or some relatives or some friends. I am asked whence I came and I answer London, because to say Southwold, Suffolk, in Russian would sound ridiculous and mean nothing at all. Now we can talk about the Great Patriotic War, ignoring the Molotov-Ribbentrop Pact and the purge of the officer *corps* (some 43,000 were shot or died in labour camps) in the late 1930s, which effectively allowed the Nazis to invade the Soviet Union so easily in June 1941.

A veteran with a flowing white moustache said: 'I was in Berlin at the end. I didn't storm the Reichstag. Wasn't lucky enough to be chosen, but I was there, alright. Saved the world, didn't we. Showed you what we could do. It was Stalin. Like your Churchill, a great leader. Man of steel. He made us great. And now... what a mess. What's going to become of us?'

Before I could answer – and nothing of what he said was new to me – an elderly woman, wearing several medals, with a mouth full of gold teeth, moves in. She announces she is the Communist Party's official observer at that polling station and her voice like a hacksaw, was only a few inches from my face: 'I am a Communist. Always have been. Always will be.'

'My grandfather was a Communist. Lenin' – and she looks into the distance in a way which reminds me of Fred Kite/Peter Sellers – 'Lenin handed my grandfather his Party Card. So my father became a Communist. So did I.'

Suddenly and curiously her voice changes and she starts to weep. 'My son was a wonderful boy and a good husband. He was a captain in the KGB. Thieves... scum... bandits... broke into his home and killed him when he defended his family. Bastards.'

She starts again confidently. 'My husband is also dead. Some thirty years ago. He was a good Communist. We are all good Communists here. The Soviet Union was a great country and' – she raises her voice so that everybody in the polling station can hear her – 'we Communists must fight to keep it that way.'

Nostalgia is all the war veteran and the women have left. Nostalgia for the order of Stalin and the supposedly dependable standard of living associated with the Brezhnev years; nostalgia for the Red Army's wartime victories and the fear that the Soviet arsenal once aroused in the heart of the Western enemy; and nostalgia for the Soviet empire – Russian greatness – which vanished overnight.

The night train from Saransk to Moscow is the longest train I have travelled on: thirty-three carriages. As the Russians say, the passengers were like sardines in a tin. It chugs at thirty miles an hour across Mordovia (Russian trains go slowly and carefully because of the ancient rolling stock and poor condition of the lines).

And it stops at a station called Potma.

Potma is a special place for me and I have to get out of the train and saviour the moment. I ask the conductor how long we stop in Potma and she says fifteen minutes. There is a camera and I need a picture of the station sign.

I climb down onto the platform which is deserted. Nobody else is getting off the train and nobody is getting on it. Potma is the junction for the trains that have taken innumerable people to some twenty or so labour camps that straddle a railway line running north for forty miles. This was never a part of Solzhenitsyn's *Gulag* – which has been entirely dismantled – but it remains Russia's biggest labour colony, consisting of sixteen camps, including one for foreigners.

And as though on cue, a policeman arrives and comes towards me as I line up the camera. He salutes: 'No photographs,' he says.

'Why not?,' I ask.

'It is forbidden,' he says.

'Who has forbidden it?' I ask.

'It is forbidden to take photographs of railway stations,' he says. 'It is the law.'

304

'I don't think it applies any more' I say. 'Times have changed, Comrade Policeman. You can go where you like in Russia today and take photographs of everything.'

He is perhaps twenty-five years old, and, by his features, of Tartar extraction. (The Tartars were one of the many nationalities repressed and exiled by Stalin.) I know a lot more than he does about the Great Experiment that exacted a staggering human toll, certainly some of the statistics. That perhaps ten million perished in Stalin's enforced collectivization in the early thirties. That some twenty-seven million died in World War II. That's as many as may have died in slave labour camps over the last twenty years of Stalin's life. That the figure of sixty-seven million has emerged as a conservative consensus estimate of the total casualties of the most murderous regime in modern history.

My young policeman friend knows nothing of this and cares even less and he was only doing his job. I give him a smile, shake his hand, and get back on the train.

The photographs never came out.

✻✵☙✵✻

Chita is 3,902 miles from Moscow on the Trans-Siberian railway, another 'closed' city now open to foreigners and I am visiting it to monitor elections to the Duma, the lower house of Russia's parliament. Once again I am not staying in one of the city's hotels and I am driven to the edge of town to the old Party-Government guest house.

Built in the 1850s, it had been the finest house in the city – famous as the place of exile of the Decembrists after their failed attempt to overthrow the absolute power of the tsars in December 1825 – and governors had lived there. It stood in three acres of tall fir trees and silver birch, and once had a large swimming pool which had fallen into disuse. It was surrounded by a high wooden fence and two police boxes stood at the gate.

There was large kitchen and dining room, a small hall for entertainment, a billiard room and several guest rooms. My quarters were clearly reserved for a VIP. I paced out the lounge – it was some twelve yards long and six yards wide.

Two magnificent chandeliers hung from the ceiling to light the room, but only one was working, and then from only two of the ten bulbs. There was a sofa and an arm chair, a huge Russian television (it needed at least two men to lift it), and a fridge, which also didn't work, even when plugged in. A fine carpet covered much of the lovely old wooden floor. It was the sort of room in which a Tsarist Governor and a visiting Communist bigwig could receive guests. I could have lined up some really long putts in this room.

Unbelievably, the bedroom was bigger. There were draped curtains, a small but antique dressing table, a modern wardrobe, a genuine Bokhara carpet covering the whole floor, a chandelier in reasonable working order, and two large eucalyptus plants in pots.

There was a single bed in the middle of the room with a polished wooden headboard and two small side-tables. This suite also had a bathroom with a modern plastic bath and a separate toilet – a sign that this area was for important people. However, this was Russia, and the wooden toilet seat was broken and the bath filled up only with brownish-coloured water.

The man from the Chita administration told me what I had suspected. Yes, this villa was for the top people – the 'big zits', in Russian slang – and Comrade Leonid Ilyich Brezhnev himself had stayed there when he visited Chita for the only time, and yes, he had stayed in my suite.

And yes, *Gospodin* Miller, believe it or not, you are sleeping in his bed...

Who says the Russians haven't got a sense of humour?

26 – Perspective

After I knocked out *All Them Cornfields and Ballet in the Evening*, I had the chance to go back to see how Mother Russia was getting on. It was the time of the first free elections – ACC. And I learned a great many things about the new Russia.

Such as, for example, the dreadful murder of a Russian acquaintance of some thirty years, Vadim Birukov. When I first got to know him in the early 1960s, he worked for the long-established *Time-Life* Moscow correspondent. Then he joined TASS, the Soviet news agency, and claimed to be their political correspondent, whatever that meant in the Soviet Union. Certainly he did not write stories about what was really going on in the Kremlin, who was shafting whom, fiddling their expenses and having a relationship with a Bolshoi ballerina. For, simply, he was also a colonel in the KGB, a man of charm and menace in equal measures.

When the Soviet Union bit the dust (and we all cheered) and there emerged overnight something akin to a free press, he became the managing editor of a new business newspaper targeted at Russian entrepreneurs and foreign businessmen. This was the time of smash-and-grab Capitalism and it was inevitable that the Mafia wanted a piece of the action, or at the very least, were prepared to offer their 'protection' services to the newspaper – the Russian word is *krisha* or 'roof.'

He declined their offer and predictably signed his own death warrant.

What followed was straight out of Quentin Tarantino's *Reservoir Dogs*, the nasty Hollywood film which clearly the Russian Mob had seen and enjoyed. He was tied to a chair, his ears were cut off and shoved into his mouth, and petrol was poured over him. To great hilarity matches were lit as if to set him on fire. Finally they shot him through the back of the head, no doubt *pour encourager les autres*.

This was, and is, a terrible story about the new Russia. And such killings have happened several times especially involving journalists, and very few killers have been brought to justice.

The Mafia have done very well out of the collapse of Communism. As it happens, I have long argued that the biggest Mafia the world has ever known was under the old regime – the Soviet Communist Party with its godfathers, in other words the ruling élite, its monopoly on power and its hit men who were the KGB. But... Russia has had to start from year zero or close to it. After seventy-five years of the grossest tyranny that prevented the emergence of a civic society, shattered institutions and attitudes associated with property and law (and it is worth recalling there was not much enlightenment before that, either) Russia is on the move. The rise from the wreckage of Communism is gradual and painful, but it is happening.

Finally, to get a few things off my chest (and if you don't already know it), the Russians are lazy, submissive, risk-averse – hence Russian roulette – and often outrageously xenophobic. They are prone to much talk and little action, And too often drunk. And they are ridden by ills and plagued by superstition.

They have done some dreadful things to each other and to others – in very recent history Chechnya comes quickly to mind – and I fear they will behave badly again.

But there is a good side to the Russian character – and I do not mean buying up Premier League football teams like Chelsea or London newspapers – and it is beginning to surface. They are creative and persistent. Entrepreneurship, thwarted for so long, is on the rise and not only by the ruthless and unscrupulous oligarchs, who grabbed anything and everything worth having and are noted for their outrageous vulgarity, tastelessness and riches beyond imagining.

And millions of Russians are discovering their national identity, history and religion, even if they have got out and gone elsewhere –there are said to be 300,000 living in and around London, and I've even heard Russian spoken in Southwold by a family who hired a beach hut along the promenade .

We are seeing the dawn of the rebirth of long-suffering Russia. Yes, it is true that as I write this in 2010, Putin's Russia lacks any ideology except a crude notion of Capitalism. But I am convinced that the day is coming when Russia will be an ordinary, normal, and – heaven forbid – boring, country. A place beset by normal problems, rather than shattering crises and disaster. A state of full civil rights, freedom of conscience and freedom of expression.

25. John Miller handing over to Frank Taylor in the *Daily Telegraph* office in 'Sad Sam'. The office walls were adorned with Soviet propaganda posters to remind Miller of where he was.

Finally, definitely finally, I would like to offer a modest piece of advice to young people who might like to take advantage of this Renaissance, to do as I did some sixty years ago.

Learn Russian. And start now.

Vsevo khoroshevo and *do svidania.*

26. John Miller leaving the Soviet Union for home in July 1983 on the Trans-Siberian railway.

Acknowledgments

I am hugely in debt to Alan Hackney, novelist and screenwriter who died in May 2009, aged eighty-four.

Alan Hackney wrote a novel *Private Life* which he transformed into a film script released in 1959 called '*I'm All Right Jack*' which satirised the British Class system and labour relations of the postwar years. It launched the film career of Peter Sellers who played the Communist shop steward Fred Kite. And Kite worshipped the USSR because of 'all them cornfields and ballet in the evening.'

This book has not been read for advice, comments and accuracy by any Kremlinologist, Soviet Affairs expert, Russophile, former or present Moscow correspondent, or, come to think of it, any Russian citizen. But some of my kith and kin looked at the manuscript such as Brenda, daughter Jane, sons Dod and Tim, my sister Joyce, my brother-in-law Bob, and my brother and sister-in-law Nat and Sylvia Tinkler. Some of them knew a thing or two about English grammar and how to spell and experienced the Cold War and their input to this end was invaluable.

One book above all has influenced me greatly over the years and my copy is well-thumbed and falling apart. It is *Inside Russia Today* by John Gunther, published in 1958, a reporter's job, readable, lively, and, of course, opinionated.

Index

Black Diaries, 57
Black Sea, 89
Blake, George, 64, 119, 123–124, 158, 215
Blunt, Anthony, 46
Böll, Heinrich, 268
Bolshevik, 69, 146, 175, 178, 219, 224, 234, 236, 246, 294
Bolshoi, xiii, 8, 46, 104, 128, 167, 197, 210–213, 266, 307
Bonavia, David, 113–114
Bonner, Yelena, 272
Brando, Marlon, 92
Brecklands, 278
Brezhnev, Leonid, 69–70, 74, 77–78, 126, 145, 148, 169–183, 199, 224, 235, 238, 240, 242–246, 254, 264, 271, 289, 297, 304, 306
Bribe, 92, 147, 165, 195.
    See also Corruption
British Ally Magazine, 124
British Embassy, 257, 259
Brooke, Gerald, 215–216, 219
Broomball, 16
Broomfield, Nigel, 263
Brown, George, 242, 246–247, 260
Budapest, 159, 188
Bug (Listening device), 100, 102–104, 108, 154
Buist, Vincent, 11
Bukovsky, Vladimir, 191
Bulgakov, Mikhail, 234
Bulganin, Nikolai, 72, 150
Burchett, Wilfred, 127–129
Bureaucracy, xiv, 70, 73, 109, 148–149, 211, 302
Burgess, Guy, 45–65, 120–124, 132
Butyrka prison, 11, 160
Byelka, 96
Byelorusski Voksal, 10
Bykovo airport, 298

C

Callaghan, James, 242–243
Casement, Roger, 57
Catherine the Great, 172

Caucasus, 117, 150
Caviar, 71, 74, 76, 96, 119, 127–128, 136, 212, 224
Censorship, 89–97, 109, 118, 176, 247
Central Desk, Reuters, 32
Central Telegraph Office, 89, 90, 95–97
Chazov, Yevgeny, 170
Cheka, 167, 215, 219
Chekhov, Anton, 4, 145, 146, 149
Cheltenham, 178
Chernenko, Konstantin, 180, 184, 235, 294
China, 24, 28, 94–95, 102, 109, 127–129, 166, 181, 195, 236, 281
Chisholm, Ruari & Janet, 153–163
Chita, 305–306
Christian Socialist, 147
Churchill, Sir Winston, 19–20, 56, 138–139, 232, 303
CIA, 112, 128, 156, 159, 161–162, 166, 280–283
Clockwork Mouse.
    See Roberts, Sir Frank
Cockney, 94
Cockroach, 40–44, 89, 101, 112, 176, 178, 300–301
Cockroach Whiskers, 19, 27.
    See also Stalin, Joseph
Cold War, 3, 15, 19–20, 27, 46, 67, 90, 119, 124, 149–150, 153, 164–166, 221, 240–241, 257, 259, 277, 279, 284–285, 286, 289, 296, 298, 313
Come East, Young Man, 128
Communal
    Flat, 9, 35, 89, 107, 192–193
    Grave, 60
Communist Party, xiv, 12, 26, 60–61, 64, 72, 78, 80, 105, 130–131, 137, 141, 147, 149, 169, 175, 177, 180, 193, 211, 222, 233, 235–236, 241, 244, 289, 292, 300, 303, 308
Congo, 33, 57, 110
Constantinople, 146

316

317

319

Lonsdale, Gordon, 161
Loory, Stuart, 226
Lopez, Roman, 180
Louis, Victor, 82, 112, 131, 176–177,
224, 270, 274
Low, Ivy, 190
Lubyanka, 60, 113, 161–162, 167, 175,
178, 189, 215–222, 236, 246
Lugansk, 236, 238
Lukyanov, Anatoly, 295–296
Lumumba, Patrice, 117

M

Maclean, Donald, 45–51, 53–54, 56,
58–66, 119–120, 124, 131–132.
See also Frazer, Mark Petrovich
Maclean, Mimsie, 47
MacManus, Arthur, 236
Macmillan, Harold, 250, 279
Maiyorovo, Natalya, 163
Marcos, Emelda, 182
Marks and Spencer, 12, 45, 154
Marsh, Ricky, 268
Marx, 21, 154, 289
Mason, Sidney, 32, 33
Matthews, Stanley, 223
Mausoleum, 8, 21, 92, 173–174,
179–180, 227–235, 238
Mazurov, 74
McCaffrey, Sir Tom, 245–246
Menzhinsky, Vyacheslav, 235
Metropol Hotel, 35
MI5, 45, 62, 123, 154, 162, 178, 218,
264
MI6, 62, 154, 161–162, 235, 246, 259
Mice, 38, 40, 44
Mikhalkov, Sergei, 22
Mikoyan, Anastas, 74, 150, 175
Milimen, 185, 204
Miller., Henry, 57
Ministry of Foreign Affairs, 47–48, 91,
110, 111, 149
Mintoff, Dom, 80
Mokhovaya ulitsa, 238
Molotov-Ribbentrop Pact, 303
Molotov, Vyacheslav, 149, 175

Morozov, Pavlik, 207
Mosby, Aline, 135–136
Moscow Radio, 28, 30, 37, 38, 49,
111–113, 279
Moskovskaya, 133, 136.
See also Vodka
Mossman, John, 57–58
Motion, Tony, 246
Muraka, Dev, 119
Murmansk, 125
Mzhavanadze, 76

N

Na levo, 13
Names.
See also Lenin, Naming
children after
Soviet children, 238
National Hotel, 156, 266
Neizvestny, Ernst, 147–149
New Maiden Monastery.
See Novodevichy
New Statesman, 125
Nicholas II, Tsar, 179
Nixon, Richard, 68
Nkrumah, Kwame, 40
NKVD, 106, 131, 215, 220, 222, 224
Norfolk, 72, 79, 87
Norfolk - Cruiser, 130
Norwich Mercury, 72
Novak, Kim, 157
Novodevichy, 54, 145–150
Novoslobodskaya, 11
Novy Mir, 125
Nureyev, Rudolf, 211

O

Oakshott, Keith, 51
Oblomov, 204
Observer, 48
October Revolution, 238, 289, 293
OGPU, 236
Okhotnichya, 136.
See also Vodka
Okhotny ryad, 238

One Day in the Life of Ivan
    Denisovich, 125, 127
Opera, 74, 211–212
Orchard, Ted, 249
Orwell, George, 21, 71
Osman, John, 176

P

Palace of Congresses, 73–74
Palace of Culture, 140–141
Palace of Soviets, 74
Parker, Ralph, 125–126, 128
Parker, Valentina, 125
Pasternak, Boris, 79–84
Pavlov, Valentin, 290, 295
Payne, Ronnie, 246
Peking Restaurant, 13
Pelshe, Arvid, 177, 287
Penkovsky, Oleg Vladimirovich, 72,
    156–163, 166–167
Pentagon, 89, 113
Peredelkino, 80, 82–83
Peters, Lana, 226
Peter the Great, 7
Philby, Kim, 46, 53–64, 119–124, 162,
    180, 235
Philby, Rufina, 123
Pioneer, Young, 207
Pits, The, 17
Plan.
    See Five-Year Plan
Playboy, 6
Plisetskaya, Maya, 211
Podbelsky, Vadim, 236
Podgorny, 74
Pogranichniki, 3–4
Pokazukha, 172
Poland, 97
Polish officers, 72
Polish resettlement camp, Suffolk, 126
Politburo, 67, 74, 169, 172, 175, 177,
    179–182, 224, 225, 239, 282,
    287
Pollitt, Harry, 129–131
Polyansky, 74
Ponomarev, Boris, 245

Portland Spy Ring, 161, 166
Poshlost, xiv
Potemkin Village, 205
Potma, 304
Powers, Francis Gary, 280–285
Prague
    Czechoslovakia, 29, 53
    Restaurant, 57
Prague Spring, 261, 288
Pravda, 15, 27, 44, 79, 91–94, 142, 173,
    189, 190, 192, 199, 240, 245
Press Department of the Soviet Foreign
    Ministry, 73, 109, 111, 116, 194
Prestwick, 51
Pretoria Prison, 165
Prime, Geoffrey, 178
Prokofiev, Sergei, 16, 22, 146, 234
Propaganda, 6, 15, 20, 30, 45, 54, 59,
    89, 112, 125, 127, 130, 142, 207,
    225, 228, 240, 246, 272, 281, 309
    Photograph editing, 246
Prospekt Mira, 10, 40, 41, 45, 99, 100
Public Record Office, 62
Pugo, Boris, 292
Pushkin, Alexander, 4
Pushkin Square, 192
Pushkin Street, 166, 266
Putin, Vladimir, xiii, 308

Q

Queue, 4, 8, 9, 14, 76, 81, 91, 130, 193,
    208, 210, 230–231, 233, 248,
    266, 296

R

Rabbit
    Floppy, 38–40
    Gorbachev's, 295
    Hat, 7
Racism, 40, 117
Rashidov, 74
Rats, 38, 101, 210, 300
Ratzin, Gerry, 33
Reagan, Ronald, 172, 245
Red Army, 3, 13, 19, 20, 22, 24, 26,

322

323

Lightning Source UK Ltd.
Milton Keynes UK
06 January 2011
165263UK00001B/233/P